Adventure Tourism

Adventure tourism is an increasingly widespread phenomenon, appealing to an expanding proportion of the population who seek new destinations and new experiences.

This timely, edited volume offers new theoretical perspectives of this emerging subset of tourism. It uses philosophical and cutting-edge empirically grounded research to challenge existing thinking and develop the conceptual framework underpinning definitions of adventure, interrogating the adventure tourism experience and further building upon recent advances in adventure education. The book brings together adventure literature from range of disciplines and applies it to focused study of adventure tourism. By doing so it significantly furthers understanding and moves forward the development of this area of tourism.

This significant volume is written by leading academics in the area, and will be valuable reading for all those interested in adventure tourism.

Steve Taylor is a researcher at West Highland College, University of the Highlands and Islands.

Peter Varley is Director of the Centre for Recreation and Tourism Research at West Highland College, University of the Highlands and Islands.

Tony Johnston is a lecturer in Development Geography at King's College London.

Contemporary geographies of leisure, tourism and mobility
Series Editor: C. Michael Hall
Professor at the Department of Management, College of Business and Economics, University of Canterbury, Christchurch, New Zealand

The aim of this series is to explore and communicate the intersections and relationships between leisure, tourism and human mobility within the social sciences.

It will incorporate both traditional and new perspectives on leisure and tourism from contemporary geography, e.g. notions of identity, representation and culture, while also providing for perspectives from cognate areas such as anthropology, cultural studies, gastronomy and food studies, marketing, policy studies and political economy, regional and urban planning, and sociology, within the development of an integrated field of leisure and tourism studies.

Also, increasingly, tourism and leisure are regarded as steps in a continuum of human mobility. Inclusion of mobility in the series offers the prospect to examine the relationship between tourism and migration, the sojourner, educational travel, and second home and retirement travel phenomena.

The series comprises two strands:

Contemporary Geographies of Leisure, Tourism and Mobility aims to address the needs of students and academics, and the titles will be published in hardback and paperback. Titles include:

Routledge studies in contemporary geographies of leisure, tourism and mobility is a forum for innovative new research intended for research students and academics, and the titles will be available in hardback only. Titles include:

Adventure Tourism

Meanings, experience and learning

Edited by Steve Taylor, Peter Varley and Tony Johnston

Routledge
Taylor & Francis Group

LONDON AND NEW YORK

First published 2013
by Routledge
2 Park Square, Milton Park, Abingdon, Oxon OX14 4RN

Simultaneously published in the USA and Canada
by Routledge
711 Third Avenue, New York, NY 10017

Routledge is an imprint of the Taylor & Francis Group, an informa business

British Library Cataloguing in Publication Data
A catalogue record for this book is available from the British Library

Library of Congress Cataloging in Publication Data
Varley, Peter, 1960–
Adventure tourism : meaning, experience and learning / Peter Varley,
Steve Taylor and Tony Johnson.
   p. cm.
   Includes bibliographical references and index.
   1. Adventure travel. 2. Tourism. I. Taylor, Steve. II. Johnson, Tony.
   III. Title.
   G516.V37 2013
   910.4–dc23   2012029973

ISBN: 978-0-415-52483-4 (hbk)
ISBN: 978-0-203-12009-5 (ebk)

Typeset in Times
by Wearset Ltd, Boldon, Tyne and Wear

Printed and bound by CPI Group (UK) Ltd, Croydon, CR0 4YY

Contents

Illustrations

Figures

Tables

Notes on contributors

Pete Allison PhD works in the Institute for Sport, PE and Health Sciences at the University of Edinburgh. His main research interests are in expeditions, values and youth development. He is co-founder of www.expeditionresearch.co.uk. He is an enthusiastic skier and regularly goes on expeditions.

Antonie Bauer is a professor at the tourism management department of Munich University of Applied Sciences. The topics of her publications range from the economics of global warming to the marketing of adventure providers. Her main research interests are currently adventure tourism and intercultural communication.

Simon Beames is lecturer and programme director of the MSc Outdoor Education at the University of Edinburgh. His research interests lie in learning outside the classroom and adventure-based outdoor education.

Paul Beedie is currently Head of Department (Acting), PE and Sport Studies at the University of Bedfordshire. His research has been driven by an interest in adventure and includes explorations of risk, identity and community. He wrote *Mountain Based Adventure Tourism: Lifestyle Choice and Identity Formation*, London: Lambert Academic Publishing (2010).

Carl Cater is a lecturer in tourism at Aberystwyth University, Wales, and his research centres on the experiential turn in tourism and the subsequent growth of special interest sectors, particularly adventure tourism and ecotourism. He has written over twenty papers and book chapters.

Terry DeLacy is professor in sustainable tourism and environmental policy at Victoria University, Australia. He was previously director of the Australian government-established, national, Sustainable Tourism Co-operative Research Centre. He is co-author of *Green Growth and Travellism: Letters from Leaders* (Goodfellows, 2012).

Dale Dominey-Howes, Associate Professor, Director of Australia – Pacific Tsunami Research Centre and Natural Hazards Research Lab, University of New South Wales, is an expert in natural hazards, disaster risk reduction. He has authored over 150 publications and is Chairman of UNESCO Post-Tsunami Disaster Working Group.

Sebastian Filep is a Lecturer at University of Otago, New Zealand, and Honorary Research Fellow at Victoria University, Australia. Sebastian is a tourist behaviour expert with an interest in positive psychology. He is a co-author of *Tourists, Tourism and the Good Life* (Routledge, 2011).

Sue Geldenhuys is the Head of the Department of Tourism Management at the Tshwane University of Technology, South Africa. Her research interests includes mega events and tourism curriculum issues in higher education. She has published in accredited as well as in other journals.

Ashley Hardwell completed a PhD in 2007 on UK rock-climbing culture. He lectures in outdoor adventurous activities at Leeds Metropolitan University. He has a particular interest in lifestyle sports, their culture, consumption and commodification. He contributed to the LSA special publication of *On the Edge: Leisure, Consumption and the Representation of Adventure Sports*, edited by J. Ormrod and B. Wheaton (2009) and has also presented papers at national and international conferences.

Tony Johnston is a lecturer in Development at the Department of Geography, King's College London. His research focuses on the cultural geographies of tourism and development. He has a particular interest in the commodification and consumption of death.

Melissa Janette Lötter is an Adventure Tourism Management lecturer and DTech: Adventure Tourism Management student at the Tshwane University of Technology, South Africa. Her research interests include adventure tourism management, marketing and practice.

Louise Munk Klint is a Research Associate at the Centre for Tourism and Services Research at Victoria University, Australia. Her current research focuses on dive tourism and climate change. Her PhD thesis established a climate change framework for dive tourism sector in Vanuatu.

Marius Potgeiter is a lecturer interested in aviation, marketing and destinations. He worked in industry for eleven years and based his doctoral thesis on marketing information systems. He is actively involved in research, presenting papers at academic conferences and publishing articles, and also provides study leadership to postgraduate students.

Tristan Semple is a lecturer on the BA (Hons) course in Adventure Tourism Management at West Highland College, University of the Highlands and Islands. He has been mountaineering for twenty years, and has carried out research into educational partnerships and professional development with the Himalayan Mountaineering Institute. His other research interest areas are experiential education and ecosophy.

Tim Stott is Professor of Physical Geography and Outdoor Education at Liverpool John Moores University. His research interests encompass fluvial geomorphology, learning through fieldwork and expeditions and technology-enhanced learning. He is a member of the Editorial Advisory Board for the *Journal of Adventure Education and Outdoor Learning*.

Steve Taylor works for the Centre for Recreation and Tourism Research at the University of the Highlands and Islands. His most recent publication was '"Extending the Dream Machine": Understanding People's Participation in Mountain Biking' in *Annals of Leisure Research*. His research interests include mountain biking, motivations for adventure, the ski industry and recreational site development.

Georgie Urry is currently undertaking a doctoral research project into the affective nature of limit experiences at Bristol University. The project questions how the vulnerable nature of the human self can infer a proximity to the material world that has hitherto been neglected.

Peter Varley heads up the Centre for Recreation and Tourism Research in the School of Adventure Studies in Scotland. Earlier research focused on tourism and liminality, and the commodification of adventure. Current work is centred on 'slow' adventure in hypermodernity, leisure Disneyization, and a Bourdieusian analysis of mountain biking.

Frank Vernon is a doctoral student at Indiana University and lead instructor for both the North Carolina and Northwest Outward Bound Schools, USA. His research interests include experiential learning, adventure education, critical pragmatism and ethnography. Recent and forthcoming publications focus on the co-instructing experience.

Kris Von Wald PhD is an independent consultant with Learning and Change Consulting. Her research interests are in personal development and organisational change. She recently co-developed the Sail Training International Model for Youth Development through Sail Training and wrote the 'Sail Training Programme Self-Assessment Toolkit'.

Introduction

Peter Varley and Steve Taylor

This book is a collection of papers generated as a result of the 2012 Adventure Conference at the School of Adventure Studies, Fort William, Scotland. The theme for that event was 'meanings, markets and magic', and it attracted a global audience drawn from a range of disciplines and perspectives. In two broad camps there were educationalists and leisure/tourism providers; in addition there were tourism, leisure and outdoor education academics, theoreticians and some other interests represented. All those attending the conference were also, or had been, participants in adventure tourism, both as consumers of commercialized experiences and/or as autonomous adventurers, and were therefore able to offer a range of insights. Emanating from this event is this diverse collection of ideas under the title of *Adventure Tourism: Meanings, Experience and Learning*.

What is clear from the papers gathered together is that there is much to be exchanged and learnt from all of the perspectives. In particular, however, it seems that adventure tourism could do worse than to return to its roots in outdoor education. The detailed attention paid to the experiential dimension, to feedback, to the dynamics of adventure careers and to dissecting the power of the expedition as a learning tool means that there are deep insights to be had here. Whilst Beames and Varley (Chapter 6) point to the analysis of the service encounter and ways in which it is constructed and controlled, Stott, Allison and Von Wald (Chapter 11) dig beneath the surface and use participant voices to uncover the effects of the experience. Whereas Bauer (Chapter 8) talks of the importance of service quality in the relationship between the entrepreneur and the adventure tourist, Vernon (Chapter 10) explores the balance, or hegemonic *im*balance, which inheres in many relationships in outdoor scenarios (although his focus is that of the formal learner–teacher one).

Woven into these texts, the reader will find some related gems about the power of narratives in the experience of adventure as resistance to the encroaching aspects of modernity and an engagement with time, or about the limit conditions of body and mind and how these are prodded, stretched and tested in adventurous activities such as skydiving. One is reminded here of Gidden's ideas about ontological security and how that can be difficult to attain in late modernity; might forms of adventure allow us a reconnection with nature, place and time?

As the arguments swing from philosophy through sociology to marketing and back again, one inevitably is wont to ruminate on the similarities of the concerns, whether they reside in the commercial sector, or the not-for-profit and educational realms. Whilst the key concerns of the business of adventure tourism might hinge on service quality, standardization and efficiency, so educationalists are focused upon the quality of experience and its repercussions, as well as the tensions between the subjective and objective responses to situations. Hardwell argues that the traditional outdoor apprenticeship is lost, and that the commercial world now offers a fast-track to notoriety and adventurer status; yet by the same token, it is the educationalists who would seek to empower learners, invert the hegemonic relationships of the classroom and foster learning by experience. Clearly, each aspect of controlled, marketed and managed adventure offers much to inform our understanding of the other – thus, feedback techniques may be borrowed from educational settings and used for tourist debriefs, and the research into tourism experiences could usefully harness the participants-as-researchers approach adopted by Stott *et al.*

To be sure, the 'fast-trackers' of the leisure and tourism marketplace do seem to have a habit of returning for the next level course, to try correlative experiences or to consolidate what they learned last time; for many the sweet and easily consumed taste of capsule adventure never quite generates the appetite for them to pursue their activities autonomously. There is a 'tick box' mentality in some sections of the adventure-consuming public, avidly seeking Facebook material and dinner party tales of derring-do. Experiential educationalists may cautiously observe the Disneyization of adventure centres and practices, and consider how best to preserve the unique qualities of these practices. Taking more time – spending time in the outdoors – might be the key. The thread which may be picked up in most of the chapters in this book shows that the adventure experience is often condensed to fit the convenience needs of the consuming public, but that the benefits for generating meaning, improving experiences and enhancing learning are all linked to the passage of time during immersive spells in nature.

But it is apparent that there *is* a concomitant interest in these deeper machinations of the great outdoors, and if primetime television is a barometer of public interest, then the efforts of the BBC's Monty Hall to recreate life on a West of Scotland croft, or attempts to live unaided and unfed in the Yukon wilderness, score highly. Likewise core viewing time and extensive broadsheet attention is given to issues such as great feats of journeying in wild places, finding, cooking and eating wild food, and so forth. As adventure tourism fragments, so it increasingly reflects the fragmentation of wider societal effects: convenience food – convenience adventure/education; and slow food – slow adventure, slow travel, slow learning (serving adventure apprenticeships).

Readers will doubtless cherry pick from this book according to their needs. We would urge you, however, to try to mix your selection, and to explore the interesting arguments emanating from analysis of adventure presented as: a learning opportunity, a product, a personal experience, a journey, a career and so forth. Tack back and forth between commerce and learning, bungee jumps and expeditions, narratives and close-to-death moments. We suggest that disciplinary fragmentation is unhelpful, and that a truly multidisciplinary approach to the study of adventure in its less-controlled and managed forms alike will benefit the field enormously. Cater, right at the beginning of this book, reminds us of the lumpy, amorphous nature of adventure and its varied histories. The notion that this subjective phenomenon could become objectified, rationalized, controlled, packaged and sold or used to educate people seems strange.

One might reasonably imagine that people whose everyday life consists of searching earnestly for food, water and shelter in order barely to survive would have no concept of 'adventure' as such. Their lives seem risk-filled and danger-ous enough. Yet many tribes and groups do have their rites of passage, and many of these include what we would readily identify as adventurous tests, somewhat akin to the Greek odysseys or the suitors' trials in fairytales. There lies, we venture, the enduring power of the *idea* of adventure: be it a learning journey, a post-experience badge of honour, a heroic tale to be told, an apprenticeship toward accomplishments in outdoor leisure or maybe just a personal reconnec-tion with something ordinarily just out of reach. Researchers must continue to search for new ways of capturing the broad field of adventure (there are some new approaches here) and also consider how adventure is labelled and inter-preted through the many lenses of geography, sociology, anthropology, educa-tion, business and so forth. The results of such studies will enrich our understanding of all elements of the subject.

Finally, delegates at the conference were reminded by practitioners at the conference, and Filep and co. (Chapter 3) remind us here too, that, for all our earnest theorizing, the late-modern adventure form is hopefully about fun; a way to happiness and to rekindle those carefree days spent playing as a child. Taking those risks and being nearer to death is simply a tactic that makes us feel more alive, while our time spent in nature has been proven to calm the psyche, lower stress and provoke feelings of happiness. So take this book outside, sit under a tree, and enjoy.

Part I

The meaning of adventure

Tony Johnston

Part I explores how we understand the adventure experience. Comprising philosophical reflections and empirical material from Carl Cater, Paul Beedie, Filep *et al.* and Georgie Urry, the section challenges contemporary thought on the consumption of adventure as an embodied and political experience.

The part is opened by Cater, who situates adventure as a complex and layered phenomenon. For Cater, adventure as a concept remains loosely defined, is negotiated differently across the disciplines and remains poorly understood by industry. While many academics have sought to define adventure in recent decades, holistic definitions are elusive due to their high dependence on context. To address this conceptual barrier, Cater explores the people, places and representations which define adventure as an experience, as a practice, as a philosophy and ultimately in much of the Western world, as a commercial venture. To fully consider this variety of actors and spaces and move towards a stronger theoretical framework and fuller definition of adventure, Cater draws upon contributions from sociologists, geographers, psychologists and anthropologists.

Cater's multidisciplinary approach importantly includes a brief analysis of the history of adventure. The chapter illustrates how dominant Western perspectives of adventure sprouted from early European travel imagination, particularly in the context of colonialism and exploration. This historical perspective introduces the theme of fluidity, arguably one of the few constants in definitions of adventure. Constantly shifting and evolving since early European exploration, Western understanding of adventure is now arguably shaped by the commodification of nature, desire for participation in dangerous sports and representations of adventure, among other mediating factors. Cater concludes the chapter by noting the dominance of Western discourses in our understanding of adventure, pointing towards the potential to challenge or rethink perceptions of play and risk in the developing world, or from an Eastern perspective.

In Chapter 2, Beedie continues the theme of fluidity with an exploration of the consumption of British mountaineering. As with Cater's chapter, Beedie begins with a reflection on the historical growth of adventure tourism, positioning early British mountaineers as agents of globalisation in late Victorian times. These great explorers demonstrated qualities commensurate with their environment; leadership, vision and determination. However, while this idealised view of mountaineering illustrates the long traditions of British exploration and the cultural identity of mountaineering, this image of the mountaineer is disrupted by Beedie as he fast forwards a hundred years to the rise of the consumer society, the focus of the chapter. Beedie posits the management of risk and the rise of the consumer society as the two dominant social developments which construct the identity of contemporary mountaineers. With ever-changing boundaries in terms of how adventure is classified and the equally rapid changes in the demographics of those who consume adventure, the argument that theorising adventure tourism could be approached from a mobility paradigm is logical and flexible.

In Chapter 3 Filep *et al.* explore the elusive concept of happiness in the context of adventure tourism. Although difficult to define, establishing core characteristics of happiness is crucial in developing our understanding of adventure. Filep *et al.* approach the leisure, happiness and well-being nexus from a psychology perspective, establishing the need to challenge the dominant view that 'holidays' or 'tourism' equals happiness. Such an approach allows us to develop our understanding of adventure by learning more about the tourist experience and how tourists understand the consumption of adventure in particular spaces, in this case the small island nation of Vanuatu. Twice ranked by *Lonely Planet* as the 'World's Happiest Country', Vanuatu has a relatively developed adventure tourism product. Filep *et al.* seek to establish the levels of well-being experienced by adventure tourists in their quest for a 'perfect day' on the islands. Usefully the chapter takes a qualitative approach, proposing innovative methodological tools to address the elusive and often highly subjective question of what constructs a positive adventure experience. Analysing rich representations of the adventure experience from a group of adventure and nature tourists, the chapter resolves that sense of engagement and developing relationships was central to creating a positive psychological experience.

The part concludes with a critical reflection from Georgie Urry on the sensory and embodied experience of doing adventure. In a chapter that may have particular resonance with readers of Patrick Laviolette's recent *Extreme Landscapes of Leisure* (2011), Urry draws upon Foucault, Deleuze, Thrift and other key theorists to rethink understandings of the life–death experience in extreme sports. Using the ethnographic experience of a skydive, Urry illustrates how the body mediates the experience of consuming adventure for the consumption of the mind. Exploring the idea of embodiment in the adventure experience, Urry argues that the situation of the body in the material world must be considered as a layered phenomenon – it is too simplistic to think of an adventure experience as a one-dimensional event experienced only by the flesh. The chapter traverses three layers: the micro-space of the adventurer and his/her embodied experience; the transmission of this sensory experience into forging relationships with place; and finally the notion of extreme sports as a challenge to ontological security.

1 The meaning of adventure

Carl Cater

Introduction

Adventure is a term that surrounds us in contemporary society, and is used in a positive sense to convey the merits of all sorts of experiences and products. Despite, or perhaps as a direct result of its reach, the definition of adventure is remarkably fluid, with Varley suggesting that it has seemingly become an 'infinitely variable, malleable construct' (2006a: 174). As a consequence it is important to take stock of its origins and interpretation, therefore this chapter will examine the varied meanings of adventure through an illustration of its context-dependent and highly mediated aspects. Whilst adventure tourism is an industry sector that has seen significant global growth as outdoor recreation opportunities have become increasingly commercialised, it also has a long history evidenced in exploration, wars and even in basic biological responses.

Adventure tourism includes a great diversity of activities, from those with little actual risk to those posing quite significant challenges to participants, although the perceptions of this may often be dramatically different. Authors agree that adventure tourism activities include specific elements such as specific skills and elements in which the outcome is influenced by the participation. However, increased commodification of the adventure experience has involved transfer of risk responsibility to commercial operators. In this realm the experience may become overloaded with high expectations, especially if the setting and perceptions of the organiser differ from that of the tourist. In order to uncover these differing perceptions this chapter poses several questions to signpost discussion and lead into the more empirical parts of this book. Given the geographical coverage of this volume it is pertinent to consider the location of adventure, as well as participation in a commodified era. The importance of technological and organisational structures in improving access is only one dimension to these aspects. However, probably the major issue that adventure tourism academics and the industry have struggled with is in achieving a definition of adventure, so we begin with the question *what is adventure?*

What is adventure?

History of adventure

Adopting a contextual approach to adventure we should recognise the importance of a historical perspective. Since adventure is closely linked to challenge, it is undeniable that our prehistoric ancestors faced some form of challenge to their very existence on a regular basis. Whilst these may not be an 'adventure' in the modern sense, particularly because entry was unlikely to be voluntary, our thirst for a thrill stems from these everyday challenges. The ghosts of these psychological inheritances remain with us in the production of various hormones within the body that heighten the experience and are often central to satisfaction in more active adventure. Sensing a threat, the fight-or-flight preparation involves the 'aminergic system of the brain stem preparing the brain-mind for action by heightening all the functions normally associated with waking' (Hobson, 1994: 161). This includes the production of serotonin, which serves to make the brain more alert. At the same time the autonomic nervous system of the body produces adrenaline to prepare for physical and mental exertion and dopamine in order to prepare the body for injury. It is clear that these processes occur when a participant is involved in many adventure tourism activities (Buckley, 2012). However, in addition to the recognition that experiences are highly contextual, it should be apparent that individuals rarely make sense of adventure in these terms, other than perhaps to refer to the 'buzz'. This desire for connection to nature within runs parallel to connection to nature without, which has been described as biophilia (Wilson, 1993). The point to be made here, then, is that adventure is part of who we are, and whilst its form has changed in terms of participation, risk and place, adventure is a factor throughout all of human development.

Culturally and historically the dominant Western meaning of adventure has been shaped by the European exploration and colonisation of the world. Phillips shows how the production of the earliest world maps in particular 'established an intellectual framework in which contemporary geographical knowledge was logged, and ignorance made visible' (1997: 6). The blank hearts of continents like those in the Mercator map of 1587 acted as an incentive both to the imagination and hence exploration of them. Of course the exploration and further mapping of these spaces was deeply bound up with the scramble to 'colonise and consolidate imperial power' (Phillips, 1997: 7). The irreducible links that lie between are highlighted by how 'science, exploration, and indeed "adventure" occupied (and, by implication, continue to occupy) a common space' (Gregory, 1994: 20). This rhetoric continues with organisations such as the Royal Geographical Society still closely linked to the promotion of adventure and exploration, through funding for adventures and annual training workshops such as *Explore*. The fact that these explorations of unmapped space are inherently adventurous is also linked to the generation of adventure tales, both real and literary, founded in this other space. Indeed the binary between objective science and emotional romanticism is a terrain where adventure may be seen to be nego-tiated and defined.

It is undeniable that adventure has an underlying masculinist imperative, although it should be noted that this is again culturally constructed. Adventure for males has also existed throughout history through war. It is clear that adven-ture in this case was not always entirely voluntary, although an idea of duty has a powerful, albeit externally influenced, part to play. However, it is undeniable that many of the concepts that can be seen to emerge around ideas of pure 'adventure' are closely entwined with those of conflict. Often it enabled the only means of escape for the ordinary man from a more traditional life, and the oppor-tunity to travel, and then return with tales of glory and heroism, was an attractive one. The Second World War was an important watershed because huge numbers of people, mostly men, had undergone some form of temporary or permanent displacement. Whilst this was not necessarily tourism, it opened up the possibili-ties and desires for travel in a way not before witnessed. Furthermore, the post-war period was an important one in terms of technology and adventure, when large amounts of surplus military equipment, such as jeeps, rafts, backpacks, scuba gear, camping equipment, skis and guns could be redeployed in the search for adventure in inhospitable places (Adventure Travel Society, 1999). River navigation, and whitewater rafting in particular, owes an early debt to the avail-ability of this hardware. Much of this surplus equipment deteriorated, however, and it was not until the 1970s that the availability of cheap new materials like aluminium, rubber and plastics enabled rafts to be marketed at a reasonable price again (Maritime Safety Authority, 1995).

Levels of adventure

This complex cultural history creates some difficulties in attempting to define adventure. Many attempts to do so have recognised that there is a scale in its interpretation, often using terms like 'soft' and 'hard' to distinguish different levels (Swarbrooke *et al.*, 2003: 32). There have also been a variety of models proposed to describe the adventure experience, many of which have focused on the interplay between risk and competence, following the work of Mortlock in *The Adventure Alternative* (1984), for example the 'Adventure Experience Para-digm' (AEP) (Priest and Bunting, 1993), or the 'Adventure Tourism Process' (ATP) (Morgan, 2000). More recently, however, Varley has shown the context-dependent nature of adventure tourism that corresponds with the growth of the adventure tourism industry in his 'Adventure Commodification Continuum' (ACC) (Varley, 2006a). It is important to note the voluntary aspect of an adven-ture, at least at the entry point, which will lead to what has been called a peak experience, or the pleasurable feeling that someone feels when they are perform-ing to their physical and sensory potential. However, there are clearly many indi-vidual definitions and levels at which adventure may operate; for one person's adventure may be another's backyard stroll. It is more useful if we consider adventure as an individual concept – and in this it is an experience that is different from that of everyday life. Official definitions of adventure focus on the uncertainty element as a vital part of the challenge. The New Zealand Mountain Safety Council defines adventure as:

> An experience where the outcome is uncertain because key information may be missing, vague or unknown, but it must appear to the adventurer that it is possible to influence the circumstances in a manner which provides hope of resolving the uncertainty. An adventure is much like leisure because it is a state of mind, is freely chosen, intrinsically motivating and may lead to a peak experience. The adventure experience is individually specific due to competence, situationally specific because of risk and chronologically specific in time. An adventure for one person in a certain place and at a particular time, may not be an adventure given a different person ... place ... or time.
>
> (NZMSC, 1993: 9)

This definition seeks to highlight the context-dependent nature of adventure, as well as to emphasise that there is some ability of the individual to govern the outcome, which itself is not some foregone conclusion. This uncertainty is often created through the presence of risk, defined as the potential to lose something of value, whether it is physical, mental, social or financial. This risk, or danger of an 'other' event, is integral to the adventurous experience, but again it is also a floating concept. As Cater (2006b) has shown, real and perceived notions of risk in adventure tourism are frequently incongruous. In many forms of commercial adventure activity the outcome is almost certain, but participants are not always fully aware of what it might *feel* like. This emphasises the embodied nature of adventure tourism pursuits, where the human body is the vehicle for engaging in experience.

Narrating adventure

Recognising the importance of context, perhaps a more useful lens for understanding adventure is from the narrative perspective (as discussed by Semple and others in this volume). Adventure is closely linked to identity for both the casual traveller and the dedicated mountaineer in the formation of narrative capital. Schiebe has suggested that adventurous tales form the basis of life stories that in turn are foundations of individual identity, whereby 'the value of such action is that the consequences of having enjoyed such thrilling experiences flow beyond the bounds of the occasion ... the life story of the participant is enriched' (1986: 136). Of course the participation in adventure and its narration needs to be appropriate in terms of risk behaviour and this is frequently defined by society (Johnston, 1989: 42). As a result it is not the risk alone that is upheld but the 'contextual significance or participation in risk for the construction of self-narratives' (Schiebe, 1986: 135).

Central to the very idea of an adventure is that it has a clear beginning and end, perhaps something that is attributable to the link made between culture and adventure in the adventure tale. Adventure stories illustrate something important to the quest for adventure, the peculiarly human ability to experience through another's eyes. Thus reading an adventure story, or more modern diversions such as film, can be seen as fulfilling the need for adventure itself, providing an escape from 'real' existence. Thus, imagination is an underlying thread to adventure, since the anticipation or within-mind adventure is as important as the adventure itself. This has important consequences for those involved in programming adventure tourism activities.

The adventure also has an inbuilt attribute of retreat as part of the experience, and this is a theme that is present in real adventure and in literature. The moments of peak experience are emphasised by the periods of tensioned calm that punctuate them. In Steinbeck's *Arthur*, a tale of the medieval king, the knights must return to a Haven when the 'wild life becomes intolerable' (Schiebe, 1986: 133). To take an example of modern adventure, a typical white-water rafting experience is likely to be one of tensioned calm for most of the time, only broken by peak activity in the rapids. The return to the castle is replaced by the retiring to a riverside lodge, with the provision of showers, saunas, tea and cakes that only the triumphant participant would deserve. Varley (2006a, 2011) has shown how the still times of adventure are, in fact, at least as important as those of high adrenaline in understanding the adventure experience.

Despite the link to imaginary narratives of adventure, there is a somewhat paradoxical search for reality that runs parallel to this. Indeed several commentators have framed the desire to travel as a search for an experience more authentic than that found in everyday existence. The work of MacCannell (1976, 1992) and May (1996) particularly focused on this idea that 'reality and authenticity are thought to be elsewhere' (MacCannell, 1976: 3) in modern existence. Despite criticisms of the concept of authenticity, the arguments that back up this debate are useful in that they do confirm the undeniable touristic trait of yearning for the untouched, and the associated prestige that goes with the experience of such. Again a clear link emerges to narration, as the experience of some more authentic other enriches the narrative capital of the traveller. This search for something different is undoubtedly a major attraction for many participants in adventure tourism. In many ways adventurers may be seen as searching for 'the space of the dream ... where everyday life is put into brackets and temporarily replaced by a different life' (Lefebvre, 1991: 353).

All of this comes with a caveat that adventure is still contextualised through the processes of everyday life. Turner (1986) argued that the place of adventure has altered from the exclusive place it held in tribal or pre-modern societies as a rite of passage, thus supporting the social order, to a more subversive character in industrial society. However, it is more appropriate to see these disruptive spaces not as apposite to the character of modern life, but more as a safety valve which is, in fact, just as much a reinforcing of tradition. As Phillips states, 'in the liminal geography of adventure, the hero encounters a topsy-turvy reflection of home, in which constructions of home and away are temporarily disrupted, before being reinscribed or reordered, in either case reconstituted' (1997: 13).

Indeed, this is no doubt true, but the very interpretation and reconstitution is always mediated through the pre-existing geographies of home. Further, despite some concerns that the commercialisation of adventure has eroded authenticity, some work would argue that the individual, active and embodied focus of these pursuits means they can only ever be 'real' to the participant (Cater and Smith, 2003). Indeed this very real aspect to adventure is geographical, with adventure tourism taking place in specific locales. Therefore we next ask *where is adventure?*

Where is adventure?

Wild places

Despite its often imaginary contexts, adventure is also a highly spatial practice, with strong ties to place. These places are continually expanding, for '*as* people become more demanding of ... adventure, society will continue to push its limits in search of new peripheries looking for new boundaries to cross and places to collect' (Timothy, 2001: 175). Drawing on the links to exploration described above, adventure may often be interpreted as the search for wilderness. Again, however, this concept is culturally specific, even between English-speaking countries. One only has to look at the different interpretation of national parks, themselves magnets for adventurous activity, to see this in action. The lack of facilities and habitation in American or Antipodean parks contrasts with those in British or European contexts for example (Frost and Hall, 2009), and these have implications for the study of adventure in these settings. Work by Klein (1980) has highlighted the way in which, particularly in US society, frontier culture has been held in high esteem, despite the fact that the 'frontiers' are of a different nature. Values such as risk-taking are seen to be socially desirable and are reinforced through institutional practices in school, family and the media.

These issues become even more complex in emerging destinations that may seek to mimic wilderness conservation practices elsewhere. In China many national parks have been designated along American lines, and yet, as Buckley *et al.* (2008) show, Mandarin-language interpretations of wilderness carry a negative connotation (the term for wilderness is *Da-Ziran*, literally 'big nature'). Indeed, there is a contradiction in the mapping and delimiting of wilderness, in that to map nature into scientific confines threatens the existence of an untamed nature in the first place. True adventure relies on nature as being an active element in the experience, unknown and unpredictable. Yet, in work on polar tourism Stonehouse and Crosbie (1995) illustrate the inherent unsustainability and falsehood of the quest to 'tread where no human has done so before' (95). Thus there may be more mileage in the meanderings and musings of Macfarlane (2007), who suggests that finding wild places is often up to individual experience.

Further proof of the culturally biased search for adventure lies in the popularity of certain lists or conquests. Often this may be in search of the physically highest (the highest summits on each of the seven continents for example). Of course these statistics are meaningless when situated within the contextual application of adventure. Although there is an argument that this might be driven by rational thought in the physical altitude of each peak, the reality is that this rarely defines the difficulty, which itself is a highly contingent aspect. This process works at a lower level to the 'bagging' of Munros in Scotland (mountains over 3000 feet). In Taiwan, mountain hikers are drawn to a list of the 'top 100' (*bai yue*) mountains, which are all peaks over 10,000 ft but are of special significance by aesthetic virtues such as steepness, beauty, unusualness or prominence (Huang, 2010). Thus, adventure is a profoundly liminal experience, but contrary to this ethic, an irrefutably spatial one (Winchester *et al.*, 1999: 60).

Wildlife

Wildlife often features in the adventure tourism experience and this does illustrate some of the crossovers with ecotourism described by Fennell (2003). In an adventurous context this may be a desire to look the predators of our past in the eye. The hype that surrounds fatal shark attacks and the growth of great white shark cage-diving in South Africa and Florida has been documented by Dobson (2006). We are reminded here of Chatwin's discussion of Dinofelis, the leopard-like creature which, it would appear, hunted our ancestors in Africa, the Austral-opithecines, some 1.2 million years ago: 'Could it be, one is tempted to ask, that Dinofelis was Our Beast?' The Arch-Enemy who stalked us, stealthily and cunningly, wherever we went? But whom, in the end, we got the better of? (Chatwin, 1987: 253). Chatwin, and many academics, have argued that overcoming our primary predator was a major step in our evolution, but that we still have a desire to come face to face with that beast (Cater, 2010). In the marine environment, the 'beasts' are still present, motivating us to seek adventurous encounters, although hopefully towards a greater respect for such creatures. Indeed, Chatwin argues that there was a sense of sublime intimacy with our predators, that there was, in some senses, a 'nostalgia for the Beast we have lost' (Chatwin, 1987: 254) that surely drives a desire to experience these animals in the wild. This does not always end favourably, as illustrated in recent fatal polar bear encounters in arctic regions (Cater, 2013).

Places of adventure

One consequence of the commercialisation of adventure has been the growth of so-called 'adventure capitals', often ski resorts or outdoor recreation hubs that have sought to diversify their product offerings. Cater (in Buckley, 2006) describes the development of the self-styled adventure capital of the world, Queenstown, in New Zealand. Building on an existing ski and outdoor tourism industry, and a high youth-tourism profile, this was allied to the development of iconic adventure tourism products. Jet boating and whitewater rafting first 'blended scenery and excitement' in the tourism experience (Pearce and Cant,

1981: 10). However, the first commercial bungee-jump site, established at Kawarau bridge in 1988 had a major impact on the destination as a place of 'crazy' adventurous pursuits as well as boosting numbers of participants in other existing adventure activities. The majority of adventure tourism destinations invariably have a wide selection of activities available that cements their reputation, as it is part of the very character of the destination that there are a number of smaller scale adventure activities also on offer. Not all of these activities are permanent fixtures, and some may only survive for a season, but all of the larger activities were once small operations, and the nature of seeking the latest craze means that the market is always present.

Of course the success of Queenstown has led to a wide degree of imitation, for whilst Buckley (2006) identified seventeen destinations that had some degree of 'adventure capital' in their destination branding, the numbers are now significantly higher than this. Notably these are well-defined tourist places that are 'legitimated regions; space that is safe, structurally separated, licensed and channelled into approved zones' (Varley, 2006a: 181). Some destinations have been successful in using an interest in events to raise the profile of adventure in a destination. In Voss, Norway, the annual *extremsports veko* (extremesports week) combines adventure spectation of activities such as BASE jumping, downhill mountain biking, skydiving and kayaking, with softer adventure tourism experiences during a 'try-it' programme. All of this is combined with a festival atmosphere with musicians and other liminal experiences, such as tasting the local delicacy of boiled sheep's head (*smalahove*) (Mykletun 2009). Adventure-film making has also reached a zenith, with adventure-film festivals becoming increasingly popular, often in adventure capitals. One of the longest established, the Banff Mountain Film Festival, now embarks on an annual world tour with stops in around 285 communities and thirty countries (2012). Outdoor film-making has also become progressively democratised with the wide availability of lightweight high-definition cameras. Therefore we should also consider a potential for adventure to take place in non-traditional settings, as described in the other chapters in this book. As well as non-traditional places, there is a trend towards non-traditional adventurers and thus to our third question, *who is doing adventure?*

Who is doing adventure?

Throughout this discussion it becomes apparent that there are vastly more people engaging in adventurous activity. In line with the 'democratisation of travel' (Urry, 1995: 130), what scholars of adventure tourism observe is a parallel democratisation of adventure. This can be demonstrated by a raft of reports that hint at the growth of adventure tourism, or through statistics from certifying agencies. For example, the world's largest scuba diving organization, the Professional Association of Diving Instructors (PADI), has issued in excess of twenty million certifications since 1967, with almost a million new certifications every year over the last decade (Cater, 2008). This points to huge numbers of people taking the opportunity to seek those unfamiliar marine spaces. Furthermore it is important to get beyond the stereotypes of adventure participation, reinforced by the media, for example the Pepsi-Max/Red Bull youth extreme-sports participant described by Varley (2006a: 180). Yet research has demonstrated that commercial adventure tourism is open to a wide range of participants (Cater and Smith, 2003), and in fact adventure pursuits attempt a high degree of inclusivity (Cater, 2000). In marketing terms, however, it is important to tread a fine line between advertising exciting experiences versus those that present a real challenge. Cater and Smith (2003) show how jetboat operators needed to apply careful language in advertising thrills not fear, and yet simultaneously they needed to use youthful faces in brochures to ensure that older participants would still be attracted to 'feeling young again'. This older market for adventure will become increasingly important as their numbers, health, and desire for experiences grows. Despite these inclusions, there are very real concerns over broad socio-economic access, and particularly over access to adventure activities for host populations in less-developed countries.

Nevertheless, emerging economies are developing as locations and markets for adventure activity. Several of the chapters in this volume describe the emergence of South Africa as an adventure tourism destination, popular with both international and domestic tourists. Likewise *Action Asia* is a dedicated high-end magazine aimed at the adventurous tourist within the region. Pearce and Moscardo (2004) found that Chinese visitors to the Great Barrier Reef were more active and more interested in learning than previous Asian visitors. However, as described above, Chinese interpretations of adventure may be culturally specific. The growth of so-called 'drifting', or passive whitewater rafting, in China points to a different relationship with outdoor activity than previously witnessed.

At the other end of adventure we have seen commercialisation of even the most extreme of adventures, for example with guided mountaineering. In Nepal nearly five hundred tour operators are members of the Nepal mountaineering association (Hales, 2006). The growth of this subsector has been dubbed Skilled Commercial Adventure Recreation in Remote Areas (SCARRA) by Buckley (2006). This commercialisation has not been without its detractors, indeed, some outdoor purists may even view adventure itself as a 'dirty' word, sullied by the commercialisation of experiences. However, this overlooks the levelling potential for adventure experiences, as Nietzsche claimed (and more fully critiqued in Varley, 2006a), 'a few hours of mountain climbing turn a villain and a saint into two rather equal creatures ... exhaustion is the shortest way to equality and fraternity – and liberty is added eventually by sleep' (quoted in Fennell, 2003: 48). Of course, with commercialisation comes more reliance on others, and in this respect we should ask *what do we need for adventure*?

What do we need for adventure?

Technology

Technological change has important consequences in tourism, for example the impact of jet aircraft from the 1960s onwards. However, as Lash and Urry

(1994) contend, it is important not to succumb to 'technological determinism' which sees 'travel as derived demand'. Instead they highlight organisational innovations as key to success of technological advances and, hence, the social organisation of travel as part of a wider 'social organisation of the experience of modernity' (253). Whilst not overlooking the importance of organisational innovations, this process of technological availability has continued in adventure tourism, for example the scientific development of bungee cord and the development of jet boats. In adventure travel as well, one only needs to look at the way in which rucksacks have changed over the last twenty years, from rigid frame designs to body-hugging creations, with the wearer clad in the latest easy-breathe fabrics. Of course the consumption of these goods is not wholly defined by the adventure itself. The consumption of consumer goods related to an adventurous ethic is explained by Riley (1995: 634), as the need to engage 'in ideal rather than utilitarian consumption; the burgeoning phenomenon of fashion-oriented consumption; and an increase of interpreted symbolism from consumptive displays'. Thus a huge consumer goods industry has grown alongside adventure tourism itself, with the adventure tourist being able to assert their identity as such through the carrying of the badges that denote such a lifestyle, with goods that 'possess qualities beyond their functional purpose' (ibid.). Johnston and Edwards demonstrated how the activity of mountaineering had become progressively commodified in the 1990s:

> Corporate sponsorship has shaped mountain experiences and even the fantasy of a mountain experience in order to sell commodities to a consuming culture. (As a result,) … many more well-equipped, stylishly dressed holiday consumers are travelling to mountain regions … sent by an ever-growing legion of adventure travel companies who advertise their services in (an also growing number) of 'Adventure Travel' magazines and guides. They arrive carrying clothing and equipment purchased at outdoor shops staffed by adventure enthusiasts; and they are guided through their mountain adventure by mountaineers turned tour guides.
>
> (Johnston and Edwards, 1994: 468)

Expenditure on 'adventure clothing' and high-performance fabrics is a multibillion dollar industry, even if little of these products ever make their way into the outdoors. This is perhaps more so given the current vogue for adventure design in urban lifestyles. This latter point highlights that it is possible to confirm the ideals of an adventurous lifestyle through the display of such consumption, without even partaking, and the superficial nature of this consumption is described by both Buckley (2003) and Cater (2005). It is interesting to see how the adventurous ideals of the Royal Geographical Society both reinforce and are reinforced by their corporate sponsors, Land Rover (Phillips, 1997: 184). More recently the discussion of the importance of artefacts in adventure has sought understandings of hybrid cultures, where the 'kit' becomes an important part of the mediation of the adventure experience (for example Merchant, 2011).

Organisational structures

Confirming the adventure experience as mediated recognises the organisational structures that play an important part in the promotion and regulation of adventure tourism. In understanding the place of adventure, the role of these organisations is paramount. It is notable that the Adventure Travel Trade Association (ATTA), currently the most globally prominent adventure tourism industry association, has had a somewhat turbulent history. Originally established in 1989 parallel to the Adventure Travel Society, this organisation grew rapidly and celebrated a tenth world congress on adventure travel and ecotourism in Anchorage, Alaska in 2000. However, by 2004 the membership and direction of ATTA had waned, and it was relaunched with new ownership later that year. Taking the world summit overseas for the first time in 2010 to Aviemore, Scotland, heralded an international focus for the organisation, with an emphasis on sustainable adventure tourism. Nevertheless, ATTA still operates within a North American trade-focused model of adventure tourism, with relationships between suppliers, outfitters and wholesalers being core to adventure tourism on that continent. In contrast, in the UK it is likely that some adventure tourism operators will be affected by the removal of the Adventure Activities Licensing Authority (AALA). Although outwardly focused on licensing outdoor activities undertaken with minors, this process would have impacted on general adventure activity provision. A new 'common sense' approach to adventure activity is supposed to replace it, but this will only work in a healthy reporting culture advocated by Bentley *et al.* (2010). This dynamic organisational and regulatory environment means that individual operators need to be responsive to the interpretations of adventure at these levels.

Adventure temptation

This chapter has not achieved a formal definition of adventure, which has been attempted by many academics, but continued to elude many in the industry. Indeed, an industry source lamented in 2004 that 'everyone we've spoken to recently has offered us their own interpretation of what real adventure travel means' (SNEWS, 2004). However, what this chapter has shown is that adventure is an incredibly diverse and diffuse concept that is highly context dependent. There are some core elements to adventure such as uncertainty, risk (real or perceived), difference, and escape, but what matters most is the individual exploration that can result. As Eassom (1993: 27) suggested, 'what price a ripe old age in the sterilised bubble, when there is the temptation of adventure on the outside and a short sharp dose of Life?' It may be apparent that this chapter has included very little discussion of danger in relation to adventure, when that may be an element that is traditionally thought of being closely allied to its practice. Indeed many of the early discussions of adventure place danger at the heart of understanding the adventure experience, and management of danger remains at the core of many adventure tourism businesses. However, as a number of contemporary authors such as Varley have shown, it is not really danger that drives adventure participation, being 'too narrow … to understand and develop concepts of adventurous leisure' (2011: 86).

Advocating a broad understanding of adventure also calls for broad participation. Indeed, as societies and governments look towards ensuring the mental and physical health of their populations, adventurous exploration has an important role to play in their future sustainability. Initiatives such as the Outdoors and Health Network in the UK underlined this aspect (Outdoors and Health Network, 2012). Certainly the adventure industry is expected to continue its growth in size and diversity and it is important that the academic and industry understanding of the adventure sector and the broader adventure phenomenon are taken seriously. This collection is part of a growing adventure tourism literature that illustrates the potential richness of academic study in this area. However, in this quest we should take care to properly situate adventure tourism within broader leisure/tourism frameworks. Contemporary travellers frequently wear 'multiple hats', engaging with a variety of touristic experiences, some of which may be deemed adventurous, some which may not. However, understanding how these experiences fit together is important for academics, destinations and practitioners alike. Indeed, failure to do may mean that we will miss the greatest potential contribution of adventure tourism study, in highlighting how marginal practices are often at the core of all tourism desires. The processes of crossing space and the desire for difference are fundamental to adventure and tourism alike.

2 The adventure enigma

Patterns of participation in mountain-based adventure tourism in Britain

Paul Beedie

Introduction

The conquest and subjugation of mountains – from the Golden Age of Alpine exploration in the middle of the nineteenth century (Frison-Roche, 1996) to the tabularisation of Scottish mountains over 3000 feet as 'Munroes' (Lorimer and Lund, 2003) – has coincided with the modernist ambition of control and organisation. The certainties of this age generated relatively stable forms of identity, notably, in the field of adventurous exploration, that of mountaineer. As characteristics of postmodernism emerge, the clarity and precision commensurate with the modernist ideal has been compromised and, as Bauman (1991) argues, replaced with an ambivalence predicated on a destabilisation of social structures that opens up a whole host of possibilities for identity formation through the promotion of individualisation. The two social developments that impact upon the identity of mountaineer are the management of risk and the rise of consumer society (Bauman, 2001; Beck, 1992). This chapter is concerned with the patterns of participation in mountain-based adventure activities generated by these two characteristics of the late modern age. The discussion has a particular concern with the phenomenon of adventure tourism because it is through the emergence of adventure products that it becomes possible to see the conflation of risk management and consumption in ways that represent this ambivalence. The modern world has become fluid and individualised so that, as the securities and stability of traditional forms of identity in the adventure field are undermined new possibilities are created generating a disruption to established social patterns. Thus, a tension exists between the 'old' and the 'new', and adventure tourism is the flux in the mix.

In adventure tourism, commercial and business interests use modern technologies and media to promote adventure activities that (mostly) offer short and intense packages of excitement with a closer proximity to certainty of outcome – because of the way risk is controlled – than the original meaning of adventure. Technology-driven access to destination and participant images reinforces traditional views of adventure as 'wildness' but the discursive rhetoric is of risk management and control. The double impact of risk controls and commercial expediency turns adventure into packaged commodities. In this way, the needs of a paying clientele are both created and met by commercial interests. However, when the social organisation of adventure activity participation is scrutinised it becomes clear that whilst there are emergent characteristics commensurate with increased mobilities in the twenty-first century (Urry, 2000), there are also many resilient characteristics that sustain patterns of social organisation from the past. In the contemporary way of thinking, adventure is promoted as a lifestyle choice, however, this can only have mass popular appeal if the risk integral to the original idea of adventure as uncertainty of outcome is controlled. The suggestion that adventure tourism products demonstrate a 'public secret' (Fletcher, 2010) such that participants can be both at risk and safe at the same time has been promoted as being consistent with the demotion of adventure lifestyles to the superficial, ephemeral and free-floating shallowness of postmodernism. However, the complex interaction of the ideological, the experiential and the virtual across the range of possibilities deployed under the catch-all of adventure tourism suggest the need for a more nuanced consideration of patterns of participation in adventure activities. To this end, the concept of the 'sociations' is developed as a conceptual framework for illuminating the modernism–postmodernism tensions that are evidenced in the rapid growth of adventure tourism. The next section sets out an example of the social patterning of mountaineering.

Social patterns in mountaineering

In his book about the famous Scottish climber John Cunningham, Jeff Connor (1999) describes how Chris Bonington 'integrated' himself into the close circle that was the Creagh Dhu climbing club. The club drew its members from Glasgow and in the 1950s and 1960s these were staunchly working-class people, rather like the English contemporary Rock and Ice Climbing Club in Manchester which could list the famous artisans Don Whillans and Joe Brown amongst its membership. Connor cites an incident at the Creagh Dhu climbing hut in Glencoe called Jacksonville when Bonington first appeared:

> Scottish climbing had Christian John Storey Bonington as the embodiment of the snotty, arrogant English, the very name being sufficient to raise sneers and snarls north of the border. Bonington's ability to make a healthy living out of mountaineering, his high profile and his comfortable, southern middle-class background certainly brought out the worst prejudices of the working-class Glaswegians ... he was definitely not a man who had come up the hard way, an unforgiveable failing in their book.
>
> (Connor 1999: 85)

The climbing world of this time was small and networked because climbers gravitated to where the new routes were to be made in Scotland (e.g. Ben Nevis and Glencoe), Wales (e.g. the Llanberis Pass and Clogwyn d'ur Arddu on Snowdon), the Peak District (e.g. Stanage and Froggatt Edges) and the Lake District (e.g. the Langdale valley and east face of Sca Fell). Everyone knew, or had heard of the prominent climbers. Rivalries were considerable, both personal and national, and competition for status commonplace. Climbing groups formed around clubs which operated from fixed bases in the big cities and organised meetings in the famous climbing locations in British mountains and often owned climbing huts in these wild places. The lifestyle choice was austere and hardship was an integral part of the climbing experience. The social organisation of climbers in this way generated loyalty, allegiance to certain locations and an acceptance of the unwritten rules of being a climber or mountaineer. The club structure often existed around class distinctions and was male dominated. Membership was exclusive of the casual climber and other non-serious mountain users because becoming a club member required nomination by an existing member and scrutiny of the applicant's credentials by committee.

Fifty years later, in the present day, there is still evidence of this resilient social organisation: the British Mountaineering Council (BMC) for example operates as the representative body for climbers and their clubs through nine local areas (BMC, n.d.). Whilst the antipathy towards Bonington by the Creag Dhu can undoubtedly be partly explained by a combination of class and nationalistic prejudices, Bonington, as arguably the first high-profile professional mountaineer in Britain, recognised the potential of mountain recreation to be more than a sport in that it could, if it was developed using business logic, support economic development. He is also an individual, not a club, and through his expeditions and climbing activities has captured the *zeitgeist* of the times. Bauman (2001: 7), paraphrasing Marx, argues that: 'the times of "life politics" demand ... that people make their lives but not under conditions of their choice'. Yet it would be overly simplistic to assume that in Bonington's life commercial expediency has overtaken his lifestyle choice – for one thing, despite finally succumbing to the 'need' to actually stand on the summit of Everest in 1985 rather than logistically co-ordinate attempts on unclimbed routes up the mountain, he has a CV of mountaineering and climbing first ascents that indicate extensive engagement with objective risk (Curran, 1999). Bauman's *conditions* under which mountaineering takes place, that is the social structuring frameworks, may have changed, but this does not necessarily mean that all forms of identity construction are destabilised by the mobile and fluid social circumstances of the present.

Paradoxically, mountaineering has contributed to the social mobilities that sustain these fluid and socially destabilised conditions. Mountaineers might be thought of as agents of globalisation, particularly in the way developed countries such as Britain spread its sporting values through its drive for economic dominance and trading preferences at the height of the British Empire in late Victorian times. Cultural confrontation was integral to these complex processes, which are ongoing, as mountaineering demonstrated its utility to the empire builders by literally exploring, surveying and mapping the great blanks on the existing maps (Macfarlane, 2003) and thus providing a catalyst for the ensuing processes of colonisation and economic exploitation. Additionally, the great Victorian explorers and mountaineers epitomised the qualities commensurate with leadership such as vision, determination, organisation and an educated rationality. Thus, mountaineering can claim a long history and this has generated a sense of tradition and a set of culturally embedded social mores. The Victorian mountaineers were a product of their age and their work – as in the conquest of high mountains – was located in the expanse of the modern world (Giddens, 1990) and its drive for organisation and rationality consistent with control of risk.

However, there are at least two limitations of this neat picture. First, the sport of mountaineering was both within and without the sporting lexicon: no 'rules' as such were written down about how mountaineers should conduct themselves in the face of a mountaineering challenge but an emergent set of ethics was a part of the tradition and fiercely defended (Tejada-Flores, 1978) by those who considered themselves to be mountaineers. But the crucial difference with other sports is that people who climb risk serious harm and, in some cases death – the history of mountaineering and its protagonists clearly shows the dangers (Frison-Roche, 1996; see Wells (2001) and Thompson (2010) for a particular focus on British mountaineers). Not surprisingly, therefore, the early mountaineers were both civil servants (e.g. George Everest) and adventurers. Second, society has moved forward in almost every sense – economically, educationally, socially and technologically – in the last 100 years and, in the context of this shrinking and accelerating world, boundaries become fluid and ambivalence prevails. Bauman (1991) identifies ambivalence as a symptom of disorder generated by the possibility of assigning an object to more than one category. Classification – a central tenet of modernism – requires acts of inclusion and exclusion. As society evolves so do the classification possibilities until, Bauman argues, boundaries necessarily dissolve in a plethora of flows and mobilities leading to ambivalence that can only be resisted by further classification. This tension, when applied to definitions of selfhood generates contestation of identity, and, of particular interest here, inclusion and exclusion from the social world of mountaineering.

To understand the way mountaineering identity construction has been influenced by social, cultural and economic change, there is a need to position mountain adventure tourism in its social context. Hetherington (1996: 42–43) suggests that: 'non-essentialist conceptions of identity recognise the idea that identities are not innate and essential but derive from a play of difference within identity positions which are articulated through a dialogue between their constituent parts'. It is Hetherington's (1996) concept of the sociation (a group of people) as *bund*, developed by Urry (2000) in his conception of mobilities for the twenty-first century, that becomes useful in explaining the new social patterns in mountaineering. In essence, adventure tourists who aspire to climb and thus align with the identity of mountaineer might be considered as a *bund* in keeping with the transitory and mobile lifestyle choices people can make. The sub-theme of this discussion is the way the relationship between risk and adventure has been influenced by risk management strategies emerging from the social conditioning of 'risk society' (Beck, 1992; Furedi, 2007), and in particular how adventure tourism has shaped this social dynamic. Varley (2006a: 185–186) captures the centrality of this underlying idea: 'in a risk society immersed in a culture of fear and insecurity regarding the hidden danger lurking in our everyday lives, people tend to turn to the licensed, risk-free marketplace products rather than attempting to go it alone'. In this respect, a combination of identity construction through *group* experiences in an environment shaped by market forces operating in a context of *risk management* forms the basis for a discussion which aims to illuminate mountain-based adventure tourism in Britain today.

Adventure forms and tourism

Zweig (1974) claims that the possibilities of adventure lie within us all; however, the use of this term is not without its contradictions as Price (2000) explains that adventures cannot be planned, they can only happen and thus the whole notion of authentic and non-manufactured experience is nonsensical in the light of adventure being defined as 'uncertainty of outcome' (Miles and Priest, 1999). Adventure is, however, a malleable term constantly being redefined as social, cultural and political landscapes change and that it is constituted of four overlapping forms: education, recreation, sport and tourism (Beedie, 2008). All four forms of adventure have a relationship with risk (Lupton, 1999) but the characteristic way that objective (hard) risk is typically managed in ways that produce degrees of (soft) perceived risk (Gardner, 2008; Thompson, 2010) is particularly evident in the adventure as tourism form.

Although there is literature illuminating adventure in all four of the forms, it is adventure education that has provided the most robust theoretical and conceptual tools for investigating adventure (see, for example Mortlock, 1984; Miles and Priest, 1999 and Varley, 2006b for a critical evaluation of much of this literature). Swarbrooke and team (2003: 3–37) devote much energy to categorising adventure as tourism but rely on adventure education precedents. This illustrates the complexity of attempting to capture the essence of this broadly defined area. This lack of consensus in the definition of adventure tourism, both academically and within the industry (TIG, 2010; Page *et al.*, 2006) alludes to Bauman's ambivalence in its quest for categorisation. British mountain-based adventure tourism is thus a broad term which spans a range of activities and interests. It can include:

- Walking/climbing: mountain walks/treks, long distance trails, rock climbing and mountaineering.
- Cycling/biking: cycle touring and mountain biking.
- River activities: canoeing, kayaking, rafting and canyoning.
- Marine activities: sailing, kayaking, surfing, coasteering and diving.
- Wildlife/nature watching: boat and vehicle excursion and walking.
- Snow activities: skiing, snowboarding, ski-touring, snow-shoeing, ice climbing.

This list shows that mountaineering is far from being clearly bounded and includes snow-based and rock-based skiing and climbing activities as well as walking, hiking and biking.

Adventure tourism and risk

Risk management is central to adventure tourism development and part of the attraction for people is that the management principle connects with the behaviours we learn from childhood. For Beck (1992), risk is the defining characteristic of contemporary society. In a 'risk society', social norms become culturally accepted practices prescribed by building structures via the processes of socialisation. This engenders the propensity to stay within normative, safe and familiar boundaries of established patterns of play; and parents and teachers become aware that they must avoid subjecting children to unnecessary risks. According to Scott (2000), adolescents in today's society are living in circumstances that differ from those experienced by previous generations, and are socialised by structures operating in the context of a risk (averse) society in which accidents are considered unacceptable rather than unfortunate events (Furedi, 2007). Furedi shows that Beck's risk society impacts at a local level because the negative mindset it generates overrides the empirical evidence which demonstrates our everyday lives are safer than ever before: bureaucratic responses of risk management multiply and we become excessively risk averse. Concern over autonomy is a reoccurring theme in the work of Gardner (2008) and Furedi (2007). Douglas (1992) argues that the shift towards a global society has freed individuals from the constraints of local community, but at the same time weakened the traditional forms of protection and support. If people are cut loose from traditional social anchors then risk assumes a more significant social place in everyday behaviours and choice. Giddens (1990) is one of many commentators to demonstrate that one of the consequences of modernity is reliance upon 'experts' generated in part by a search for ontological security in an individualised risk society.

Bauman (2001: 68) takes this argument further when he suggests: 'needs creation is today taking the place of normative regulation, advertising replaces ideological indoctrination and seduction is substituted for policing and coercion'. He argues that our social integration into contemporary society is through our role as consumers. Bauman (2001: 69) further suggests: 'we speak of risks whenever it is impossible to precisely predict the outcome of actions we intend to undertake'. His argument suggests that the consequences of being 'free-floating' in the ambivalence of postmodernism is that we are forced to turn to the market of commodified goods to seek out a sense of identity. Adventure has immense appeal as a neo-tribal sociation that has the potential, by drawing on traditions that are discursively developed, to reduce 'risk' in its broadest sense and provide an 'anchor' or secure base in a world of free flowing lifestyle choices. This can only happen if the participant feels 'safe' in undertaking the adventure activity: herein lies a central paradox of participation in adventure activities.

The freer we are to operate agency and make lifestyle choices, the less certain we become about dealing with the social risks inherent in that choice. Being less sure of ourselves, we are more likely to defer to experts in the field. In a key study concerning adventure as business, Robert Fletcher (2010) reinforces the importance of this circumstance for the efficient functioning of adventure tourism. Fletcher (2010: 7–8) argues that: 'adventure tourism involves a *public secret* in which both providers and consumers discuss their experiences as an authentic adventure while at the same time all maintain that the experience is not "really" an adventure at all'. By developing Taussig's use of the concept the *public secret*, Fletcher is able to argue that the risk management controls commensurate with adventure tourism as an industry today means that adventure tourists do not have to choose between security and risk but can actually: 'sustain the contradictory ideas that they are safe and in danger at once' (Fletcher, 2010: 10). Drawing upon his own research into white water rafting, he argues that public secrecy in adventure tourism comprises three dimensions: first, providers and clients construct the trip as an adventure when it is not an adventure at all; second, providers and clients speak as if the trip is both dangerous and safe at the same time and third, both providers and clients describe the clients' active participation as integral to the trip when it is irrelevant.

Whilst there is some utility in using this conception to illuminate adventure tourism participation, there are reasons for caution. Fletcher is recounting his experiences in rafting, a growing adventure activity precisely because it offers a veneer of adventure in a situation of visceral experience over which the raft guide (instructor/expert) has almost complete control. McGillivray and Frew (2007), who investigated a white water rafting company in Scotland called Splash, support Fletcher's claims for this particular activity, but it would be simplistic to assume this circumstance transfers to other adventure activities. For example it has been shown (Beedie, 2010) that mountaineering adventure tourism requires levels of skill acquisition from its 'tourist' participants that locates each person on a sliding scale with tourist at one end and mountaineer at the other. The extent to which a client becomes a mountaineer is a variable predicated on that person's experience, propensity to learn and the technical and scale challenges of the mountaineering trip. It is much harder to control variables in some mountain-based adventure tourism when the weather and other mountain conditions may be volatile and a mutual dependence might emerge between guide and client(s).

A further critique of Fletcher concerns the constituents of the 'adventure' itself. Part of the malleability of the term is that 'adventure' is subjective and personalised: as Ogilvie (2000) succinctly argues in relation to the expedition component of the Duke of Edinburgh Award Scheme, just because British wilderness places (particularly the national parks) have become sanitised with car parks, valley campsites with hot showers, engineered paths and signposted trails which make fewer navigational demands upon hikers, this does not mean that the young participants are not having an adventure. In this circumstance, despite the risk management controls integral to the safe organisation of these expeditions the emotional feedback from stretching the physical demands put on the body, together with decision making – sometimes in the face of unpredictable weather – might generate a sense of adventure that most definitely exists but is *relative* to the risk managed environment in which the expeditions are taking place. The same argument can be extended to adult participants: the conditions under which adventure is experienced are changing but the activity can still appear to be an adventure to the participants. In effect the participant constructs a sense of adventure that is *subjective* whilst at the same time adventure providers manage the *objective* risks in that particular setting. In adventure tourism, the participant transfers the risk from self to operator and in doing so changes the constituent elements of identity formation: when it is no longer essential to engage with the gravitas of being a mountaineer (including skill acquisition, technical handling of navigation, ropes and harnesses, judgement of objective dangers, incremental gaining of experience over time, understanding of weather and many other elements) to enjoy mountain-based activities, a participant has fewer social 'anchors' and more room for social manoeuvre as identity moves from the collective to the individual.

Adventure tourism mobilities

Urry (2000: 35) explains that accelerated reconfigurations of time and space have created mobile social patterns. Flows consist of movements of people, images, information, money and others that move within and across national borders. Urry argues (2000: 36) that this creates, for people, new opportunities and desires but also risks. Nevertheless, these developments include cheap overseas travel. Urry summarises:

> These flows thus produce the hollowing out of existing societies, especially as a plethora of 'sociations' have developed, concerned to reflect upon, to argue against, to retreat from, to provide alternatives to, to campaign for, these various flows, often going beyond the limits of the societal region. This generates within any existing 'society', a complex, overlapping, disjunctive order, of off-centredness, as these multiple flows are chronically combined and re-combined across times and spaces often unrelated to the regions of existing societies.
>
> (Urry, 2000: 36)

The consequences for tourism are self-evident as its central concerns are with the socio-spatial practices involved in travelling. Urry's discussion of collective identity, as in community (2000: 133–135) promotes the notion as problematic. Communities may be created by geographical proximity but with limited or no social relations, or by a bounded set of interrelationships between local groups and institutions, or by a shared sense of 'communion', that is, a sense of personal ties and belonging amongst members. Each conception is problematic primarily because it does not consider mobilities of senses, times, objects and discourses. Pursuing such a critique creates an opportunity to see communities as something that bears little relation to 'ascribed geographical propinquity' (Urry, 2000: 142).

Alternatively, neo-tribal communities are not necessarily geographically bounded but are bonded and networked in ways commensurate with their

common sense of purpose and thus belonging: these communities include voluntary organisations, travellers and leisure groups. Many are premised on a culture
of resistance as in environmental pressure groups such as Surfers Against
Sewage. Hetherington (1996: 40) likens these sociations to *Bund* or *Bunde* as:
'an elective, unstable, charismatic, intensely affectual form of sociation that provides its members with a community of feeling'. The term is drawn from early
German youth groups, the *Wandervogel*, who roamed Bohemian forests in small
groups bonded by a fellowship, mobile communion and a search for an authentic
recreation. Hetherington goes on to explain that such *Bunde* set a context for
identity formation but are a form of sociation that requires: 'intense emotional
identification with others and offers a high degree of a sense of belonging'
(ibid.), and, crucially, because these *Bunde* require social maintenance their affiliation, and therefore their cohesive capacity: 'is a transitory sociation liable to
break down or be routinized into more stable forms over time ... the group is
held together through subcultural forms of identification' (ibid.).

Thus, although they may leave at any time, people remain in such sociations in
part because of the emotional satisfaction they derive from common goals and
shared social experiences. Additionally people might feel empowered by inclusion
and they might provide relatively safe places for identity building. People are freed
from compulsory work to pursue their 'enthusiasms' through such sociations and
can utilise technologies of communication to do so. The conceptualisation works
well for new age travellers (Hetherington, 1996) and a multitude of other groups
which might include free festivals, rural fairs, rave culture, historical re-enactment
groups, peace conveys and animal rights groups (Urry, 2000) but is the concept a
useful way of thinking about adventure tourists, especially those concerned with
walking, biking and sailing amongst and climbing mountains? Of particular note is
the notion of 'belonging' because the elective dimension of potential adventure
tourist sociations requires admission to a long-standing and more established tradition of mountain-based adventure activities.

Ad-sociations and adventure tourism

In her book *Wild: An Elemental Journey* Jay Griffiths (2007: 84–85) reminds us:
'We were not born for pavements and escalators but for thunder and mud. More.
We are animal not only in body, but in spirit'. As technologies and mobilities
increase the speed at which we live our lives and the levels of comfort therein so
we become more distanced from the visceral and the elemental. Yet the enduring
appeal of adventure activities suggests that atavistic forces might still be a
human driver: it is social activity and cultural sophistication that has distanced
us from these primal motivations. In the modernist ambition to be risk averse,
adventure has been reformulated as something that can be controlled, and this, in
turn, is creating new ways that people can organise themselves in their sport and
leisure choices.

The concept of the *bund* works when applied to sociations that are lifestyle
choices predicated on a person's commitment to a cause or social field such as

Hetherington's (1996) study of new age travellers. The affiliation is clear and the person is free to leave at any time, presumed to move permanently back towards the centre of mainstream social life. However, in adventure-based pursuits the affiliation is the experiential dimension in which a person has to engage: 'being' has to be demonstrated by 'doing'. Additionally, in keeping with the fluidity of contemporary social patterns, the affiliation might be defined by intense periods of action interspersed with time spent in quotidian social regimes. In this respect the adventure lifestyle choice has itself become ambivalent and its sociations more loosely defined in various ways.

When a person is introduced to outdoor climbing by buying a guided package from a qualified adventure tourism operator such as Jagged Globe or Foundry Mountain Activities, that person commonly builds skills and experience through participation that facilitate independent trips with friends who may or may not be members of a climbing club. One of the crucial differences between climbing as an adventure product and activities such as bungy jumping and white water rafting is the progression that is built into the activity. Put simply, there are more opportunities for progression, advancement and (adventure) career development in activities such as climbing, mountaineering and kayaking than there are in the intense 'buzz' experiences of abseiling, bungy jumping and zip-wires/aerial ropes courses. This might be explained by the established longevity and the gravitas of history that shapes the traditional adventure sports and, in particular, the resistance of those whose identity is deeply established as climber, moun- taineer, caver and so forth to any developments that might threaten the value system of the activity and diminish its adventurous appeal. Commercial develop- ments are thus viewed with caution precisely because commercial activity only flourishes in adventure activities that are almost completely risk managed.

The implications of these differences are important for the sociations that develop through participation in adventure tourism products. Because of the dis- tinctive experiential experience of adventure activities such groups might be con- ceived as 'adventure sociations' (ad-sociations). These temporary social groupings are emotionally bonded by the experience but people do not change their lives to become members, rather, unlike the original concept of the Bund, having had the experience they return to normal life until such as time as a new gathering of the ad-sociation can occur. The strength and durability of the ad-sociation comes from the potential progression the central or core activity can offer to its members. Thus, the ad-sociation might be seen as the mechanism that both links the past with the potential development of that adventure activity in the future.

This might be understood as a sliding scale which extends Varley's (2006a) 'Adventure Experience Continuum'. At the left side there are individualised experiences of manufactured adventure, commonly short lived but adrenaline surging activities such as bungy jumping, abseiling and zip-wires. Here the experience is so brief and singular that, although the symbolic exchange poten- tial of the photographs, videos and memorabilia is high (McGillivray and Frew, 2007), enduring ad-sociations are unlikely to form because to have accom- plished the activity is to 'tick the box': the experience is diversionary and not socially binding. Moving rightwards brings activities such as white-water rafting. The activity is (certainly in a British setting) highly managed and risk controlled but the participants, although needing minimum skill and experience, are at least paddling as a group and sharing the challenge. The potential exists for *ad-sociations* but, as the activity is commonly set up as a commercial business – with similar symbolic exchange potential to other activities at the left end of Varley's continuum – and progression is limited, the commonest way that rafting is used in a socially constructive way is via management training courses, executive away days or friendship reunions. These are not *ad-sociations* because there is nothing sustainable *through* the engagement of adventure.

Moving to the right end of the scale means to engage with high-risk activities that are problematic to sell as a commercial product because of the scale of the undertaking, the skill and fitness levels required, the location and the objective dangers of the setting. The people who operate in this frontier of adventure exploration have a strong propensity to form *ad-sociations*. This can be illustrated in a British context by the example of caving. Apart from the highly tourist orientation of short strolls into show caves such as those of Cheddar Gorge in Somerset, and acknowledging that there are short adventure education caving journeys regularly made by outdoor centres in limestone areas such as the White Peak of Derbyshire, the Mendip Hills and parts of South Wales, Lancashire and Yorkshire, there are no British commercial caving businesses through which adventure tourists can buy an adventure caving experience. There are reasons for this, including the potential for caves to flood, access difficulties above and below ground, the delicate nature of the cave environment and its formations, the technical demands of working ropes and ladders and the sheer unpleasantness of grovelling around in the dark. Yet the caving communities (somewhat regionalised because of the geographical distribution of porous rock) are among the strongest *ad-sociations*. Perhaps because of the lack of commercial potential for adventure caving, its participants are genuinely following a lifestyle choice and building an identity that through a shared experience of exploration (mapping the underground frontier) and physical graft (as in digging out passages to allow human entry). In the 'Three Counties' exploratory link up (Wainwright, 2011), several teams worked on different contact points to make the breakthrough; long hours were spent underground in cold, wet and muddy conditions that bring to mind Griffiths' (2007) allusion to humans as 'wild' ('born for thunder and mud'). These people are networked and organised but, following intense days together, return to their normal lives and spend days or weeks or sometimes months and years without doing any caving: but the *ad-sociation* remains robust and is sustained by a value system and a team spirit bonded to the common ambition of cave exploration which implicitly engages the original concept of adventure as uncertainty of outcome.

Somewhere in the middle, between the left and the right of the scale, lies the potential for other *ad-sociations* but the extent to which these are realisable in practice will depend upon a person's view of adventure and their sense of adventure 'career'. For an *ad-sociation* to form there is a need for sustainable endeavour and a form of bonding capital drawing on the shared experiences of the past and the potential to extend these experiences in the future. Adventure careers can take a number of forms. When adventure is seen as a symbolic experience to be purchased and transferred to other forms of capital (e.g. social or cultural capital – commonly seen in the guidance set out in the plethora of books on the '1001 adventures to have before you die' theme) then the career becomes the aspiration to accumulate 'hits' that can be ticked off a list: a bungy jump, an abseil, a coasteering trip, a coast-to-coast cycle ride, walking the Pennine Way, an ascent of Ben Nevis. This form of adventure is catered for by adventure tourism operators and does not lend itself to *ad-sociation* formation. When adventure is sparked by the desire to do more in a particular activity following an introduction via an adventure tourism experience then this offers much more potential for social cohesion. Climbing and mountaineering illustrate this well. A person may be introduced to the activity at an indoor climbing wall but then want to progress to real rock, and then to bigger climbs and mountains: given the ethical code set out by Tejada-Flores (1978), risk and challenge can be retained in climbing by electing to climb to a certain set of 'rules' and thus the possibilities for progression are theoretically limitless. Climbers and mountaineers, like cavers, eschew commercial developments and resist risk management strategies that limit the adventure of what they might plan; for example, it is not yet a requirement to register with an authority before journeying in British National Parks, which is not the case in other countries. The bonding that provides the affiliation for the *ad-sociations* comes from the shared adventure.

When it is the adventure itself that forms the bond this can become a career in its own right opening up the possibilities of multi *ad-sociation* membership. It is not uncommon in Britain to find activity crossover amongst adventurously orientated people – cavers who climb, fell runners who paddle and parachutists that BASE jump. This is well illustrated by the British climber and mountain guide Andy Cave who recently undertook some technically demanding caving trips and then wrote about his experience in a way that showed he had been reminded of what it meant to be a relative novice in an adventure activity (Cave, 2011). However, such people are well networked into the outdoor community – some have websites, many others contribute to blogs and tweets in ways that circulate ideas, images, plans and reflections on the adventure experience. This is not the same as self-promotion, although by definition to be networked in this way does raise a person's profile in the network. Adventure careers, then, can utilise networking technologies and other mobilities but it is the interpretation of the term adventure that becomes central to the social organisation commensurate with the activity. In this respect *ad-sociations* might be seen as a continuation of the social exclusivity that Christian Bonington found difficult to penetrate in his overtures to the Creagh Dhu climbing group.

Conclusions

The central premise of modernity in clarity of social structure, integration and identity has been overtaken by a consumer society that purports to deliver autonomy, freedom and choice but actually generates ambivalence and uncertainty. The social mobilities made possible by time–space compression and technical innovation have an impact on all aspects of social life. A sense of community based on geographical proximity and shared interests has been replaced by patterns much more fluid and mobile which, while providing a temporary refuge from the risks generated by the uncertainties of postmodernism, only offer degrees of identity security because identity is defined by consumption. Consumption is ongoing as our life-projects must also be and in this respect the accumulation of capital becomes a form of career that is as evident in leisure as it is in work.

Adventure recreation is a social field where there is evidence of social structures that are both *resilient* (in that they reinforce existing social boundaries) and *emergent* (in that new forms of adventure activities can be experienced, notably those promoted by commercial interests). This modernism–postmodernism tension can be illustrated by the development of the concept of the *Bund* or sociation through an application to this social field. It has been suggested that the experiential nature of an adventure experience provides for the possibilities of *ad-sociations* to form, that is, a *Bund* that does not require a full immersion in a lifestyle choice (however temporarily) but rather is an alternative social identity that becomes one of several hats that are worn as the person moves between different social settings. The *ad-sociation* is potentially revisited over long periods of time but only becomes sustainable if there is sense of ongoing progression for the person evidenced by the emotional bonding commensurate with engaging in non-manufactured adventure activities. The commodified adventure products that offer an individualised experience with a limited or no sense of adventure career development in a risk managed setting cannot sustain *ad-sociations* and therefore rely on the novelty of creating 'new' attractions (such as longer and faster zip-wires) to sustain the market of mass thrill seeking that become attractive to many because of the passive and mundane lives that most people lead. It is these heavily managed and controlled settings that support the suggestion of the 'public secret', i.e. that adventure participants can be both at risk and safe at the same time.

In this respect, it is the level of engagement with risk – indeed the whole idea of personal challenge – that becomes the variable that determines the existence and durability of *ad-sociations*. Paradoxically, the stronger the engagement by the individual in real objective risk and danger the greater the sense of security generated by membership of the *ad-sociations* defining such groups. Such groupings, and the way the members organise themselves are more fluid and mobile than the more rigid social forms that are gradually being replaced (e.g. the climbing club structure). However, although there has clearly been considerable growth in the commodification of adventure through an expanding adventure tourism industry which has challenged the original idea of adventure as uncertainty of outcome, there are indications that resistance to this momentum exists and that the spirit of adventure is alive in British wild places. However, because of the way 'scapes' are configured and flows (e.g. of images, money and people) facilitated, one consequence is a reinforcement of the iconic (and therefore desirable to visit) status of existing hubs of adventure. Commercial interests are therefore still able to shape social configurations of adventure as in competitive economic concerns with establishing an 'adventure capital of the UK': market forces are the drivers of adventure tourism and the latter is about much more than access to an adventure activity, it is about the infrastructure of support for the activities (e.g. accommodation, restaurants, equipment and clothing suppliers and other retail outlets) that collectively facilitate the generation and reinforcement of adventure identities.

3 Discovering what matters in a perfect day

A study of well-being of adventure tourists

Sebastian Filep, Louise Munk Klint,
Dale Dominey-Howes and Terry DeLacy

Introduction

If our lives are dominated by a search for well-being then perhaps few activities reveal as much about this quest as our travels (De Botton, 2003). This chapter deals with the following question: What psychological value do tourists get out of adventure holiday experiences? This is a complex question which few psychologists or tourism experts can answer with conviction. For the purposes of this chapter, the term psychological value refers to an individual sense of well-being or happiness – two terms that can be used interchangeably (Seligman, 2002). Clearly, the core difficulty in answering the question is in defining well-being (Seligman, 2011). Another difficulty in answering the question is that adventure tourist experiences are very diverse (Pomfret, 2006; Weber, 2001). Weber (2001) highlights this heterogeneity noting that they include pursuits involving risk and uncertainty (such as kayaking, hang-gliding or rock climbing) and more passive tourist pursuits (such as individual overland travel). Pomfret (2006) similarly highlights this diversity and differentiates adventure tourist experiences into land-based (e.g. mountain biking), water-based (e.g. scuba diving), air based (e.g. parachuting) and mixed (e.g. gap year travel). So each experience is different and would have different psychological impacts on individuals.

Nevertheless, there is a sound basis for arguing that individual, psychological well-being can be explained in terms of common elements, such as positive emotions, meaning or engagement (Seligman, 2002, 2011). Hence, tourist experiences can be investigated in the context of those common well-being elements (Kler and Tribe, 2012). Researchers in neurology have established motivational drivers of play and lust, which are common for all humans and which can be recognised in human brains (Panksepp, 2005). Fredrickson's (2001) seminal work on positive emotions similarly points to four core universal emotions of love, interest, joy and contentment, which are experienced by all humans. In this research, there is an underlying assumption that there is a difference between what is experienced and how something is experienced. While everyone may experience a positive emotion of joy, there are many different situations for experiencing this positive emotion. Similarly, while everyone may gain meaning (a sense of purpose in life) about an activity at some stage of their life (Steger *et al.*, 2006), there are multiple contexts for deriving that sense of meaning. Hence, while a formulaic definition of well-being may not exist, researchers in psychology have started to argue for broad and uniform elements of happiness or well-being (Seligman, 2011). Sociological and anthropological analyses may embellish this individual and almost clinical focus on well-being. These non-psychological analyses are, however, outside the scope of this chapter.

Specifically, we report on an exploratory study that investigated the experiences of a group of adventure tourists and linked them to the established elements of well-being (engagement, relationships, meaning and achievement; Seligman, 2011) to understand the psychological value of the holiday experience. The focus of the investigation was on 14 adventure tourists visiting the Republic of Vanuatu (Figure 3.1), which were selected from a larger group of 22 international tourists. Vanuatu has one of the world's most accessible volcanoes (Yasur volcano, Tanna) and popular wreck dive sites (e.g. President Coolidge shipwreck, Espiritú Santo) making it an important adventure island destination in the Pacific (Harewood *et al.*, 2006). The research study was part of a project

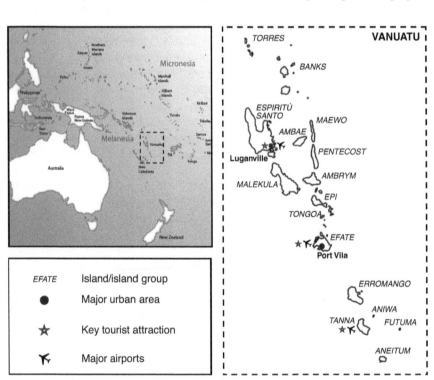

Figure 3.1 Locational map of Vanuatu (source: adapted from Pacific Peoples Partnership, n.d. and World Atlas.com, n.d.).

on visitor experiences and risk perceptions for the Ministry of Tourism of Vanuatu. The fieldwork underpinning this study was conducted in August 2011.

Land-based, air-based, water-based and mixed adventure tourist activities, such as hiking in volcanic and jungle areas, helicopter rides and scuba diving are popular activities by Western tourists in Vanuatu (Vanuatu Tourism Office, 2012). The country has twice been voted the happiest country in the world (Lonely Planet, 2010; Nadkarni, 2007) and the country's tourism slogan is 'Discover What Matters'. No known research, however, exists on the experiences of adventure tourists in Vanuatu using psychological well-being models. This study aims to provide the Ministry with in-depth data on the psychological value of the Vanuatu tourist experience – information that could later inform destination marketing strategies. Although the adventure study component was a minor part of the entire project, the study aimed to provide new information on the experiences of adventure tourists in Vanuatu. Before the study is discussed, a rationale for the choice of well-being elements is provided with reference to previous adventure tourist experience studies.

Tourist well-being and adventure tourist experiences

For a long time, people have assumed that holiday trips make people well or happy. If this were not true, millions of people, despite occasionally feeling frustrated on holidays, would not re-engage in tourism so frequently (Pearce, 2011). Yet, relatively little research exists to substantiate this anecdote or to explain how a holiday experience may be linked to common elements of well-being (Corvo, 2010; Nawijn, 2011; Nawijn and Mitas, 2011; Kler and Tribe, 2012). Part of the problem is the lack of agreement about what common elements constitute well-being. Nawijn and Mitas (2011) highlight this lack of agreement and point to two core distinctions: the eudemonic interpretation, which is typically known as psychological well-being (PWB), and the hedonic interpretation, which is known as subjective well-being (SWB) (Sanjuán, 2011). Christopher and Hickinbottom's (2008) review, similarly, shows that that there are two dominant conceptions of well-being in psychology: the SWB theory, which suggests well-being is mostly pleasure; and second, the authentic happiness theory (Seligman, 2002) and its extension PERMA (positive emotions, engagement, relationships, meaning and achievement) (Seligman, 2011). Seligman's conceptions integrate the hedonic aspects (positive emotions) with the eudemonic aspects (meaning and sense of achievement). In contrast, the SWB view focuses on the hedonic aspects, but is a more established conception of well-being (Diener, 2009). Literature on SWB has flourished since the 1970s. In this tradition, people identify and talk about happiness or well-being in terms of feeling good and feeling bad (Layard, 2005). SWB, thus, includes evaluations of people's moods and feelings and people's judgements of life satisfaction (typically on a scale from zero to ten) (Cummins, 2009).

Both SWB and authentic happiness/PERMA models have been applied to investigations of tourist well-being (Nawijn, 2011), including applications to investigations of well-being of tourist scuba divers (Kler and Tribe, 2012). However Seligman's (2002, 2011) conceptions of well-being have received less attention in adventure tourism contexts (Kler and Tribe, 2012). Researchers in tourism have mostly adopted the emphasis on pleasure (or feeling good) from SWB instead of evaluations of meaning, engagement or achievement (Gilbert and Abdullah, 2004; Corvo, 2010). While SWB's satisfaction with life scales touch on aspects of life meaning in their assessments (for example a rank from zero to ten on satisfaction with spirituality) (Diener, 2009), SWB theory is mostly about what makes people feel good. Recent tourism research has revealed that vacationers are happier than non-vacationers, but that such happiness effects typically do not last long after a holiday ends (Nawijn *et al.*, 2010) as the pleasure effects quickly dissipate.

There is room for Seligman's authentic happiness theory and PERMA model to receive more attention in adventure tourism research. It can be argued that the authentic happiness or PERMA conceptualisation includes more relevant theoretical constructs (positive emotions, engagement and a sense of meaning) that better explain well-being in relation to adventure tourist experiences than SWB. The emphasis on SWB in tourism does not suggest that tourism authors believe that adventure tourist well-being is only pleasure, but that the scales used to analyse well-being through the SWB lens cannot sufficiently assess experiences that are meaningful or engaging. There is a tradition in tourism research of understanding special tourist moments (Mannell and Iso-Ahola, 1987; Hom Cary, 2004) and powerful, engaging, on-site experiences (Han *et al.*, 2005). Some time ago, Botterill (1987) suggested that these unpredictable events and moments often end up being most memorable and gratifying for tourists and should be studied separately. For example, fulfilling mountaineer adventure tourist moments identified in Pomfret's (2006) study were characterised by a sense of flow (high state of engagement – an element of PERMA) in mountaineering. Similarly, Laing and Crouch's (2011) research highlighted the importance of existential authenticity (resembling the meaning element of PERMA) that adventure tourists derived from their frontier tourist experiences. Likewise, in research of independent female tourists and their experiences, Wilson and Harris (2006) showed that meaningful travel centred around three key themes: a search for self and identity; self-empowerment; and connectedness with others/global citizenship – themes that are clearly much less about pleasure and much more about the nature of one's being and existence (meaning).

So it appears the PERMA model is more appropriate than the SWB theory in evaluating the psychological value of adventure tourist experiences in Vanuatu. PERMA allows for a more thorough examination of well-being beyond pleasure. While there is evidence of some elements of PERMA studied separately in evaluations of adventure tourist experiences, the new model has not yet been applied to investigations of the psychological value of adventure tourist experiences. The exploratory study reported in this chapter addresses this literature gap.

Study aim

The aim was to understand the psychological value of the Vanuatu adventure tourist experience for the surveyed group. To address this aim, we sought to examine which PERMA well-being elements were most influential in explaining this value and how the fulfilling experiences were expressed by the adventure tourists. Key attractions and activities that motivated tourists to visit Vanuatu and individual tourist characteristics (such as age, gender and country of origin) were also investigated to gain a profile of the adventure tourists.

Study methods

Twenty-two respondents (11 females and 11 males) agreed to take part in the anonymous study; all participants were over the age of 18. Those who selected that they were motivated to come to Vanuatu for nature and adventure tours were classified as adventure tourists and their responses were chosen for this analysis. There were 14 respondents who selected this option. Out of the 14 (six female and eight male) adventure tourists, 36 per cent were 36–45 years old, followed by the 26–35 age category (27 per cent). Half of the respondents were Australian (seven), while the rest were from New Zealand, the United States, Germany and Finland. Most visitors to Vanuatu are from Australia, New Zealand and other Western countries (Vanuatu National Statistics Office, 2012), so the study's respondents fit this typical visitor profile.

To address the aim, the researchers asked the 14 respondents to describe in writing and then sketch their 'perfect' day in Vanuatu. 'Perfect day' descriptions have been used in the medical field where patients, families, doctors and nurses construct a shared vision of the perfect day for a patient. This shared vision then becomes the foundation of change for the treatment of the patient (Gruber *et al.*, 2003). In the psychology field, perfect-day descriptions have been used to study the well-being of university students. Kurtz (2006) asked her student respondents to describe their perfect days using the following instructions:

> Describe in detail what you would do and how you would allot your time. Attempt to live that day. How did you feel throughout the course of the day? Did you feel happy? How do you feel as you look back over your day? Would you have changed anything? Can you incorporate things that made you happy on that day into your daily life?
>
> (Kurtz, 2006: 4)

Justification for using the perfect-day approach for this study is also found in the psychology literature on fantasies (Roy, 2011). A perfect-day description is a fantasy, as it is an imagination in its extremes and shows how far our minds can stretch beyond the normal and the natural. Roy suggests that fantasy, like imagination and associated creative processes aids us in our mental journey and fantasies trigger positive emotions that help in productivity. Fantasies can also bring out repressed emotions and desires (ibid.).

In our study, the adventure tourists were first provided with a two-page blank writing template and invited to write about their perfect day. As with Kurtz's (2006) study, further written instructions were provided to guide the respondents. But in this case, the instructions more closely resembled PERMA elements and were based on Seligman (2011) instead of Kurtz (2006):

> Think of at least three special, engaging or memorable events or activities during that perfect day. Describe in detail what you would do. This doesn't have to be a real day. You can imagine what your ideal day in Vanuatu would be like.

As opposed to the commonly used in-depth interviews (Patton, 2002; Phillimore and Goodson, 2004), short written descriptions such as these do not need to be transcribed, hence improving the efficiency of data collection. The problem of interviewer bias is reduced or eliminated, as a researcher does not need to construct interview questions and probe his or her respondents (Veal, 2005). The personal written descriptions, thus, allowed for greater spontaneity of expression than structured interviews (Stamou and Paraskevopoulos, 2003). Following the written descriptions, the adventure tourists sketched their perfect day in Vanuatu. The value of the sketching exercise was that unarticulated feelings of well-being could be drawn. A similar visual method has been successfully applied in tourism research. In a study of beach images, tourists were asked to draw their ideal beach (Falco-Mammone, 2007). The particular advantage of the sketching activity is to access the data through 'another language'; that of visual images.

Data collection and analysis

Convenience sampling was used (Gray, 2004) and respondents were approached at a tourism establishment frequented by international adventure tourists in central Port Vila. The data was analysed thematically using 'nodes' in the NVivo software (Crowley *et al.*, 2002). The positive emotions element was, however, not assessed. The emphasis of this analysis was on understanding other PERMA elements (engagement, relationships, meaning and achievement), differentiating the analysis from SWB work on moods, feelings and pleasure (Nawijn, 2011). A set of quotes was identified by each co-investigator that resembled the engagement, relationships, meaning and achievement elements. The final set of quotes emerged following a discussion. The concept of theoretical saturation guided the analysis (Strauss and Corbin, 1990; Krueger, 1994). The dominant themes consistently re-occurred after the analysis of the first ten written descriptions.

Study results and discussion

The perfect-day analyses were preceded by analyses of demographic questions and of questions about motivations to visit Vanuatu. Table 3.1 specifies the

Table 3.1 Characteristics of international and adventure tourists

	International tourist		Adventure tourist		All tourists*	
	N = 22	Percentage	n = 14	Percentage	n = 93,960	Percentage
Gender						
Female	10	45.5	6	42.9	—	—
Male	12	54.5	8	57.1	—	—
Age						
18–25	2	9.1	2	14.3	—	—
26–35	6	27.3	3	21.4	—	—
36–45	8	36.4	6	35.7	—	—
46–55	2	9.1	2	14.3	—	—
56 and older	4	18.2	1	7.1	—	—
Nationality						
Australian	12	54.5	7	50.0	57,843	61.6
New Zealander	1	4.5	1	7.1	11,399	12.1
Other	9	40.9	6	42.9	24,718	26.3
Highest level of education achieved						
Masters/PhD	5	22.7	9	64.3	—	—
Bachelor degree/ Honours	11	50.0	2	14.3	—	—
Other tertiary education	3	13.6	1	7.1	—	—
Secondary education	3	13.6	2	14.3	—	—
Primary education	0	0.0	0	0.0	—	—
First visit?						
Yes	17	77.3	12	85.7	—	—
No	5	22.7	2	14.3	—	—

Note
* All international tourists arriving by air to Vanuatu for the year 2011 (based on Vanuatu National Statistics Office, 2012).

demographic characteristics of the adventure tourists and compares them with the other international tourists, who were also surveyed, and all visitors to Vanuatu for the year 2011. As can be seen, the sample was very well educated – 64 per cent of respondents have a Masters or a PhD degree. Twelve out of 14 adventure tourists were on their first visit to Vanuatu and all expressed intention to revisit the country.

Questions about attractions and activities that motivated the visitors to Vanuatu followed. The list of attractions and activities was based on input from the Vanuatu Tourism Office and the Ministry of Tourism. Ten out of 14 of the adventure tourists were attracted by warm sunny beaches, beautiful weather, diving and snorkelling in Vanuatu (in addition to nature and adventure tours). This suggests that the sample most closely resembles Pomfret's (2006) water-based adventure tourists, due to references to diving and water activities. Eight of the adventure tourists were also attracted by the relaxed atmosphere of the destination, possibly suggesting that the friendliness of the local people and the laid-back lifestyle further played a role in the motivations to revisit Vanuatu.

The perfect-day investigations then followed. Results from the sketches and the written descriptions suggests that the engagement and positive relationships elements were the key PERMA well-being elements in understanding the psychological value of the adventure tourist experiences.

Engagement

Engagement (a sense of involvement in an activity or task) was the most common well-being element in the written descriptions. The element was identified 17 times in the 14 written descriptions. Engagement was coded by searching for references to fascination and interest in an activity, based on the definition of this element in Seligman (2002, 2011). In two-thirds of the engagement descriptions, tourists referred to closely observing the natural environment (flora of Vanuatu, the ocean and the waterfalls). This is how a male American adventure tourist described his sense of engagement in the Vanuatu tourist experience:

> Vanuatu is known for high volcanic activity, so my first activity would be to visit Tanna or Ambrym. I would expect to hike through jungles, pass by waterfalls and come to an active volcano. I can imagine watching the lava as the sun sets.

The reference to imagining watching the lava suggests engagement. The women were equally fascinated with the marine natural environments:

> Game fishing – a day or several nights and days fishing from Vila and outlying islands on game fishing boats crewed by Ni-Vanuatu staff. Love being in the ocean, watching land change and birds working bait schools, plus catching fish and eating them.
>
> (Australian female)

For others there was a sense of fascination and interest in the local culture. An American female described her ideal day in the following manner:

> My ideal day would be on a rural island. I would want to stay at a local bungalow that serves local food. During the day, I would want to visit a close-by attraction (such as a village, waterfall or volcano depending on the location) and experience the culture at the same time, either through a guide that can tell custom stories, knows the history of the area and can demonstrate custom arts (sand drawing + custom music) or through a separate cultural event.

Relationships

The tourists also sought to connect with close friends and travel companions and establish positive linkages with the local communities. There were 14 references to this element in the written descriptions of the perfect day. In a recent review of literature about tourists' positive relationships, Pearce (2011: 128) suggests that 'the building of new relationships and the enhancement of existing social bonds are key personal growth opportunities associated with tourism'. The exploratory findings of this study lead to similar conclusions. The tourist group wrote fondly about contact with the locals. This contact created an opportunity for personal development and learning:

> I'd like to visit a local artist or business to make contact, exchange & learn about local life. (e.g. a carving workshop, a coconut oil factory, etc.). In Port Olry we had a 10 year old girl show us fruits/nuts we had never seen before & how to open them. A great one would be to learn/participate in basket weaving & cooking/making lap lap, etc.

Others wanted to connect with fellow travel companions and the locals without necessarily participating in a personal development activity. An Australian female adventure tourist said:

> I would like to be amongst my close friends, and experiencing a shared holiday with them, but also being able to have alone time and meet with the locals.

An American male respondent similarly referred to interactions with the local community, in this case a tribal chief:

> Wake up to a beautiful sunny day in Port Resolution. Dinghy in to the village and speak with Prophet Fred about what he's up to. From there have a nice walk over the mountain to Sulfur Bay. Meet chief Isay & Vitel. Have lunch with them.

Meaning and achievement

The last two coded PERMA elements were meaning and achievement. Achievement can be defined as a sense of accomplishment in an activity or task; and meaning is a sense of purpose in life (Seligman, 2011). The meaning and achievement themes were often expressed in a similar manner and in relation to the same tourist situation. Nevertheless references to meaning were more common (it featured seven times in the 14 written descriptions) than achievement (the theme featured only five times).

This quotation from an Australian female adventure tourist shows how the themes of meaning and achievement were expressed in her perfect-day descriptions:

> Our adventure continues. We fly to Tanna and Mt Yasur. We have free range to explore the areas, finding amazing pockets of red raw nature seeping from the ground. Rumbles under our feet, plumes of smoke against the bluest sky, the addictive smell of sulphur, the knowledge that this is a very special place + what a privilege & lifelong dream it is to be here. We dawdle around, picking up unusual rocks that have long ago spewed from the earth. I scoop up some coarse black sand and let it trickle through my fingers. Nature's caress. I am in heaven. The day lasts forever in my mind. I freeze it and commit all my sensory experiences to memory. I never want to forget this moment. But, we must move on to our tree-house castle. We wander back down, through the lush forest to our magnificent banyan tree-house – we climb the tangled natural ladder, feeling the rumble of the volcano echo through the branches. We curl up together, with the last vision of the day being our view of the streaming volcano out our wooden window. I smile to myself – let's do it all again tomorrow!

Meaning was coded by searching for references to memories (Seligman, 2011): *'The day lasts forever in my mind. I freeze it and commit all my sensory experiences to memory. I never want to forget this moment'*; achievement was coded by searching for references to accomplishment (Seligman, 2011): *'what a privilege & lifelong dream it is to be here'*.

There was a desire for experiences involving risk in the adventure tourists' written references to achievement and meaning. For example, the reference to *'plumes of smoke and the addictive smell of sulphur'*, and feeling the *'rumble of the volcano echo through the branches'* relate to Tucker and Kane's (2004) motivators for the experience of adventure tourism: risk, danger and adrenaline. A male American respondent similarly wanted to *'watch eruptions for a bunch of hours'* during his perfect day in Vanuatu, suggesting a desire for a risky experience. An important implication of this exploratory finding is that pleasure alone did not explain the psychological well-being of the tourists. Experiences of smelling sulphur or smoke were hardly pleasurable but were meaningful. As Jayawickreme *et al.* (2008) point out, people (and hence tourists) are not simply experience machines and, thus, a lifetime of artificially induced positive emotions (pleasure) would not be chosen by many people.

Sketches

Following the (P)ERMA evaluation of the written descriptions of perfect days, an analysis of the sketches was undertaken, based on De Bruycker (2007). Despite arguably helping researchers understand unarticulated sense of well-being, insights from the sketches were limited. The sketches were not very detailed. They are shown in Figure 3.2.

For this group of adventure tourists, sketches of the perfect day consisted of: (1) people, people's possessions and human behaviour (smiley faces, people's belongings and people holding hands); and (2) sketches of environmental characteristics (village houses, volcanic mountains, boats, the sea and local food). This distinction into environment and people features guided the analysis of the sketches, as in De Bruycker's (2007) work on children's perceptions of tourists and their environment.

The sketches show the following. Ten out of 14 respondents sketched images of marine activities. These included images of people (presumably tourists) diving and swimming and environmental characteristics of images of boats and water. In fact, an image of a boat featured in eight sketches. This finding complements the quotes that explained the engagement element – engagement was linked to descriptions of marine activities (sailing, fishing, swimming, snorkelling, diving etc.) and to mindfully observing the natural marine environments (e.g. the ocean and waterfalls). As in the written descriptions of meaning and achievement, there is evidence of depictions of risk. Six out of 14 adventure tourists drew volcanoes erupting with lava and in half of these sketches people were shown climbing the erupting volcanoes. The sketches also resembled the written descriptions about positive relationships. Images of people (presumably both tourists and locals) were found in seven out of the 14 images. People were drawn in groups of two or three indicating interaction (De Bruycker, 2007). Three tourists' sketches of the perfect day showed either a smiley face or a smiley sun, possibly suggesting the friendliness of the locals.

A limitation of the sketch analysis was that the abstract, intangible characteristics (friendliness, safety and atmosphere) were challenging to directly observe in the sketches. Thus, these intangible characteristics of the perfect day were mainly expressed in the written descriptions. Nonetheless, according to Tversky (2002), additions of small arrows or short words that name parts of the sketch could help the researcher extract the unseen from the seen. Nine out of the 14 respondents included short explanations in words to help the researcher understand the ideas behind the sketch. A male New Zealander, for example, only used words and arrows to illustrate the progression of his perfect day in Vanuatu, involving passive activities, such as sleeping, eating and resting, and more active activities, such as running, swimming and walking. Eight respondents included word labels for environmental characteristics (a boat, the ocean, a cafe, local

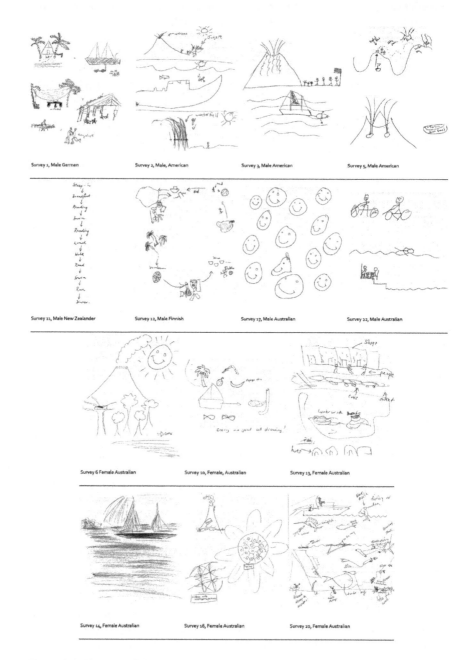

Survey 1, Male German   Survey 2, Male, American   Survey 3, Male American   Survey 5, Male American

Survey 11, Male New Zealander   Survey 12, Male Finnish   Survey 17, Male Australian   Survey 22, Male Australian

Survey 6 Female Australian   Survey 10, Female, Australian   Survey 13, Female Australian

Survey 14, Female Australian   Survey 16, Female Australian   Survey 20, Female Australian

Figure 3.2 Sketches of the perfect day in Vanuatu.

food, volcano, jungle, waterfall, fish) and labels for human behaviour (dancing together, having lunch, hiking, swimming and scuba diving).

Conclusions and implications

The results point to some interesting conclusions in terms of understanding the psychological value of the holiday experience for adventure tourists. Our analysis of the written descriptions of perfect days has shown that engagement and relationships are the dominant well-being elements in the experiences of these tourists. The results are largely in agreement with previous research, although this previous research did not use the PERMA model.

First, as in this study, Ryan's (1995) analysis of white-water rafting experiences of adventure tourists in New Zealand, showed that the state of flow (sense of focus and engagement) was central to explaining the psychological value of tourist experiences. A related concept is mindfulness, characterised by active absorption in an activity, sensitivity to the context and a sense of learning (Langer and Moldoveanu, 2000). Second, as in Jennings *et al.*'s (2008) work, the element of positive relationships featured strongly in the sketches and the written descriptions. Seven out of 14 images contained depictions of people eating food, dancing with the locals and interacting. Lastly, the importance of meaning and achievement in explaining the psychological value is in line with the recent research that applied Seligman's (2002) authentic happiness theory to study tourist experiences of scuba divers. In their qualitative analysis of scuba diving experiences, through in-depth interviews, Kler and Tribe (2012) uncovered eudaimonia (*daimon* being a Greek term for true self) as a core benefit of such experiences. This suggests the fulfilling scuba diving experiences were not just about pleasure but also about a deep sense of meaning.

There are, however, some important limitations to this study. First, while the methods employed were more appropriate than the SWB methods, they are not widely established despite being used previously to study well-being (Kurtz, 2006). The PERMA model (Seligman, 2011) is still in its infancy at the time of writing and its ability to explain the psychological value of tourist experiences needs to be strengthened through future research. Despite the specific instructions to respondents, it was not possible to ascertain from the data if the respondents were referring to a real or an imaginary perfect day in Vanuatu. In other words, this investigation examined both travel motivations and the actual satisfaction with the Vanuatu experience in explaining the psychological value. Diener (2009) suggests one of the ongoing challenges of well-being research is methodological rigour. This leaves room to implement more explicit measures of the individual PERMA elements. For example, for engagement appraisals these measures could include flow state methods (Jackson, 1992; Jackson and Eklund, 2004) or experience-sampling assessments (Schimmack, 2003) or for evaluations of meaning, Meaning in Life Scale (Steger *et al.*, 2006) or autobiographical methods (Duckworth *et al.*, 2005). In addition, Diener *et al.* (2010) have recently proposed a scale that measures all five PERMA elements together

– the Flourishing Scale – albeit further validation and testing is required. The research sample was small with only 14 respondents and the results reported are exploratory. The study was conducted during the tourists' holiday in Vanuatu. Future work could employ similar research strategies to analyse adventure tourists' reflections after the holiday or to assess well-being in the anticipatory travel phase. There is also room for comparative studies with different adventure tourist groups.

Nevertheless, it is hoped that the research has shed new light on the intangible value of adventure holiday experiences. Understanding how intangible factors such as visitors' sense of engagement and sense of meaning are expressed is increasingly seen by marketing experts as more relevant than previously thought (Oh *et al.*, 2007). The consistent, high level of service quality in many visitor contexts can simply no longer be used to differentiate choices for consumers (Mehmetoglu and Engen, 2011). Destinations need to understand and develop a distinct value-added provision for services that have already achieved a consistent, high level of functional quality (Stamboulis and Skayannis, 2003). Tourists, therefore, need to be understood at a deeper, psychological level and this study of visitor experiences addresses this marketing knowledge gap. Methodologically, this exploratory study replaced quantitative motivation appraisals and standard appraisals of visitor satisfaction. The standard satisfaction appraisals typically use service quality scales and ask respondents to rate their levels of satisfaction with parking facilities, signage, toilets and similar instrumental features on a seven-point Likert scale (Archer and Griffin, 2005). While useful for managers, these appraisals cannot uncover the psychological well-being aspects, which were investigated in this study. In this study, the positive relationships that tourists want to build through their contact with the locals, a sense of interest and fascination with the natural environment, and the risk, danger and adrenaline that gives tourists a sense of meaning and achievement were core themes of the perfect day. The adventure tourists' drawings and words helped uncover the psychological value of the adventure tourist experience. They helped us *'discover what matters'* (Vanuatu Tourism Office, 2012).

4 Pushing life to the edge of life

The ability of adventure to take the individual into the world

Georgie Urry

Introduction

Once upon a research project I found myself sitting at the edge of a plane door with only faith that a line was attached to the plane and would pull the ripcord on my parachute the moment I tumbled out. 'Terrified' does not begin to portray the state I was in at that moment. Words simply can't describe it. And what was I researching? My concern as a geographer and social scientist more broadly is with our individual material engagement with the world. So why look to extreme sports to articulate some of the threads running through this politically charged debate?

Extreme sports (as a type of adventure tourism conducted for recreation outside of the realm of the everyday) plug into a huge array of social scientific concerns. Economic questions might vary from how 'adventure' or 'extreme' are defined and packaged for a captive audience to the commoditisation of the environments in which adventurous activities take place. Ideas of journeying might think about where we are escaping from and to in adventurous travel or what we are doing when putting ourselves in extreme situations. Identity considerations might tease apart the social groups formed around certain sports or the gender and age trends seen amongst participants. Further, what identities are constructed or performed through taking up such activities? As a topic for empirical research, extreme adventure is rich with discursive points, many of which feed tangentially into what I want to look at here.

Most importantly for me, though, extreme sports bear certain elements that prompt discussion surrounding how it is that the physical fleshy body plays mediator between that which is outside and that which is commonly referred to as 'thought', overcoming a dualism that has pervaded Western tradition for centuries. Two subsidiary points follow from this. First, our body is finitely capable of conducting lively engagement with the world. Death is an unquestionable part of life. In activities such as skydiving we seek out the adventure of pushing to the edge of life before withdrawing to safety. How is this limit point pertinent to a perception of being in the world? Second, the porosity of our body to 'an outside' leaves it vulnerable to subjectifying forces that seek to control life, that which Foucault terms biopower (1990). Biopower seeks to proliferate life and this is evidential in safety technologies that are widespread throughout Western institutions. Again, then, a question arises, what is it about life now and its conflict with what it is to be human that is encouraging individuals to step outside safety norms and fabricate risk in such sports?

This chapter travels through three stages to tease out these important questions and uses an ethnographic study of a skydive to illustrate the debate. It also, however, has the underlying aim to bring together, one, the idea that basic sensory engagement with the materiality of the world is fundamental to the individual and, two, the political space that this opens up for the finite being at a societal level. With this in mind, it begins by looking at our individual experiencing of the world and thinks through the non-conscious, pre-language encountering of the world through the body. It moves on to consider this external world more thoroughly and how the body might be thought of as being more than the fleshy, limited human body that is traditionally perceived as being distinct from the material world in which it is situated. Throughout, the discussion uses the highly sensory experience of the skydive to spotlight both the individuality and yet externality of the sensing being. This opening out of the body permits a move to the final section of the chapter in which the negative aspect of 'being open', namely our ability to be exploited by subjectifying forces, is attended to before the way in which extreme sports, when thought of as a push against the limit point of power, can be seen as being productive escapism from such limiting structures.

Affect, sensation and the skydive

One concept in particular that has been predominant within the social sciences in recent years seems an appropriate place to begin in a discussion of such a sensory activity, the concept of affect. The turn away from language and representation in the last decade has seen a renewed attentiveness to that which is often written out of humanities discourses by way of interrogation of how it is that feeling, embodiment, emotion and materiality affect our ontological status within the world. Discourses around affect tease out these different elements to ask what they mean for our being-in-the-world in a way that acknowledges, first, the individual basis upon which we experience and, second, that there must be something beyond us (our mind) to experience such sensation ahead of representation. Definitional accounts of affect are ambiguous and a variety of uses for the concept can be found running through the social sciences (Thrift, 2004). Here I follow a Spinozean/Deleuzean thread which facilitates an understanding of how it is that the body opens to the external world through being affected. For Spinoza, a body is a set of relations and it is our capacity to forge new relations or to interact that is where affect inheres (Deleuze, 1988). To intensify affect is to productively increase one's capacity for relation building which, following this line of thought, is beneficial to our power to act. In order to explicate this further I first want to think through adventure sports, the motivations for doing them and the all-important question of death as a limit point. I will then exemplify some of these ideas by looking at empirical work conducted at a sky-diving 'drop zone' and thinking through the visceral and cognitive 'thoughts' that occur before, during and after the act. This will move on to look at how sky-diving can be considered to be an activity in which affect is placed into motion by the individual. After this somewhat singular perspective, I will discuss the manner in which the body is opened to externality by such an affectual experience before considering the implications of such notions for social frame-works. For now though, it is the individual, and the body, that is at stake in such a sport and this that must be addressed first and foremost.

What denotes that a body is performing an 'extreme sport'? There is no clear definition of what an activity needs to involve in order to be called an 'extreme sport' given their relatively recent evolution through modification from often military techniques and each other. Tomlinson and Leigh (1996) note three ele-ments that are widespread throughout extreme sports and that segregate them from normative competitive sports: individuality; the forces of nature; and tech-nology. Regarding individuality, without wishing to fatally push themselves beyond their body's capabilities, individuals participating in extreme sports are able to go beyond conventional understandings of 'what is safe' because they have 'consistently challenged themselves to redefine what those limits are' (Tomlinson and Leigh, 1996: 6). There is competition amongst individuals but training is through and by the body in action so the competitive element is more often both proposed by and against oneself. It might also be said that this is the reason that nearly all so-called extreme sports are solo performances (exceptions include white water rafting). Bringing us onto Tomlinson and Leigh's next aspect of extreme sports, there is, of course, another competitor in the activities in question: nature. In climbing a rock face, surfing a wave, or gliding on a thermal air current one is both going against and using the Earth's forces to accomplish astonishing feats of human endeavour. But not just 'human' endeav-our. Tomlinson and Leigh's third characteristic of extreme sports and one that is key for me is the use of technology to make the human more than its body, for example adapting it to be able to survive underwater or through the air. There are obvious exceptions to this and it is true that some of the most extreme ver-sions of these sports are often ones with pared down equipment, such as boulder-ing or cliff diving, but for the most part the extreme sports category readily makes use of technological advances to push further and further towards the limits of human endurance. Thus the suggestion emerges that it is the individu-al's limit point that is the undesired target of extreme sports participants, 'unde-sired' because death is fended off through safety precautions and 'target' because of the trajectory along which these bodies travel. Further, this limit point is moved towards through an open relation to that which is outside of the human body.

So what about a skydive? As an extreme form of adventure sports, during a skydive the individual places themselves in a situation which would be physi-cally fatal without the aid of training and technology. A skydive involves a human body leaving an aircraft at an altitude of between 1000 m and 4000 m with a parachute that should ensure a safe descent to the ground. There are several types. First, there are jumps that involve 'free fall'. These are conducted from greater heights so that the skydiver is able to experience falling at terminal velocity before deploying their own parachute. They are often conducted as 'tandem jumps' whereby an inexperienced skydiver is able to experience the thrill of free fall whilst an attached instructor takes care of the procedure itself. In terms of the individual experiences that both passenger and carrier go through, they are very different. For the instructor the other person is redundant to the action itself. For the attached novice, on the other hand, the instructor becomes an essential piece of equipment without which the experience would ordinarily not be viable or safe at this stage in their skydiving career. Another way to begin skydiving is the static line method. During a static line jump the skydiver's parachute pack and, more specifically, the ripcord is attached to a point in the plane so that upon exiting the plane the parachute is automatically deployed. Due to the lack of free-fall time these jumps can be conducted at a much lower height and given that one is not responsible for one's own ripcord they are a solo endeavour from the very first jump. It is this type of jump that I draw upon throughout his chapter, for two reasons. Primarily, I want to move away from the idea of a passenger jumper having an experience that is comparable to the solo jumper. We might here draw distinction between a rollercoaster rider and street luge participant whereby the latter requires skill and technique whilst the former passively experiences. The static line jump enables the novice to partake in two days of training regarding how to control the canopy (parachute), how and where to land, and malfunction safety drills before performing the jump itself. Of course this experience differs from the skydiver who has hundreds of jumps logged. But this goes hand in hand with Tomlinson's assertion that the extreme sports participant continually pushes their own limits. The experienced jumper might push their limits of free-fall time or landing precision whilst for the novice simply getting out of the plane door might be limit enough. And here we stumble upon a key point. There is an active decision in crossing the threshold of the plane hatch to position oneself in an extraordinary state. My second reason for drawing on static line jumping is, and for the above reason also, it is the experience that I undertook as part of my ethnographic research into extreme sensory engagement.

Three things stand out for me when thinking through my original experience of skydiving. First, the visceral, bodily reaction I had to the anticipation of what was about to happen. The final aspect of training was a test that we had to pass on the morning of our second day before being allowed to jump. It was imperative that we passed but also not difficult and passing meant that we were done, we were going up. Whilst marking the test, the activity that we were about to do was confirmed. There had always been a chance up until that point that weather or lack of ability might prevent it from actually happening. But now it was certain:

> Am I ready? John [instructor] returns and we mark the test. I feel unbelievably nauseous. I've experienced this feeling with extreme nerves before. I

tell myself that it was the tea I had on an empty stomach but I know it isn't. My mouth salivates and I nearly have to leave the room. I try to hide it. I'm relieved when John brings up nerves. I tell people that I am nervous and he assures me that nerves are good. I ask John what happens if we are sick. He makes a joke. I tell everyone I'm often sick when I'm nervous and they joke that they don't want to be in front of me in the plane. This makes me more at ease and clears the nausea.

(Urry, 2010)

There is a relation here between my understanding and the abnormality of what I am about to put myself through but, further than being a cognitive understanding, it is bodily also. My body does not want to give itself over to floorless gravity. The second aspect of the jump I want to draw attention to is what has been mentioned above – sitting at the edge of the plane door. Retrospectively it is remembered and imprinted on me but difficult to describe. Looking out of the plane you see exactly what you see when coming in to land on a normal passenger jet and yet there is nothing between 'you' and 'it'. You balance precariously on an edge as the rapidly moving air tugs at your legs which you strive to keep in the position you have been taught. You wait for the moment the instructor gives the pilot the call to 'cut' the engine because that will signal that it is your time:

I edge forward. I'm terrified.
'CUT'. Oh god.
'In the door'. I move to the door, my legs hanging over the edge.
'Where's the drop zone?' I call. John points it out. He keeps looking at me. I keep staring back, looking at his eyes, trying to convey my fear.
'Keep looking at me' he says. There is not a chance I won't. He is reassuring, his eyes are reassuring.
'Don't go too far down wind. Those guys are miles away'.
'Ok'. But I'm not ok.
'Keep looking at me'
'I will'
'GO'
I look at him to check that's what he's said. It is.
I tip off the edge.

(Urry, 2010)

Revisiting this moment I tingle with the memory of how it felt to have to get myself outside of the safety of the plane, how it felt to not want to believe that John had told me to 'GO' and to have to tell myself that there's no getting out of it now, to have to do it, myself. I had not really considered how I would feel throughout the experience of learning to skydive but something that was truly surprising was the third element I want to think through and that will lead me onto the next section: how I felt after the act. The sense of 'self' I experienced was immense. What do I mean by sense of self? Simply that there was a realisation of the solitude of the act and how I placed my life in an apparently counter-life situation and dealt with it successfully. Nobody could have swooped down to tell me what to do or conduct an emergency procedure had I needed it. I pushed myself to my limit of sensing and returned to tell the tale.

But there is a gulf in this tale and that is the journey between the door and the ground. For the most part it consists of a recantation of drills and procedures learnt the previous day but for a second, if that, after the immediate tumble there is really not very much at all. A blur, a confusion, a jostling and then an awareness that I need to take control, that I let it slip and now it's time to re-grasp it. This in-between moment is loaded with connotations regarding experiencing the extreme and how it is that our mind, body and outside world are intimately engaged with one another to a more inseparable extent than is often perceived in Western tradition. This will be attended to in the next section of the chapter but for now I want to dwell on the solitude of the experience. What does it mean that my body reacted so explicitly against the cognitive idea of something that should induce physical fatality and how did my rational thought overcome this in order to shift my body beyond the plane door? Here I recourse back to affect in order to respond to such questions.

As alluded to earlier, the definitional account of affect is vague. This apparent weakness in the utility of the concept is actually wholly appropriate to the elusivity or 'slipperiness' with which it creeps throughout being. This becomes clearer in drawing upon four aspects which build upon the Spinozean/Deleuzean foundation of affect and that I believe are important for the discussion around extreme sports. First, affect pertains to forces and could be determined as the transition of those forces or intensities or, thinking in the Spinozean sense of a body's capacity to make relations, the increase or decrease in intensity (Massumi, 2002; Seigworth and Gregg, 2010). Second (and a key reason why affect is so difficult to put into words) affect is prior to language and hence different from emotion or 'feeling'. Affect is non-represented feeling or feeling before it has become signified. As Massumi elaborates, equating affect with intensity: 'Emotion is qualified intensity, the conventional, consensual point of insertion of intensity into semantically and semiotically formed progressions, into narrativizable action-reaction circuits, into function and meaning. It is intensity owned and recognized' (Massumi, 2002: 28). And here we come across the final two aspects of affect that are pertinent to this project. Affect is an in-between-ness (Seigworth and Gregg, 2010). It resides (although not statically) in the gap between language and occurrence whereby it provokes reaction prior to acknowledgement (or that could in itself be acknowledgement). And it transgresses between the body being affected and the body affecting whether this is human or nonhuman. Lastly, affect is autonomous. It does not adhere to rules of causality or expectation but infiltrates a being through the sensing body.

This body is crucial for affect to act upon. It plays the role of mediator, transmitter, for affect. The idea, then, of jumping out of a plane provoked a bodily, highly charged, visceral reaction of nausea and salivating. This is a key point for our understanding of how we, as humans, conduct our material worldly being but it is important to not get tangled in the representation/non-representation dichotomy as affect slips between the two. Affect is neither the idea of jumping out of the plane nor is it the feeling of sickness. Affect is that these two things are connected, beyond the idea and prior to acknowledgement. The materiality of affect is testified by the nausea in my stomach. But it is the body that plays host to both these things, permitting the idea to manifest itself and reacting against the cognitive understanding of the proposal of the task in hand. The individual, singular nature of this experiencing must not go unnoticed. It is my fleshy, human body that I am about to place in an extraordinary position which my understanding cognates as being highly dangerous (despite contrary statistics), and it is my fleshy body that physically reacts against this idea.

So there is nervousness (terror even) about the idea of engaging in a life-threatening activity. So why do it? What is it about the idea of physical destruction, this limit point that extreme sports push against, that is exhilarating and enticing? An interesting reaction of extreme participants is that it is not the adrenaline rush that they seek to emulate so why constantly play around death? When thinking to apply the concept of 'affect' to extreme sports, the American sociologist Stephen Lyng's early writing on 'edgework' (1990) proves a useful substantiation of certain parallels and insights to this question. Aside from his sociological and psychological contextualisation of extreme sports (here I am using more philosophically ascribed texts for a more vitally material conceptualisation of the human's 'being') Lyng's empirical findings are exemplary of the affectual nature of such activities. In describing the type of sensation typical of all experiences where the human pushes itself to the edge of physical or mental limits (1990: 857), Lyng notes six interesting commonalities extracted from primary and secondary data: self-realisation, empowerment, poor gauge of time, oneness with objects or environments, hyperreality, and an inability to capture these experiences with language. Given my ethnographic experience these are certainly familiar to me. But what I want to suggest is that they all, in themselves, point towards the same thing: a change in relation to that which is 'outside' of the individual being. It is here that affect is at its most active under the Spinozean/Deleuzean depiction and here where we can see the four elements of affect discussed earlier come into play. To recall and exemplify, an increase in intensity (affect) in an activity which tests the human's limit autonomously provokes a reaction prior to language or meaningful cognition which, importantly, reconfigures the being's relation to itself and the world. In a more ontologically attentive passage Lyng goes someway to acknowledge this:

> in edgework imaginative rehearsal is disrupted, the 'voice of society' ceases to speak, and the individual is left with a residual self. Although it would be incorrect to designate this residual self the 'I,' it does possess many of the same characteristics: it is an 'acting' self that responds without reflective consciousness, it is spontaneous and creative insofar as the dictates of society and culture are absent, and it is 'nonpersonal' and 'noninstitutional' because the 'me' component of the self is missing.
>
> (Lyng, 1990: 878)

So, to draw apart the threads some more, let us suggest that there is a two-way process at work here. On the one hand, the skydiver is pushing to the edge of life, undoing the relations established by affect. This is what Deleuze and Guattari would call de-stratification – a disorganisation of those relations inscribed upon me. Complete de-stratification would mean an annihilation (death) of the individual. On the other hand, however, this undoing of relations opens the individual up to the potential to productively forge new relations, to re-stratify, and, according to Spinoza, this increase in capacity is how affect is increased. So there is, if you like, an overhaul of the individual's relations, a movement between de-stratifying and re-stratifying. The 'me' is dissolved and the being feels affirmed and empowered, united with the environment, as if they can capture reality in a different light and an inability to describe this.

Upon jumping, I underwent a reconfiguration of my worldly relations. The activity and the world (and my material engagement with it) had forcefully acted upon me to make me encounter 'things' afresh. These 'things', perhaps myself, perhaps conceptual ideas regarding life, or perhaps nonhuman entities, appeared differently as a result of the movement of affect. Affect, then, opened aspects of the world to me. It is this opening that will be discussed next.

Inside, outside and the parachute

The focus thus far has been on the experiencing individual. But this individual is affected by (normatively speaking) things external to the human body. Alluded to earlier were the implications this has for our understanding of our material engagement with the world and I now want to dwell on this a little further by looking at how affect facilitates an opening of the human body to this external world both in the sense of conceptual (but very material) ideas and in the sense of actual physical objects.

Returning to the example of nausea, the material reaction my stomach underwent was caused by something external to it, namely the increasing certainty of the proposal of jumping out of a plane. My body, then, opened itself to this idea. The idea became a material part of my body. For Deleuze:

> What defines a body is this relation between dominant and dominated forces. Every relationship of forces constitutes a body – whether it is chemical, biological, social or political. Any two forces, being unequal, constitute a body as soon as they enter into a relationship.
>
> (1983: 40)

The relation of my human physicality to the idea of jumping out of a plane constituted a body. The reaction of nausea might be said to be evidential of the transmission of forces. The idea of skydiving, then, is affectual. So the body begins to become other than what we ordinarily understand as our human body. And it is the transfer of forces (affect) that permits these bodily relations to take place.

This is perhaps better explained by looking at the actual physical items that might be said to constitute a body throughout a skydive. Where does the body end and the outside begin? Without the technology of a parachute the body would not be able to conduct this activity without 'wildly de-stratifying' and killing oneself. The parachute is, then, very much a part of the body in question. We might compare this to the common example of a blind person with a stick. The person's senses are extended through use of the stick. The same is true of the parachute. The body would fail and no longer be able to affect and be affected if the parachute were absent. Interestingly we might recall the moment of jumping prior to the parachute opening, or, indeed, not recall it. It is significant that for that moment no cognition adhered. The senses were so de-stratified that affect, or a relation of force, was not present. The climber Lionel Terray upon finding himself in some difficulty claims:

> My personality left me, the links with the earth were severed: I was no longer frightened or tired; I felt as though transported through the air, I was invisible, nothing could stop me, I'd reached that state of intoxication, of dematerialization that skiers seek on the slopes, pilots in the sky and divers on the high board
>
> (quoted in le Breton, 2000: 9)

To continue on the path of no-cognition or intoxication would mean the end of cognitive relations for that individual, what we might call a human death or perhaps brain-death. However, the parachute or return to safety prevents this, extending the body into a space where it is able to regain relations that will protect it from annihilation.

But the idea of the parachute being the only bodily extension seems rather limiting. How about the air that creates pressure beneath the canopy to prevent plummeting at too rapid a speed? This may appear farfetched as surely air is merely a medium. But if we are looking at a vital materiality (such as that found in the work of Deleuze and Spinoza) in order to blur the boundary between the human individual and the world then creating another category for air runs contrary to the aims of the project. We might push this externality further still, in terms of the affectual nature of the experience, how about the sight of the earth as a tiny version of itself getting larger and larger as being implicative of 'falling'? Here we might think of sensory tricks to spotlight the importance of that visual recognition – the train next to yours pulls away and you feel as though you are moving or, in more adventure sports terms, a diver surrounded by nothing but blue swims down instead of up due to the disorientation of a lack of visual referencing. The world as it is sensorially perceived, then, contributes to the affectual nature of the skydive. More than this, though, the new way in which it is perceived when carrying out such sports is testimony to an affectual occurrence of changes in relations. The materiality of the world becomes much more fully realised as le Breton explains:

Certain physical or sports activities are developed in the passionate search for emotion, sensation and physical contact with the world and they provide intense moments of pleasure and a sense of fusion with the world.

(2000: 8)

The climber, Messner, wrote:

The effort and concentration required, the tension and the stress resulting from the anguish, all increase the climber's awareness of both the immediate and more distant environment; everything is seen in a new light, with a clarity and the spiritual mobility, for example, that is also acquired through meditation. But most of all the climber sees himself in a new relationship with the world, for a limited period he enters into a state of greater seeing.

(Messner, 1975: 14–15)

The body in such sports is opened to the world, de-stratified to let it in. Or, more accurately, the body is always sensorially open to the world but these sports illuminate such exposure and heighten the awareness of this through an explicit exchange in forces. The dichotomy of inside and outside the human body becomes blurred or even redundant as the confines of the body are expanding to encompass anything with which it is in relation.

The next step to make here might be to ask: how does this new perception of the world or our bodily engagement with the world move from the micro-space of extreme sports to the social and political arena? And we might return to the example of nausea as being triggered by an idea to probe at this further. The idea that my body reacted against is a construct of human comprehension that to jump out of a plane is dangerous and detrimental to our physical existence. It is an abnormal practice that defies the human instinct to stay safe and hence caused a feeling of illness. But it is not, therefore, just my relation to the single idea of jumping out of a plane that becomes a part of my body but the entire web of understanding that this act is not normal and that physical harm is not good. If you like, the entirety of socially constructed ideas regarding safety is called into question in this act. To remove relations that keep me safe is to attempt, then, to realign my relationship to normative social constructs of what death and physicality mean for the human. First, then, the skydive adjusts my relations to myself and my physical perception of the world. Second, though, it serves to problematise the social strictures that are placed upon us on a day-to-day basis. In the next section I want to look at this idea more closely having set up a foundation of understanding regarding our highly individual and yet externally present being. What is it about our 'safe-society' that has caused individuals to want to test the limits of their bodily capacities and re-educate themselves about their position in the world?

Safety, biopower and escape

It is not profoundly shocking to draw attention to the current trend to make the world safe. The idea of 'safety' as an important delimiter of all activity is now so widespread that we wince at occurrences which appear to be detrimental to the human's physical health. This can be seen on a day-to-day basis and in almost all spaces of society. For example, all institutions now have a dedicated 'health and safety' department or certainly copious guidelines for safety procedures and break- ing the rules of such documents is a punishable offence. Of course this has led to subsidiary industries springing up such as personal insurance companies for which the blaming of someone who has not made something safe enough has become a lucrative pursuit. These structures of society can also be seen to be affecting the way our physical bodies are dealt with, both by ourselves and others. For example, marketing companies play on our desire to postpone death and all things associ- ated with aging by suggesting that anti-aging products or cosmetic surgery will in some way improve us. This change in our relation to death has been acknowledged by the sociological writer on climbing, Neil Lewis, who claims that 'death has been made unreal, an event of extra-ordinary "bad luck" instead of inevitable and universal' (Lewis, 2000: 60, emphasis original). The idea of death as weakness and something that must be staved off is given gravitas by the medical industry whereby life support machines are able to keep a non-cognitive body technically 'alive'. The extreme sports industry appears to be working in two different direc- tions here. On the one hand, it agrees, it wants to keep the human safe. After all, it is an 'industry' and its components would not be successful as commercial ven- tures if there was a reasonable chance of not coming out of such activities alive. This nods to a different set of issues regarding the commodification of adventure (see Beedie and Hudson, 2003; Cooley, 1999; Fletcher, 2010; Hudson and Beedie, 2006). Wrapped up in the notion of practicing these sports 'safely' is often a mon- etary fee. For example, many of these sports, including skydiving, you cannot practice until you have been 'signed-off' for accomplishing the relevant training and gaining the appropriate certification for the level at which you wish to partici- pate. These levels are measured against tried and tested standards and are main- tained by authoritative organisations. The key point here, though, is that participants willingly pay these costs and go through the training to affirm a happy and benign outcome. On the other hand, however, what are we doing in extreme sports if we are not attempting to go beyond our normative sense of what is safe, our 'comfort-zone'? We tease or trick ourselves into the sensation that we are unsafe (as in skydiving or bungee-jumping) and become enchanted by the idea that we are trespassing in a world in which we should ordinarily be unable to survive (as in scuba diving or gliding). So what is going on in this tussle between society's desire to keep us from harm and the extreme sports participant's desire to play with death? Here a political space opens and to theorise this seeming contradiction I turn to Deleuze's contemporary, Foucault.

Foucault notes a change in the human's relation to death and this comes about through a change in how the state exercises power over the individual. Put simply, in a bid to propagate many bodies for the purposes of capitalist production, the state has made a transition from sovereign power (the power to kill or let live) to a method which controls by nurturing life or withdrawing provisions in order to let die; what Foucault terms biopower (1990: 138). Where the state (the king or sovereign) once maintained its power by wielding the threat of death over those individuals who made up society, power now takes the form of protection. There are two things to draw out from this and each one will be investigated further below. First, this 'alive body' has been captured in contemporary power relations as an object of capitalist production. Second, this change in the treatment of death by the power forces governing society alters death's positioning both in relation to the individual and within society itself.

Let us deal with the first concern here. The sensory experience delivered in a skydive has shown us to be open bodies. We are open to the world that affects us and that we affect. We are enmeshed in relations that constitute what we are. In a skydive, the change in these relations, or de-stratification, increases our capacity to forge new relations which, under Spinozean terms, makes us more powerful or more affectual. This is caused by a movement towards total de-stratification, the Deleuzean death. So, what are we de-stratifying from? Foucault makes the claim that the development of capitalism not only needed bodies but needed docile bodies that would labour and were easy to govern. To this end, institutions of power emerged in the late eighteenth century to control the labour force and facilitate economic processes. The techniques put in place operated to secure the body's productive potential but they did this in a way that adjusted the individual within the society:

> They also acted as factors of segregation and social hierarchization, exerting their influence on the respective forces of both these movements, guaranteeing relations of dominations and effects of hegemony. The adjustment of the accumulation of men to that of capital, the joining of the growth of human groups to the expansion of the productive forces and the differential allocation of profit, was made possible in part by the exercise of bio-power in its many forms and modes of application. The investment of the body, its valorization, and the distributive management of its forces were at the same time indispensable.
>
> (Foucault, 1990: 141)

Biopower, then, uses its own promise to protect life together with a removal of the primary concern with bodily survival to insidiously control the population of labouring bodies: 'it was the taking charge of life, more than the threat of death, that gave power its access even to the body' (1990: 143). So here we come up against the suggestion that the body's porosity permits it to be managed or manipulated in ways that stultify difference and individuality. The power instruments emerging out of a need for increased productivity within a commodity-driven society have taken advantage of the ability of the body to be affected in order to transform such malleability into docility. Additionally, affectual activities that might harm the healthy, mechanical body have been managed out of working life under the guise of keeping the individual 'safe'. But what this reduction in the movement of affect has done is stultify the individual's subjectivity, disabling its ability to de- and re-stratify and closing down its open relation to the outside world. Furthermore, this inhibition is perpetuated ever more so as the body stagnates and fails to resist. Whilst, then, the introduction of control via biopower has the ability to contract the body's capacity to affect and be affected, practices that instigate an element of sensory worldly engagement, such as extreme sports, can be seen to be trajectories away from such stasis. But why is this relation to physical death so appealing? It is here that the conceptual idea of death found in Deleuze and Guattari (total de-stratification) meets the repositioned societal perception of death as proposed by Foucault.

This change in the exercising of power from threatening death to protecting life has had the effect of altering the visibility of death and dying within everyday living and not only with respect to how we perceive aging as discussed above. Iterating this transition, Foucault claims that:

> In the passage from this world to the other, death was the manner in which a terrestrial sovereignty was relieved by another, singularly more powerful sovereignty; the pageantry that surrounded it was in the category of political ceremony. Now it is over life, throughout its unfolding, that power establishes its domination; death is power's limit, the moment that escapes it; death becomes the most secret aspect of existence, the most 'private'.
>
> (1990: 138)

For the individual, then, death comes to represent an escape from being controlled as a hegemonic component of a labouring society. Foucault expresses the increased astonishment with the act of suicide around the time of this change in power tactic given that 'it testified to the individual and private right to die, at the borders and in the interstices of power that was exercised over life' (1990: 139). Death, then, as well as being suggestive of an escapist element is also a proponent of the assertion of individual power. But individual power in what capacity? It is prudent to think this through: 'death was ceasing to torment life so directly' (1990: 142). The sensing being becomes abstracted away from the materiality of the physical body and world with which it is in relation as forces (under the new power regime) work in two ways. First, the body's affectual capacity is sedated as the reading of sensory forces that are mediated through the body becomes less urgent for living under the new 'safe' structure. Second, other dominant capitalist forces take hold and stratify the being, seizing up the motion of de-stratification and re-stratification that is so important according to Deleuze and Guattari. What death does here, and we might go so far as to suggest a movement towards death such as that which is found in extreme sports, is to affirm the individual's ability to take leave of the stratifying relations in which they are enmeshed in the biopolitical capitalist agenda and open themselves to more worldly attuned relations, relations that pertain to life itself and that are all the more powerful for it.

Conclusion

In short, this chapter has evolved through three levels. It addressed the micro-space of the individual as a recipient of affect who senses their being and orien-tation of the world through the body prior to language or conscious acknowledgement of such sensing and used the empirical example of nausea from the anticipation of conducting a first skydive to illustrate this. It then sought to take this sensing being into the world by showing how affect acts to forge relations with other-than-human 'things', for example, the idea of the skydive or, more materially, the parachute. It is these relations that constitute what the body is. And it is the changing of these relations, de-stratification and re-stratification, that increases our active power and prevents us from being subjectified and exploited by organising forces. These 'organising forces' signify the third level which the chapter confronts – the political. In thinking through why it is that individuals are taking up extreme sports the idea of the predominance of 'safety' in contemporary society was spotlighted using Foucault's depiction of what he terms biopower. Biopower (as a method of control that seeks to preserve life rather than threaten death) serves to stratify the individual and closes down the ability of the being to unmake and remake relations. In turn it diminishes the sensing being's capacity to be in relation to the world and 'life' understood in a broader more encompassing way. Activities such as extreme sports whereby an individual is testing the limits of physical human endurance might be said to be challenging these modes of power through de-stratifying towards total de-stratification (Deleuze's death) in a very real and literal way.

This idea of sensory engagements as opening new imaginings of political actions is important as it questions the ethics of life itself, asking what it is that is worth living for. By interrogating these social structures in this way we are at the same time realigning our worldly presence and demonstrating a fundamental need for material sensory engagement with life, making trajectories away from power technologies that separate out subject and object, being and world. One key point to emerge from the debate is that we are open beings but also that this porosity can be put to use in different (and potentially good or bad) ways. We are able, on the one hand, to be manipulated into docile workers for the purposes of the capitalist labour force. On the other hand, however, we are able to reclaim our relation to that which surrounds us through affective sensory engagement so that an ethics of care towards others (human and nonhuman) might be more firmly established. To this end, extreme sports work in two very important areas. First, they work on the bodily individual to reconfigure their relation to the world, making them see it in a 'new light'. Second, extreme sports translate to the political arena to prompt investigation into why it is that individuals are taking leave of the constructed safety of day-to-day life. In this way, discussions around extreme activities and adventure tourism more broadly offer a space for politically charged discourse around the positioning of the subject in relation to themselves and society.

Part II

Delivering the adventure experience

Steve Taylor

Adventurous experiences can encompass a range of motivations, from the obvious seeking of thrills to the more subtle pleasures associated with mental catharsis. This section examines aspects of how these adventurous experiences are delivered. Adventure tourism is often cited as one of the fastest growing tourism sectors – the interface between the experience provider and the customer is critical in terms of both delivering a great service and encouraging more people to add excitement, even if ephemeral, to their lives.

The core hypothesis of Tristan Semple's chapter proposes that many people's motivations for taking part in adventurous pursuits stem not from an accepted desire to take risks or face uncertainty, but from other deeper, intrinsic and ostensibly less likely motivations, such as the desire for loneliness, exposure to unforgiving environments or discomfort. In exploring these practices, Tristan introduces the concept of fast and slow adventure, through which elements of adventurous typologies can be examined, as well as how and why people choose to partake in these activities as a way of both developing and enacting their narratives and constructing their self.

The changing nature of many commercialised adventure activities forms the focus of Simon Beames' and Peter Varley's chapter. Rather than leisure settings merely being places where people go to recreate, many are now presented as integrated, multifaceted leisure arenas, where the recreation experience is augmented by, perhaps even usurped by, a range of associated products and services. Using Scottish adventure centres to illustrate this trend, the authors examine how these operations conform to Bryman's (1999) concept of 'Disneyization', from the hybridised nature of consumption practices to the associated merchandise sales that so often accompany contemporary commercialised adventure experiences.

In order to better understand the adventure tourism market in South Africa, Melissa Janette Lötter *et al.* examine a range of key demographic variables that help to define the sector in Pretoria. Although the difficulties inherent in defining the adventure tourism market are acknowledged, understanding the characteristics and preferences of potential customers is central to developing products and services that will appeal to these target markets. It is by segmenting the potential market, the authors argue, that adventure tourism businesses can position themselves and target their marketing activities much more effectively.

Finally, Antonie Bauer takes a look at the Irish adventure tourism sector, and assesses the service quality provided by the companies operating in the sector. Service quality is a subject that has received a great deal of scholarly attention; the majority of academic articles have confirmed the link between the level of service quality and the consumer experience, and the consequent purchasing intentions of those customers. Researching the level of service provided by 70 adventure providers in southern Ireland illustrates how the adventure sector operates and what its strengths and weaknesses are, as well as an insight into the nature of entrepreneurship in what may be perceived as a lifestyle tourism sector.

5 The semiotics of slow adventure

Narrative and identity

Tristan Semple

Introduction

This chapter extends the notion of adventure as a subjective (Weber, 2001) and socially constructed (Beedie and Hudson, 2003) practice by investigating the relationship between adventure narratives, the performance of adventure as leisure and the processes by which identity is constructed. The notion of *self* or *selfhood* is engaged with as a creative project which is externally realised through symbolic acts and internally shaped by imaginative devices. Moreover, the performances, thoughts and feelings which constitute adventurous leisure, are presented as emerging in direct relation to the motifs and meanings embedded within certain narratives. The notion of *slow adventure* is introduced to help characterise this distinct sub-genre which articulates a particular constellation of emotions and semiotics.

In extending the notion of the 'self' as a raft of co-constructed selves (Goffman, 1959) and identity as a developmental project (Baumeister, 1986) the literature has proposed that the performance of tourism and leisure is set against a backdrop of identity experimentation (Desforges, 2000; Neumann, 1992). As a strand within this theoretical web, this chapter builds upon the work of Moscardo (2010) and brings greater focus to the central proposition that the tourist experience is concerned with the enactment, creation and recreation of stories. Moscardo's framework (2010: 51) will be extended to include the influence of archetypal roles, mythologies, cultural scripts and narratives. Furthermore, McAdams's (1985) concept of life chapters and Singer and Salovey's (1993) theory of self defining memories are incorporated to explore the tripartite relationship between narrative, identity and adventure experiences.

(Hi)story

The history of the story is one which has incited wars, founded religions, shaped the contours of societies and cemented their norms, immortalised heros and ensured the passage of knowledge from generation to generation (Ransome, 2010). The etymological roots of narrative and story (Latin *narrare*, 'to recount' and the Latin *historia*, 'to inquire') demonstrate a close and complex relationship with memory, the passage of knowledge and the construction of reality. This cyclic relationship is essentially creative, whereby the past is selectively and imaginatively engaged with by (re)constructive recollection (Barclay, 1996; Thompson *et al.*, 1996). Put simply, the past is remade by the act of remembering and retelling. Similarly, the present is also contingent, held together and given form by our journey from, and understanding of, the past (Geertz, 1973). Whilst the material culture of architecture, tools and sculpture provide some concrete form of continuity, it is through stories that meaning and understanding have evolved through the generations.

The particular types of narrative which constitue the shared story: legend, allegory, myth, fable, saga, epic, fairy tale, parable and chronicle all depend upon an important and profound verisimilitude or 'imaginative truth' (Green, 1980: 52). That is to say that however fantastical the embellishment and climactic events of the story, there must remain a kernel of truth at the centre. Thus the portrayed feelings of even fictional protagonists: the lover, the risk taker, the aggressor, the victim, the libertine, provide society with important reference points. Narratives thus provide 'knowledge structures' (Adaval and Wyer, 1998: 208) which act as conceptual maps, facilitating existential navigation. It is apparent then that many of the rules which construct our shared reality are contained within the 'official literature of a nation' (Inglis, 2000: 75) as well as its informal transactions and artistic projects. Consequently, individuals have access to a cultural library from which they can both borrow and adopt: as such, a reservoir of identities and archetypal roles (see Campbell, 1990, 2008; Jung, 1990).

Wherever there are humans there are stories (McAdams, 2001: 114) and it would appear that stories have been central to both the survival of the human species and to our understanding of the world (Cobley, 2001; Sugiyama 2001). The most hegemonic form of story is that of the grand narrative (Lyotard, 1984) which traditionally took the form of a societal myth or religion. Campbell (1990) has proposed that modern societies change too rapidly to allow any new and meaningful mythologies to replace those now outdated narratives. Within the industrialised societies of late modernity, with their multicultural and technocentric networks, the singular voice of any grand narrative has been drowned out by the variety and volume of individual narratives accessed through films, podcasts, ebooks, iPlayer, smart phones etc. A postmodern lens would offer the view that stories no longer function as socially integrative grand narratives, but rather provide a rich palette of texts from which we can paint and script our many individual worlds and selves. Whilst the political and socially integrative power of narratives is arguably less hegemonic in modern society, their proliferation, and ease of digital access ensures their centrality within our everyday worlds. Similarly, whilst mythology no longer has the power of exclusive governance, the 'literal-fundamental mythological motifs' can still be seen as the 'social cement' in many cultures and segments of society (Wilber, 1995: 251). It is proposed that the adventure scene is such a subculture, infused with its own heroes and myths.

Storied landscapes

Macfarlane (2007) explores the importance of narratives in our relationships with and movements within landscapes. He proposes that there are fundamentally two types of map: the grid and the story. The story map records the sedimentary layers of place (Greider and Garkovich, 1994; Tuan, 2003) and imbues locations with values and meanings which are 'embedded in historically contingent and shared cultural understandings' (Gieryn, 2000: 473). The stories which are anchored within the physicality of a place shape its character and define its 'aura' (Tuan, 2003: 4). This reflects a humanistic approach to geography, whereby knowledge of place resides in how it feels and is experienced rather than the abstract spatial geometries of Cartesian framing. The significance of this to adventure tourism is revealed through the individual's desire to explore both the physical and the emotional geography of wild and extreme environments; to explore both the surface textures and the mysteries beneath the Earth's skin.

Tim Ingold (1993) brings our attention to the dynamic aspect of narratives from the discipline of the anthropologist, examining the role of stories in passing on traditions and connecting people with their environments. He asserts that in traditional cultures, stories are a means of awakening new perceptions within people as a way of pulling them 'into the world' (p. 153). This critical notion of being pulled *into* the world through narrative has direct relevance for the adventure tourist whose physical encounters with the forces of nature may well be framed and intensified by the stories they have read and carry with them as framing devices.

It is necessary to acknowledge the temporary nature of place-identity, how it is recreated and expressed through emerging cultural perceptions, new forms of usage and the (re)telling of place through constantly shifting articulations and narratives (Massey and Jess, 1995). In this sense the adventure tourist is not only engaging with natural environments through the historical events and personal biographies which are embedded in those landscapes, but also through the imaginative process of creating their own stories. As such, we can describe the tourist's 'successive explorations' as the discovery of the primacy of place (Abram, 1996) and as a process of anchoring themselves within a particular place through the fusion of action and narrative.

Travel and the story are thus intertwined for 'the journey is a symbol of narrative' (Curtis and Pajaczkowska, 1994: 199). In the context of slow adventure there is also a crucial correlation between the familiar structure of narrative and the physical act of passage, both moving towards some climax or unknown horizon. This parallel is reinforced by the extended flows and the steady rhythms which are experienced during multi-day sailing voyages or glacial treks. The passage of body, landscape and time are synchronised along an unusually linear transit which speaks of the sequential chronology of the story. Furthermore, the deepening familiarity and acuity which arises from extended immersion within a relatively wild environment suggests a kind of *sinking-into* an *other-worldliness* which again reflects the way in which we can lose ourselves, both figuratively and tangibly, in stories and adventures. This relationship between adventure travel and narrative provides a means of organising our lived experiences to create meaningful and temporally organised plots (Polkinghorne, 1988).

The storied self

As a psychologist, McAdams (2001) argues that narratives are central to our functioning and that individuals creatively author themselves through the notion of a 'self' which is expressed and embodied within a 'life story'. We each have our own stories to tell. The events of an individual life are woven together and recounted with the structural threads of narrative, thus sowing a personal and reflexive chronology of experience and memory. It is important to recognise that they are also under constant revision, shifting and reweaving the past to portray a particular side of the story that most suits the occassion (McAdams, 2001).

Postmodernist perspectives on the notion of the self argue that there is no fixed, unified, coherent identity, but rather a multitudinous combination of selves that constitute the individual; selves that are adopted and constructed to suit the social milieu (Hall and du Gay, 1996; Sarup and Raja, 1996). In this sense identity is a continually metamorphic composite, ever shifting and responding to external pressures. Tomkins' (1987) 'script theory' imbued this fragmentary perspective of identity with the notion of the individual as dramatist, selecting scripts for particular scenes. The collective store of narratives, a cultural catalogue of feelings as such, provides society with a multitude of roles to play and scripts to plagiarise. Hermans (1996) extended this link between narrative and the many-faceted self through the notion of the polyphonic novel, where many internal dialogues narrate the self.

Paradoxically, despite or perhaps because of this playful, polymorphous self, the individual still strives to integrate their disparate elements and experiences into a coherent sense of identity which is, according to McAdams (2001), driven by a need for unity and purpose; some linking thread which signals our true self or in Wang's (1999) terms, our existential authenticity. McAdams (2001) integrates the postmodernist angle with more classical perspectives on identity, presenting a complex mid-ground, which balances the psycho-social tensions between the fluid, adaptive self or selves and the 'strong urge to find some coherence in the self, to fashion a self that is more or less unified and purposeful within the discordant cultural parameters that situate their lives' (p. 115).

This need for coherence is presented as the creative, biographical integration of dissonant selves into a more unified life story which is itself a 'nesting' and layering of stories; an 'anthology' rather than a grand narrative (McAdams, 2001: 116–118). As such, identity is the process of writing the self as a succession of selves, linked by plot and intentionality (Bruner, 1986; Ricoeur, 1984). Identity thus emerges from the past as a creative process of drawing together previous encounters, fusing and forming new connections, re-framing the enacted roles and scripts of past events through an autobiographical memory system (Barclay, 1996; Thompson *et al.*, 1996). Similarly, identity extends into the future, steering our 'life story' through 'imaginative anticipation' (McAdams, 2001: 117) towards certain scenes and roles that the self might play.

Narrative and tourism

The adventurous self is perhaps one such archetypal role people might wish to enact or embody whilst performing tourism. The notion of adventure, whilst a malleable construct, also encompasses shared and recognisable values, meanings and feelings which rest upon a foundation of social norms. As language embodies a particular, cultural way of understanding the world (Belsey, 2002: 10) it can be argued narratives provide adventure with its particular, culturally grounded, forms and feelings. Adventure then is a product of narrative, being both a social construction and an inherently individualistic project. Urbain's (1989: 116) argument, that all tourism and recreation is a form of 'identity adventure', leads to the assertion that adventure as a form of leisure is in essence a manifestation of a desire to play with an adventurous identity. The character of this adventurousness is dependent upon not only the physical challenges undertaken but also the narratives which surround and shape the experience. These texts arise from both the stories and nuanced idioms of the particular activity subculture and from the historical accounts and fictional stories which constitute the adventure genre.

Recent academic attention has focused on the experiential dimension of leisure and tourism (see Morgan *et al.*, 2010) and is extending Pine and Gilmore's (1999) proposals regarding the importance of sensations, emotions and memories in the new 'experience economy'. A growing economic recognition of the spiritual, physical, emotional and intellectual dimensions of tourism and leisure has thus been established, as is the notion that the experience of place or self in place may drive and shape the tourist quest (Noy, 2004, 2007). The ways in which stories and narratives frame the tourist experience is similarly recognised as needing further academic attention (Moscardo, 2010).

Notions such as performativity in tourism (Edensor, 2001) lend weight to the argument that leisure practices are playful experiments with identity and furthermore that tourism is bound to the fictional worlds of literature and to the realm of imagination (Hennig, 2002: 170). Similarly, the playing out of archetypal roles (Woodside *et al.*, 2008) is of consequence. Moscardo (2010: 49–55) proposes a systems framework to aid analysis into the role of stories within tourism. At the centre of the model is the tourist experience, presented as the 'enactment, creation and recreation' of stories (p. 51). There is however little exploration of how stories are performed, their relationship with identity, or of the role film and literature play in providing narrative themes.

Besides the performed, enactment of stories, it is likely that tourists also engage in an imaginative, internal narration of their experiences (see McAdams, 2001). The architecture of this self-authoring, both in terms of its structure and its character, is likely to be influenced by the common ground of popular narratives. These themes and motifs will shape the tourist's perceptions and feelings

(Inglis, 2000). Furthermore, individuals may well search for, and expect to encounter, those emotional landmarks common to the genre. In this sense adventure narratives become ontological framing devices, influencing the tourist's motivations, experiences and memories.

The significance of narrative in structuring tourist 'reality' is inevitably, relative and subjective. This is further complicated by the propensity for role-playing within a newly established communitas, and the argument that simulation, fantasy and enactment are for the participant 'existentially authentic' (Wang, 1999). Consequently, tourist reality or experience, must also be viewed from the perspective that individuals may imaginatively change or frame experiences to match the references of chosen narratives. Thus the nightly squalls flapping at a tent's flysheet, become by degrees, the battering winds of a storm, threatening shelter and perhaps survival. The adventure is perhaps less in the doing and more in the recounting; in the story.

Adventure experiences may therefore be selected by the tourist due to their likelihood to shape and imbue identity with symbolic value. Equally, the unusual situations, levels of exposure and risk, deep immersion and powerful sensory stimulation all instil these episodes with a high potential to become 'self defining memories' (Singer 1995; Singer and Salovey 1993). The level of identity impact that such experiences have is dependent upon the 'autobiographical memory system' (Conway and Pleydell-Pearce, 2000). This theory attributes greater identity formation to those events which are personally significant, life changing, intense and of extended duration. Challenging, multi-day journeys in wild terrain provide a relatively high match with these criteria and as such suggest that adventure tourists may come away with identity-forming memories. It is reasonable to hypothesise that this phenomenon is not entirely subconscious, and as such individuals may actively seek adventure experiences with this in mind. This motivational aspect of identity and memory formation may influence the individual's choice of tourist product as well as their *in situ* perceptions and later recollections.

This relationship between identity, memory and significant events is given further definition by McAdams' theory of 'nuclear episodes' and 'life chapters' (McAdams, 1985). In borrowing and appropriating these concepts it is possible to position the bungee jump, the abseil, the zip wire and white water rafting as nuclear episodes, forms of *fast adventure*, all displaying the characteristic ingredients of kinaesthetic overload, speed, instability, adrenaline rush, thrill and fear. The writing of a life chapter, however, is usually a more stabilised and complex phenomenon. The structural web has longer and more interconnected strands. Evolving contexts deepen through extended immersion within a situation or environment. It is here that the qualities of *slow adventure* emerge, where the tourist can immerse themselves within an environment and adventure experience for a number of days. This slower form of adventure will likely encompass the intensity of not only one, but perhaps several 'nuclear episodes' such as the moment of reaching a summit, watching an alpine dawn, hearing an avalanche, crossing a glacier. However, these episodes are interlinked within a larger journey and connecting storyline. This particular temporality corresponds with the notion of life chapters.

Similarly, there is extended time in slow adventure for adaptation or acclimatisation to the environment, to daily discomforts, hardships, risks and the unfolding patterns of a new kind of daily routine. The supporting context, slow pace, natural rhythms and extended immersion provide time to play with identity and develop relationships to place and others. As such it is the temporospatiality of journeying and exploration which character adventure as much as its hazards and moments of peak adventure. The open horizons and vast landscapes reinforce the spaciousness of such experiences. Their unhurried nature coupled with periods of quiet and solitude suggest that slow adventure may be as much an endeavour of reflection and imagination as it is of physical challenges. It is proposed that this imaginative dimension; of framing experience, daydreaming, introspection and self-invention, will in part reflect the individual's exposure to particular types of narrative.

Tales of adventure

For many of us our first encounters with the notion of adventure is through childhood stories (Swarbrooke *et al.*, 2003: 7). Enid Blyton's *Famous Five* and Arthur Ransome's *Swallows and Amazons* provide classic examples of the way in which childhood social relationships and identity formation may have been influenced by narratives and the imaginative dimensions of play and adventure (Thomas, 1987). Whilst children's entertainment has evolved into a global industry, encompassing a wide range of forms and media, the continuing popularity of the adventure narrative is evidenced by the international success of J.K. Rowling's *Harry Potter* series.

Tales such as *Little Red Riding Hood*, with their origins in the oral folk traditions of the European Middle ages, contain such rich, profound and disturbing symbolism that scholars continue to analyse their psychological and cultural importance (see Zipes, 1993; Dundes, 1989). Whether overtly expressed or implicit within their imaginative devices, the violence, vulnerability and darkness of these tales is balanced by the promise of adventure, heroism and romance that transports the protagonist and the reader away from the world of everyday preoccupations. Fairy tales may have originally served complex social functions, providing warnings and deterrents when woodlands were the refuge of pariahs and the hunting grounds of outlaws. Paradoxically, such tales also plant an incongruous, magnetic attraction towards these landscapes of fear. Despite our rationalised education systems, such narratives seem to still be very much a part of our childhood worlds.

The imaginative voyages of the young mind, however immature and fantastical, may lay a significant, if buried, foundation upon which future identities, fantasies and fetishes are constructed. These enduring echoes of romance and adventure may resound in certain adult domains, particularly those associated with leisure, where ideals of freedom, experimentation and self-expression are accommodated. The continuing popularity of Tolkien's *Lord of the Rings* provides but one example of this extension of fantasy into the adult world. As a classic of its genre, it establishes itself as a piece of modern mythology (Chance, 2001). Having been translated into 'dozens of languages' and 'sold over eighty million copies' (Thompson, 2007: 2), its success is partly attributed to a social need for escapism, adventure and mythology, but also in giving a voice to the dispossessed and in providing a more modern hero with which to replace those of the Arthurian genre (Chance, 2001).

Perhaps some of the success of Tolkien's work lies within its ability to blur the usually clear distinction between the world-views of children and adults. Ken Wilber's (1995) comprehensive work on evolutionary philosophy, argues that all children go through a mythic stage in their development, and then experience the pain of losing this to the adult world of rationality. He observes that despite the dominance of the scientific paradigm in Western society, there is still continuing tension between the mythic and rational, and as such a need for a more evolved philosophy which will find accommodation for both ontological perspectives. It is perhaps these complex tensions which lead many into fantasy and fetish. If groups of adults around the globe come together to re-enact and role-play scenes and scripts from *Lord of the Rings* (Kreeft, 2005: 19) then how many more might internally and privately play with similar kinds of imaginative framing when engaged in adventurous leisure and tourism?

Martin Green's (1980) wide-ranging study of adventure narratives, as a serious piece of literary analysis, not only neatly detours around the profound impacts of folklore and childhood stories, but also distances itself from the romantic, adventure ideology epitomised by the Arthurian legends. Green (1980) positions Defoe's *Robinson Crusoe* as the birth of the adventure narrative in a modern sense. That is to say, that unlike its predecessors, it no longer held at its literary core notions such as 'ideal love ... archaic war with fantastic beasts ... courtesy and chivalric honour ... the marvellous as manifested by magicians and fate' (pp. 49–50). The spirit of adventure was thus metamorphosed from the realm of fantasy to that of industry, being presented as an expression of the capitalistic and bourgeois desire for mobility, wealth and expansion (Nerlich, 1987). These emerging notions were entrenched in the colonialism and imperialism of the British Empire and reflected in part the diaspora and mobilities of mass immigration, missionaries, prospectors and deported criminals during the eighteenth and nineteenth centuries. Alongside *Robinson Crusoe* can be placed Robert Louis Stevenson's *Treasure Island*, London's *The Call of the Wild*, Mowat's *Lost in the Barrens* and Kipling's *Kim*. Novels such as Verne's *Twenty Thousand Leagues Under the Sea*, Conan Doyle's *The Lost World* and Melville's *Moby-Dick* also fit closely to this more modern form of the adventure narrative, where the adventure ideology merges both romance and industry.

Green suggests the genre of adventure is composed and defined by its motifs and references Claudio Guillen's *Literature as a System* citing that genres are 'mental codes' or maps that guide the writer in a kind of symbiotic process which reflects and also influences dominant cultural perspectives (1980: 53–55).

In this sense genres exert a reciprocal and cyclic force on author, reader and society alike. This lexicon and its symbolism can then influence an individual's internal dialogue with which they record and organise their perceptions. This is particularly likely whenever a situation appears to resemble those forms and cues that have been woven into the archetypal narratives. Similarly these genres may influence imaginative constructions, such as the expectations of a tourist.

The *National Geographic*'s list of the '100 greatest adventure books of all time' (Brandt, 2004) includes titles such as Marco Polo's *Travels*, Herzog's *Annapurna*, Thesiger's *Arabian Sands*, Krakauer's *Into Thin Air*, Heyerdahl's *Kon-Tiki*, Cherry-Garrard's *The Worst Journey in the World*, Harrer's *Seven Years in Tibet* and Worsley's *Endurance*. It is important to note that this list of adventure tales provided by the *National Geographic* has the stamp of authenticity; they are factual, biographical accounts and as such slightly distinct from those discussed in the preceding paragraphs. There is a seriousness and legitimacy which elevates these particlar narratives into the world of rational, adult affairs. As such this body of literature can be seen to satisfy what Baudrillard (1983: 148) termed our 'nostalgia for the real'.

It is also significant that the temporality and pace of these accounts is far removed from the fast-paced action and thrill of the adventure genre epitomised by Ian Fleming's *Bond* novels or the Hollywood movie with its focus on action, adrenaline and climactic moments. Almost without exception, the *National Geographic*'s 100 best adventure narratives are epic struggles of hardship which stretch accross considerable measures of time and space. Extended periods of endurance and suffering are occasionaly disrupted by moments of intense effort or sublime elation. The extreme environments which loom large in these stories, menace and threaten day after day in a gruelling game of patience and tenacity, which in its slow progression often leads to the protagonists developing a complex attachment to their surroundings. These embodied landscapes are regularly portrayed by the adventurer as a noble adversary and existential testing ground, or as a sacred setting for a form of ascetic suffering and transcendence. These recurring themes suggest something close to, yet somehow distinct from, the 'buzz' and 'rush' of fast-paced adventure. It is from this basis that the notion of slow adventure is proposed, to establish a continuum between extended journeys of exploration and adrenaline-charged moments.

Contemporary accounts of slow adventure abound in both film and novel. Examples such as Wilson's *Blazing Paddles* describes the trials and tribulations of a kayaker's four-month circumnavigation of Scotland. Joe Simpson's *Touching the Void*, Andy Kirkpatrick's *Psychovertical*, Ranulph Fiennes' *Mad, Bad and Dangerous to Know*, all very much continue the tradition, if somewhat more introspectively and psychologically focused. In these accounts, the original ideology of the hero is played down, but certainly not discarded. These are anti-heroes, villains and chancers. What is important however, is the common theme that extensive hardship is the measure by which merit is awarded. Suffering is worn as a badge of honour, often more so than the achievements themselves.

Popular films such as *The Perfect Storm*, *The Beach*, *Castaway* and *Into the Wild*, whilst subsumed within the cultural processes of Hollywoodisation, have retained something of the mood and form of the slow adventure narrative, despite their compression and the disruption of natural chronology. A wide range of independent films and small-scale productions tour the world each year with showings at a range of events for aficionados and enthusiasts such as the Banff Mountain Film and Book Festival. Despite the high impact of cutting-edge, adrenaline climaxes, a large proportion of these films focus on exploration, wild landscapes, cultural interaction and the personal stories of the protagonists. Besides the books and films, other vehicles through which such narratives are circulated include the social interactions of various subcultures, blogs, tweets, YouTube, news stories, advertising slogans, commercials and radio interviews.

Motifs of slow adventure narratives

Having thus explored some typologies within the body of what will be termed the slow adventure genre, it is necessary to extract the individual elements which compose and define it and in turn bestow its acts and actors with significance and symbolic value. A thematic analysis of texts from the cultural archive of exploration biographies, novels, folktales, children's stories, adventure films and interviews reveals both recurring motifs and an underlying, semiotic framework. This framework, which codes and structures these narratives, has been established by a cross-textual search for common *signifiers* (see Saussure, 2011; Baudrillard, 1983). The various ways of 'doing' adventure (its *signifiers*) are presented as the performances by which individuals mark their actions as belonging to the body of adventure. These collected acts, in their many guises, constitute the corporeality of the canon of adventure narratives; providing as such the hard evidence. Each of these performances is assigned particular value and meaning (that which is *signified*) by the mood and tone of the particular narrative as well as by reference to the broader codes and norms of the genre.

The *signifiers* which constitute in their varying correlations the slow adventure include: overcoming natural barriers and frontiers through mental resolve and ingenuity; long, slow and arduous journeys which hinge critically on navigational skill; the exploration of new horizons and distant goals; quests for *ultima Thule* and wilderness. These motifs are importantly qualified by the protagonists being progressively stripped back to a raw and primal focus on survival and shelter. Similarly, hardship and discomfort, pushing the limits of human endurance, isolation, weathering the elemental forces of nature, risk and uncertainty are core *signifiers*. The physical aspects of performing adventure are importantly driven and unified with a sense of overarching purpose.

Exactly what is *signified* by these acts is, however, more problematic. A pragmatic analysis illuminates a set of competencies which demarcate a general self-sufficiency and independence. Similarly a certain type of character is signified; courageous, self-willed and daring. The pathos of the narratives, however, allude to deeper rooted significance. The acts themselves are often portrayed as quests for authenticity and self-realisation which in turn idealise the primitive and as such seem to signify a sense of anomie within modern society. These acts of escapism or remonstration against the luxuries and materialistic excess of Western culture are regularly counterbalanced by a steering towards an ascetic kind of spiritual salvation or self-transcendence. Endurance, hardship, risk and suffering most notably signify heroism and the symbolic valour of battle, yet without the ethical dilemma of armed conflict. Victory is signified in both the conquest of natural frontiers and in defeating inner fears and weakness. The act of survival is perhaps the most symbolic of all, marking out for both the protagonist and society that a liminal rite of passage (Turner, 1982) has been endured. The epic motif of the homecoming provides the stage for this newly formed self to be expressed and possibly re-accommodated within their social sphere.

Whilst any such attempt at reductionism should invite criticism for its limitations and generalisations, it may nethertheless prove useful in identifying some of the significant, symbolic markers in the landscape of slow adventure. In respect of Bruno Latour's warning that 'nothing can be reduced to anything else, nothing can be deduced from anything else' (1988: 163) as well as his stance against overarching theory and metalanguages this analysis is presented not as a theory, but as providing an infralanguage (1988: 179) which codifies the genre. Put simply, it provides a set of possible lenses that individuals might bring to the adventure experience and use to interpret, steer, reconstruct and remember those events. It is interesting to note that few of the identified signifiers of adventure are traded at their exchange value within the commercial market. This may stem from the industry's often myopic focus on the speed, risk and thrill of adventure.

This analysis of the genre's motifs provides the underlying architecture which characterises the stories of slow adventure. These elements chart the experiences and feelings that the readership may be expecting or searching for. As such they describe an unlikely set of pull-factors which might also motivate the slow-adventure tourist. The paradox then is how can this proposed set of motifs find any translation into the lexicon of the travel brochure, with its focus on luxury, comfort, relaxation, sensuality and pampering? Wilfred Thesiger's (1959) well-cited phrase that 'the harder the way the more worthwhile the journey' is perhaps then one motto of the slow adventurer. In the case of the slow-adventure tourist, this motto is played with (particularly in terms of its signified value) and yet kept within the safe parameters of expert dependency, instant rescue, quality assurance and proximity to certain luxuries. That the adventure tourist invites a certain level of hardship (physical effort, camping, basic sustenance, discomfort, exposure to weather) into their leisure time becomes less problematic when situated within this semiotic framework. In this way, such practices can be seen as carrying value which has been authored by a genre and yet is written by the individual in their own subjective interpretation of challenge, loyalty, heroism and survival which are themselves recurring and cross-cultural themes in stories (Davis and McLeod, 2003; Sugiyama, 2001).

The apparently irrational proposition that some tourists may acively or subconciously seek the antithesis of luxury in their free time is according to Inglis (2000) partly that people wish for alterity to the comforts and 'well upholstered security systems' of modern technoloy (p. 76). The sociological literature which positions such lesiure practices as manifestations of a desire to escape a sense of anomie (Dann, 1977) may in part explain the urge for such alterity. Authors on escape attempts (see Cohen and Taylor, 1992; Rojek, 1993) posit that as there is no singular overarching reality, and no concrete unified self, there can in the end be no escape. Baumeister (1991) however contests that at least a temporary escape may be possible through a shrinking back of the self to its raw minimum. This phenomenon has been identified as a core motif of the adventure narrative and as such can extend the notion of adventure as an identity experiment to encompass the idea of authenticity.

The power of narrative not only to substantiate but also to illuminate the authentic self is a central tenet in Jacob Golomb's (1995) authoritative work on authenticity. Golomb states that to attempt to argue a rational justification of or for authenticity is self-defeating, as the notion itself defies the rational and positivist stance of dualism (p. 18). In response, Golomb demonstrates that it is through the narratives of 'short stories, novels, plays, poems, aphoristic essays, fiction, diaries, biographies and even autobiographies' (ibid.) that philosophers such as Sartre and Nietzsche have dealt with authenticity. This is precisely because we are best made aware of and enticed towards authenticity not by a rational description of *what* it is, but rather by a powerful and insightful description of authentically lived lives. That is to say that the *how* of authenticity resides in the 'pathos' of poetic narratives which portray the 'sublime and heroic patterns of authentic life' (ibid.: 18–19). The correlation with slow-adventure narratives is precisely this ability to entice the reader or the tourist towards a particular and temporary way of being; into a new landscape of feelings and values which extends beyond the reach of rational argument.

Golomb goes on to pose the question of why authors on authenticity fixate upon and glorify extreme situations (1995: 22). He finds answers in Joseph Conrad's penetrating question: 'Can you pull your authentic self together when you lose all support? Will you survive or go under?' (cited in Golomb, 1995: 23). This pushing of the self to the limits of endurance and to explore the outer limits of the world are also core motifs in slow-adventure narratives. It is possible the weekend adventurer and the adventure tourist are in some small measure motivated to at least get close to the experiences portrayed within the narratives of those who captured a sense of the 'heroic patterns' of an authentically lived life.

Patrick Laviolette's (2011) exploration of extreme leisure, presents the notion of 'wanderlustrous landscapes' and the need in society for 'heroes' to venture into the 'non-hallowed territories; the "wild", untamed, unexplored areas at the edges, margins and peripheries of the known world' (p. 30). The view from this *edge* is atypical, it is expansive, facilitating what Nietzsche called the 'horizon of infinite perspectives', a rare chance to survey our life pulled free from the detritus and normative blankets of the safe and familiar. An infinite and adventurous perspective which brings new insight (see Walle, 1997) and a horizon of innumerable possibilities where we might possibly mould a new path for ourselves (Golomb, 1995: 23) or shape a new sense of selfhood.

Outlook

The notion of *slow adventure* narratives has been presented as a genre constituting a particular constellation of emotions and semiotics. This is presented as a starting point for empirical research into the subjective dimension of adventure tourism, leisure motivations and the framing of experiences. Importantly, this chapter has suggested a pattern of connections between the themes and motifs of this genre and the ways in which adventure tourists both enact and internally narrate their performances as significant events. It is this co-constructed significance that is appropriated by the individual as a part of the fabric of identity.

These narratives, which constitute a cultural library of feelings and values, provide an imaginative palette from which individuals may construct their own stories. Likewise they offer lenses through which to interpret and give meaning to the emotionality of an adventurous landscape. These culturally anchored texts translate the significance of adventure; they lend authority and authenticity to such apparently irrational leisure pursuits.

McAdams (2001: 115) states that 'in modern life, constructing one's own meaningful life story is a veritable cultural imperative'. In accepting McAdams theory of 'life stories' it has been posited that adventure enthusiasts and tourists may be motivated by a desire to write their own life stories, through the creative integration of adventure narratives. Furthermore, individuals might search out specific types of adventure experiences due to their particular potential to become memories by which they can come to define themselves (Singer and Salovey, 1993).

The extended duration of slow adventures makes them likely to be incorporated in identity formation through the autobiographical memory system as 'life chapters' (McAdams, 1985) within a larger 'life story' (McAdams, 2001). This extended temporality allows for an incorporation of elements of the everyday, for the quotidian and natural rhythms, as well as the thrills of sublime scenery and peak adventure. Significantly, it has been proposed that the paradox of adventurous leisure and tourism extends beyond risk taking to include a profound and unlikely motivation for elements such as discomfort, loneliness, brevity, immersion in sublime environments, weathering harsh conditions and suffering hardship. These constitute some of the motifs that we have come to almost unquestioningly associate with adventure and heroics. Thus, rather than being the antithesis of leisure it has been posited that such experiences, framed through a narrative lens, may be sought for playful experimentation with an adventurous identity or perhaps as a means of feeling or being a more authentic self.

The notion of the story map (Macfarlane, 2007) has provided a possible framework to explore the synergy of landscape, sensory immersion and narrative, both from the perspective of the tourist's expectations arising from extant folklore and mythologies embedded in the sedimentary layers of place (Greider and Garkovich, 1994; Tuan, 2003; Seremetakis, 1994) and in the creative process of story making. In this sense, adventure can be viewed as an experiential domain of subjective encounter and as a conceptual framing device which diffuses the boundaries of physical geography, emotional geographies and imaginative landscapes. The environments of adventure are thus animated, becoming more than just arenas or backdrops for action scenes. They provide not only the challenge and the mood, but through their residual stories and those which the adventurer brings with them, the landscape and the protagonist are entwined in a phenomenon perhaps best described as embodied imagination (Castoriadis, 1998).

The sublime dimension of adventure experiences, particularly those attributed to wild and remote landscapes has been discussed in relation to the role of archetypal narratives in popularising such aesthetic sensibilities. The *ultima Thule* may call to the adventure seeker through the voices of its first explorers, both as a means of self-transcendence through stoic weathering of the elements to experience the raw, authentic self, but equally to understand what it is that society protects them from, to realise the value of home. Likewise adventure tourists may wish to play with such serious tones of identity and yet not wish to get too close to the reality of the original adventure.

6 Eat, play, shop

The Disneyization of adventure

Simon Beames and Peter Varley

Introduction

The nature of adventurous recreation is steadily changing. The places that we go to climb, ski, and mountain bike are becoming more than merely places to recreate; they are places where one can order a club sandwich with fries and a Coke, gain access to an artificial indoor or modified outdoor activity venue, and buy the latest brand-name clothing and equipment. In these places, members of the public can eat, play, and shop – often all under one roof.

A theoretical framework was sought that would foster a better understanding of the inner machinations of these leisure spaces at a more sociological level. The most useful body of literature that was found comes under the label of *Disneyization*. This chapter will outline the key features of the concept of Disneyization, as conceived by Alan Bryman (1999, 2004). These features are illustrated with examples that are found within the 'adventure cathedrals' of Scottish leisure markets. Before exploring the usefulness of Bryman's framework, and in order to make further sense of this emerging area of inquiry, the broader body of commodification literature will be interrogated, and followed by a particular focus on theoretical frameworks for services marketing and the precursor to Disneyization: McDonaldization. The chapter concludes by considering the implications that this discussion offers to practitioners and to researchers.

Background

Recent attention has been given to the commodification and consumption of recreational adventurous activities (see Cloke and Perkins, 2002; Varley, 2006a). Naturally, much of this recent discourse has drawn from a wider body of sociological and sales/marketing literature. By way of setting the scene for a discussion on Disneyization, the broader context of people paying for products and services that have been crafted by sellers and providers for this purpose must be explored.

The world of adventure tourism occupies a fascinating niche, as it blurs the line between purchasing a product and a service. Furthermore, the 'adventure' part suggests uncertainty and danger, yet the modern business world is ill at ease with either condition. The commodified form of 'adventure' is provided in the marketplace as a particular type of convenient service and, as such, this new commodity form exhibits significant differences to physical goods in terms of its production and consumption. We now explore the intersection between products and services.

The 'marketing mix' is known as the *4Ps*, and is expressed in marketing theory as product, price, promotion, and place, which Booms and Bitner (1981) extended to a *services* marketing framework by adding a further three dimensions: people, physical evidence, and process. The 'people' element encourages a focus on selection, training, performance, and personality, but also recognises the importance of the consumer themselves in the co-creation of the experience. 'Physical evidence' is often what is lacking after an adventure experience, in that the service experience rarely allows take-home evidence of what was purchased. It is for this reason that many adventure companies take photos and sell t-shirts and mugs as memorabilia, thus supporting post-consumption reflections. 'Process' calls for a recognition that service experiences in general, but particularly adventure tourism experiences, are effectively linear, and have peaks and troughs of intensity, anticipation, action, and reflection. These additional dimensions have arisen in response to four key challenges facing the marketer of services, as identified by Parasuraman *et al.* (1985).

1   Intangibility: This is the primary source from which the other three characteristics emerge. Services cannot always be physically encountered in the same manner that physical products can. The physical ownership element of many services is often limited, and therefore the service experience is invariably anticipated as an emotion only, and recalled as a memory. The environment, behaviours, and interactions with service personnel and other customers' behaviours (on a river rafting trip for example) may be crucial to the experience and its memory after the fact, but there is little to take home other than photos and memorabilia.

2   Heterogeneity: Unlike the mass-production standards of reliability and predictability applied to physical goods, services are produced for, and enacted between, individual people. Inconsistency is inevitable, as people on either side of the (real or imagined) shop counter have mood swings, problems, and triumphs. If an instructor at an outdoor centre is having personal problems at home, this may impact upon their demeanour at work, and the same goes for the consumer in the consumption setting.

3   Inseparability: This aspect of the service phenomenon is considered to have three key aspects: (a) the service provider's physical connection to the service being provided; (b) the customer's involvement in the service production process; and (c) the involvement of other customers in the service production process. All of these are particularly true for the commodified adventure. Take for example a course in winter mountaineering: the personalities of the other clients as well as the moods and life situations of the instructors will all have a bearing upon the subjective experience of the service.

4   Perishability: Services cannot be stockpiled. The service is produced and consumed in the same moment. A hotel room that has remained unoccupied for a night cannot store up the vacant time during which it has not been used. The moment of its 'saleability' has passed. Similarly, if a mountain guide has no clients to use up her available paid time, she may be losing money.

To counter some of these problems, service industries have increasingly adopted the standardising processes originally developed as part of the mass-production techniques for material goods. The performative labour evidenced by the scripted 'have a nice day' greetings at McDonalds was developed in an attempt to counter the inter-subjectivity and unpredictability of service encounters, and provoked Ritzer's (1993) extended Weberian critique of such practices.

The sale of services as commodities had therefore simply fallen into the same trap as physical commodities. Consumers got bored, in simple terms, as regulated consumption experiences were produced for the masses; the purchase of a standardised burger, accompanied by a standardized statement from the service operative, would fail to provide opportunities for creative social interaction, and, ultimately would diminish feelings of 'satisfaction'. Indeed, these experiences may be considered more likely to deepen feelings of alienation, disenchantment, and distance (Ritzer, 1993: 25). Standardized services had thus entered the 'commoditization trap' (Schmitt, 1999), in which they are consumed in the same way as standardized products, and the mystery and magic of human interaction is rationalized out.

McDonaldization and adventure in a bun

Our own awakening to the influence of corporate financial agendas on outdoor education was inspired by Chris Loynes' (1998) paper entitled 'Adventure in a bun'. Loynes' argument (following Ritzer) was that residential outdoor centres in the UK were offering programmes that were increasingly packaged and uniform. The same kinds of products were being delivered to older teenagers in Scotland that were being run for primary school children in the south-west of England; despite contrasting landscapes and clientele, the product was the same. Loynes likened outdoor education provision to the rationalizing processes Ritzer identified in his work on the creeping influence of what he termed the *McDonaldization of Society* (1993).

Much more than an explanation of what the consumer gets when they buy a hamburger or an outdoor experience, Ritzer's thesis was that broader economic circumstances were forcing businesses of all kinds to rationalise their sales models in attempt to decrease production costs, reduce risks, and increase profits by assuring customers of a standardised experience. The McDonaldization framework outlines how more and more companies are focusing on increasing the efficiency, calculability, predictability, and control of the products they are selling. A fifth characteristic is the replacement of human labour with technology. We will explain each of these concepts in turn.

The drive for *efficiency* concentrates on achieving intended aims with less cost and energy. Take the example of a mountain biking operator, where they can bring prices down for the customer by buying bicycles that are very easy to maintain and quick to accommodate customers of different shapes and sizes. The operator will not have to spend a lot of time 'fitting' the client; he will just take the money and give the customer a quick talk on how to adjust the seat before setting them on their way, unsupervised.

The second feature is *calculability*, or the increasing emphasis that is placed on quantifying operations. In many cases, this is reflected by valuing quantity over quality. So, 30 mountain bikes may be purchased at a low cost, in the knowledge that if a bike gets overly damaged it will not be repaired; it will be cheaper to replace it, in terms of replacement parts and labour. Whatever the scenario, calculability ensures that decisions regarding practice will be directly influenced by mathematical formulae, rather than a company's ethical guidelines. Similarly the time taken for a particular adventure experience can be assessed, and thus an operator can calculate how many trips can be undertaken per day, week, and month, and how much profit this would realise, given a particular staffing ratio.

The third feature of Ritzer's framework is *predictability*. People running companies can lose income through unexpected events, and people buying products and services have a need to feel comfortable in the knowledge that they will be getting exactly what they paid for. It reduces the perceived risk in the eyes of the consumer. In order to keep events and occurrences as predictable as possible, we might do everything we can to ensure that varying factors, such as the weather and the economy, have as little influence on profits as possible. This is, of course, a paradoxical requirement of adventure companies, where the promotion often suggests 'the unknown', 'risk', and 'danger' as part of the experience on offer.

Control refers to the control that the organisation has over its employees and its customers. For example, customers may have a limited choice of what is on offer and how it can be consumed (e.g. you can choose between hiring two different mountain bikes, and you can only ride in specifically delineated areas). Similarly, control is also exerted upon the employees, in terms of how they are expected to dress, conduct their particular tasks, and interact with others. Perhaps most telling is the degree to which employees are not required (or allowed) to think; they are often given careful instructions to follow, and are not expected to use their judgement. Rules and regulations (think of climbing walls or rafting rivers) control the behaviours of service personnel and consumers alike.

The final feature of McDonaldization is the substitution of *non-human for human technology*. Organisations in an increasingly rationalised society demand a certain degree of subordination of humans to machines. Put simply, more and more tasks that used to be done by humans can now be done by machines, such as the automatic belay devices in climbing walls, ticketing machines or ski pass readers.

Having now outlined the basic characteristics of McDonaldization, it may be apparent that, apart from explaining them as a means of 'laying the foundation' for a discussion on Disneyization, they also serve to provide a helpful lens through which we can consider all kinds of adventure tourism practices.

Disneyization

Soon after Ritzer's work was published, Bryman (1999) developed his own related perspective on Western society's penchant for managed consumption experiences: Disneyization. Bryman defines Disneyization as 'the process by which *the principles* of the Disney theme parks are coming to dominate more and more sectors of American society as well as the rest of the world' (1999: 26). While Disneyization may have elements of McDonaldization, it also has its own distinct features. Bryman refined the Disneyization framework for his 2004 book on the subject and refers to four defining properties of Disneyization: theming, hybrid consumption, merchandising and performative labour.

Theming is said to be the 'most obvious dimension of Disneyization' (1999: 29). Bryman cites examples of restaurants such as the Hard Rock Café, where diners are immersed in the sights and sounds of all things rock and roll. The ubiquitous Irish pub in every big foreign city is perhaps another illustration of this trend. A crucial concept within theming is that the various elements of the experience have a high degree of coherence: the décor, the name of the dish, the music. The consumer is made to feel as if they have been transported to that 'place'.

The second feature of Disneyization is *hybrid consumption* (also referred to as the *de-differentiation of consumption*). This trend is harder to define, but can be understood as the blurring of lines between 'playing' and 'buying stuff'. When we are in certain themed environments there are frequent opportunities to buy goods while partaking in the activities. For example, while at Legoland with our children, there will be countless opportunities to purchase Lego products in-between (and perhaps even during) rides. A key point here is that different forms of consumption (e.g. playing, eating, drinking, sleeping and buying souvenirs) are 'inextricably interwoven' (Bryman, 1999: 34).

Closely related to the de-differentiation of consumption is *merchandising*. If you have ever been in to a Starbucks café, you'll know that apart from the obvious corporate theming, there are also all kind of things for sale. Bags of coffee, French presses, CDs, mugs, cups, flasks, and espresso makers are all available for purchase – and quite often these marketing stands are adjacent to where one waits for the coffee to arrive. In some themed businesses it is the merchandising that provides a stream of revenue that matches or exceeds that from the principal activity (Bryman, 1999: 37); returning to our Irish pub example, the profits often come from selling t-shirts and not from selling Guinness and Steak and Ale pie.

Bryman's final aspect of Disneyization is *performative* (formerly *emotional*) *labour*. As Ritzer (1997) points out in his more recent work on 'McJobs', these jobs do not only demand fewer skills and use less judgement, but, drawing on work by Ashforth and Humphrey (1993), they also require expressing certain emotions and ways of interacting with customers. In its simplest form, it involves employees exhibiting cheerfulness and even friendliness towards customers as part of the extended service encounter. Certainly in America, and increasingly in the UK, having a dedicated 'greeter' at the entrance to a large store is not uncommon. This person, the sales person, and the cashier might also encourage you to 'have a nice a day'.

Analysis and discussion

Now that we have outlined the four themes of Disneyization, we will explain the approach employed to do a preliminary investigation into the ways in which this framework can help us understand current (and perhaps future) adventure tourism practice in Scotland.

We have chosen three adventure centres, each of which focuses on a distinctive set of activities. They are EICA Ratho near Edinburgh, Snozone in Glasgow (now run by Snow Factor), and Nevis Range Mountain Experience in Fort William. Ratho concentrates on indoor climbing (including bouldering and an 'aerial assault' course), Snozone on indoor skiing and snow-boarding, and Nevis Range on mountain-biking and skiing/snow-boarding (lately also offering a high ropes course through the tree tops). These three venues were purposefully chosen for their differing physical locations and principal activities.

Theming

There was evidence of theming at all venues. This was perhaps most obvious in the names of certain services within the centre. The climbing theme is obvious at Ratho, with the Belay Café offering cappuccinos and panini, and the 'Rock Tots' nursery providing child-minding services for recreating parents (Ratho, 2011). Snozone had its own 'alpine themed' Sno!bar that sold food, hot drinks, and alcohol (Snozone, 2011). Nevis Range draws themed inspiration from the landscape on which it is located; diners can enjoy food at the Snowgoose restaurant and Pinemarten café/bar.

Hybrid consumption

The hybrid consumption theme is perhaps the most dominant in this investigation. There are plenty of examples of how playing, eating, and buying material goods are activities that are intertwined in complex ways. Apart from the bouldering, climbing, abseiling, aerial course at Ratho, there is also a café, gear store, gym, spa, and ceramic centre. A more telling tale is apparent at the physical complex within which Snozone was located. Called 'Xscape', it boasted that people can 'Play, eat, and shop under 1 roof' (Xscape, 2011); there were at least ten retail stores and 15 restaurants and cafés to choose from, and this is in addition to the cinemas, 'fan drop', and mini-golf. Even though we sought to examine Snozone itself, it was clearly part of the larger, over-arching leisure cathedral that is Xscape. The emphasis on consumption is relatively muted at Nevis Range, except for its gear and souvenir shop at the top of the gondola.

Merchandising

While the merchandising at the three chosen centres may never measure up to EuroDisney, it certainly exists. From what we can tell, there is little venue-specific merchandising at Nevis Range, but there are Ratho t-shirts, water bottles, mugs, and even pencils for sale. Related gear is definitely for sale (as highlighted above) and it usually involves marketing brand-name merchandise. The Snozone's Snoshop sold apparel and offered 'everything you need to look even better on the slopes!' (Snozone, 2011, para. 3; Snoshop, 2011). Ratho has its own Tiso outlet within the complex and is very much climbing-focused with the gear it stocks.

Performative labour

Of Bryman's (1999) four trends, we find few indicators of performative labour at the three centres. There are virtually none of the 'scripts' or deliberately pleasing phrases that we might expect at a Disney-type park or in American shops like Walmart. As one would hope, an organisation like Nevis Range asks for prospective employees to have 'good customer care skills and a sense of humour' (Nevis Range, 2011). We would argue, however, that performative labour is occurring here, for this is service work and they may be situations in which the client is stressed, frightened, tired, or sore. Irrespective of the service being rendered, there is an expectation that staff provide a consistent manner and appearance for their audience (see Goffman's *Presentation of Self in Everyday Life*, 1959).

One phenomenon that all three adventure centres have in common is the invitation for members of the public to be connected to their virtual social networks. RSS feeds, Twitter, and Facebook are each means by which individual consumers can keep abreast of events that may provide further opportunities to engage with the adventure centre and, almost inevitably, spend more money. All of the examples cited have very active virtual communities and regularly regale these communities with the best stories and photos of the day. In a sense, these sites serve to overcome the intangibility issues which are a challenging aspect of marketing services – there is no physical 'thing' to take home, in contrast to when a consumer buys a new television or motorcycle. With social media, experiences can be relived, narrated and shared, thereby expanding the important word of mouth element of the marketing mix and encouraging post-purchase satisfaction for the client.

Conclusions and implications

An increasing number of people in Western society are taking part in adventurous leisure activities. Some people may choose to purchase predictable packages in climate-controlled environments under the watchful gaze of expert instructors. At the same time, there appears to be another group of people that is simultaneously traditional and part of a counter-culture – one that is resisting the march of rationalisation and Disneyization. This group prides itself on the pursuit of 'authentic' adventure (if that is possible) as pursued by the 'originals'. These consumers may choose to deliberately avoid the packaged sensations, and are instead drawn toward self-directed, extended adventurous journeys by ski, kayak, or open canoe. These leisure practices ostensibly defy packaging, avoid scripted performative labours, and potentially offer existentially authentic experiences for the participants. Yet, it is intriguing that often the same adventurers will visit climbing walls and ski centres as well.

Perhaps there is rather more to the adventure experience than the confrontation with risk and danger on one's own terms? It is suggested here that, in fact, the rationalised, Disneyized packaged leisure experiences are at once enabling – for the time poor, cash rich consumers of late modernity – and disabling, as they highlight people's need for protection, expert knowledge, and risk-containment in these activities. However, this is a rather essentialist stance; many hone their strength and skills indoors prior to launching out onto the rock or the slopes, and many who might never have had a taste of outdoor adventure are inspired by their packaged experience to take things into their own hands and to venture further out. Further, as much of the tourism literature clearly shows, 'adventure' as an experiential category is both personality, context, and experience dependent (Varley, 2006a), and notwithstanding clearer definitional work being conducted and widely adopted, the indoor and the outdoor versions of adventure have equal potential to deliver existentially authentic experiences; it is simply the content and quality of those experiences which will vary.

If we accept this set of circumstances, how do less experienced members of the public distinguish between what is a socially constructed and socially valued activity and one that is inherently adventurous and personally relevant? Perhaps it does not matter. Recently, there has been greater recognition of the totality of outdoor experience, as opposed to a deep focus on rock climbing or extreme skiing or whatever. Indeed, the whole idea of European skiing has long been predicated on the 'Eat, Play, Shop' principle, as tourists focus on the importance of the quality of the après ski as well as the slopes. Answering this question likely entails addressing the question of 'What is adventure?' This is, of course, material for a book in itself. Perhaps, then, this chapter's implication for the reader is to use the McDonaldization and Disneyization frameworks as a means to make more informed choices about how adventure (theirs and others) is framed, consumed, experienced, and interpreted. As Warde (2002: 17) suggests, there may be nothing wrong with consumption that 'can provide comfort, pleasure, self-esteem, escape and decontrol'.

Following on from this, future research might examine how members of the public are being advantaged and disadvantaged by these transforming social arrangements. If leisure in general, and adventurous leisure specifically, can provide the pressure release valve that allows us to let off steam from lives lived in rationalized societies (Elias and Dunning, 1986), then perhaps the convenience of hybrid consumption, flavoured with some ersatz adventure, is a perfect respite, while simultaneously providing off-season training grounds for the sporting elite.

7 Profiling adventure tourists in Pretoria

A comparative analysis

Melissa Janette Lötter, Sue Geldenhuys, and Marius Potgeiter

Introduction

The exact size of the adventure tourism market is still debated because of: the lack of a standard adventure tourism definition; the fact that the phenomenon of adventure tourism is both new and complex; the majority of available research on adventure tourism is kept confidential as it is collected for individual companies' marketing purposes; government and industry awareness of adventure tourism is not equally developed worldwide; and the available data on adventure tourism are difficult to use due the lack of comparability. Although it is difficult to measure the market, Fluker and Turner (2000) explain that the adventure tourism market is a newly emerging, fast-growing sector of tourism. Swarbrooke *et al.* (2003) further concur that although the adventure tourism market appeals to an expanding population who are seeking self-fulfilment and excitement through participating in physically and mentally stimulating activities, the patterns of consumer behavior are in a constant state of flux.

Loverseed (1997) suggests that in the 1990s satisfaction and self-actualization appear to be crucial in understanding a tourist's engagement with an activity or a product for a specific purpose to satisfy his/her specific interest and needs. Furthermore, Fluker and Turner (2000) propose that when trying to understand adventure tourists, the research should focus on the distinct travel psychographics emphasizing specific needs, motivations, and experiences or on individuals' subjective experiences and perceptions of adventure. Lastly, Weber (2001) recommends than when analyzing the decision-making process, researchers should obtain information regarding the tourists' characteristics and their consumer and travel behavior because anticipating and meeting a tourist's needs is the key to success.

However, understanding tourists and their motivations is not easy. For instance, Laws (1991) argues that however convenient it is to categorize tourists, not all individuals fall neatly into behavioral models or typological classifications. Moreover, it is not realistic to assume that accurate descriptions of tourists' reasons for travel gained at the time of purchase will remain constant throughout the travel experience. Despite such concerns, by identifying different ypes of tourists and classifying them into groups or market segments, tourism companies would be able to direct their products/services more effectively at an identified target market.

Against this background, the primary objective of this study was to compare significant demographic descriptors of adventure tourists in Pretoria, South Africa, with essential psychographic preferences, in order to assist adventure tourism companies to promote and sell specific activities and experiences that will meet the specific needs and wants of their identified niche target markets.

Literature review

Consumer involvement is a major factor in the decision-making process (Sung, et al., 2001). Consumer behavior in tourism focuses on the relationship between the components of consumer involvement and the tourist behavioral variables specific to a tourism niche market. Therefore, leisure involvement occurs because consumers expect personal meaning in leisure pursuits and realize rewards from such involvement. Sung (2004) indicates that the involvement theory's focus is on the individual, specifically his/her lifestyle, which according to Hsu et al. (2002) is based on a personal value chain which identifies how and why (why not) individuals become involved in leisure products or activities. Sung (2004) indicates that for rare bird and animal species for wildlife viewing, for example, suitable natural resources for adventure participation or wild and rugged destination environments are major motives for adventure tourism (pull factors). Moreover, socio-psychological factors (push factors), for example, risk taking, excitement, escapism, personal development, socializing, self-discovery and self-actualization also indicate the motivations that shape the nature of the adventure experience.

In addition, every adventure activity has its particular forms and amounts of risk, which is a stimulatory motive to participate in the activity (Swarbrooke, et al., 2003). Positive risk refers to risk that a person can control and this is perceived as a challenge, whilst negative risk refers to risk that a person cannot control and this is perceived as danger. These risk levels are linked to an individual's skills, experience, and knowledge of the adventure activity. There is often a disparity between a person's perceived risk and the actual risk involved in adventure participation and the absence or presence of risk can influence a person's experience. It is widely accepted that risk taking is an important component that contributes towards a rewarding adventurous experience.

There are numerous other motives that are intertwined with the element of risk. One of these is sensation seeking. Sensation seeking, according to Woicik, et al. (2009), is (1) the *seeking* of varied, novel, complex, and intense experiences and (2) the *willingness* to take physical, social, legal, and financial risks for the sake of such an experience. Other motives that stimulate people to engage in risky adventure activities are driven by needs, for example the need to enhance self-esteem, to become more competent, to face a challenge, to develop a skill, and/or to experience novel situations.

A correlation exists between the degree of experience an individual has in a particular activity and changes in an individual's motivation. This implies that if people have a positive experience, or the more experience people have in a particular adventure activity, the more likely they will feel competent. Experience and competence are important in situations where some degree of skill is required to participate successfully in adventure, for example abseiling.

Lastly, it is important to consider the number of types of adventure experiences beyond those solely related to physical risk, because this aids understanding the motives of adventure tourists. Suppliers of adventure products/services could benefit from recognizing that there are different classes of adventure tourists, ranging from those who seek activities that offer physical challenge and risk to those looking for adventures that are intellectual, spiritual, or emotional.

As adventure tourism is associated with specific activities as a primary motive for traveling, various types of adventure tourists have emerged. These include, for example: eco-tourists, sport tourists, wildlife tourists, charity challenge tourists, gambling tourists, independent travellers, hard and soft adventure tourists, hidden adventure tourists (sex tourists), religious tourists, and gay tourists. Exploring adventure tourists' motives, as explained above, can be useful to some extent. However, the deeper motivation is often overlooked.

This is especially visible in adventure tourism research as it has received relatively little attention in academic literature. For example, authors such as Christiansen (1990), Fennell and Eagles (1990), Beeh (1999), Fennell (1999), Page and Bentley (2001), Page and Dowling (2001), Wilks and Page (2003), as well as Weed (2008), include adventure tourism typologies within their publications. However, it appears to be only Hudson (2002), Swarbrooke, *et al.* (2003), as well as Buckley and Cater (2007), whose books specifically focus on the concept of adventure tourism. In addition, research studies with an adventure tourism focus have been published by Bentley and Page (2001), Bentley *et al.* (2001), Weber (2001), Beedie and Hudson (2003), Callander and Page (2003), Gyimothy and Mykletun (2004), Page *et al.* (2005), Cater (2006a), Buckley (2007), Bentley and Page (2008), as well as Williams and Soutar (2009). However, none of these publications solely focuses on the deeper motivation when targeting adventure tourists, as this study proposes to do.

When targeting a specific market it is important to create an understanding of tourists' needs, desires, and personal goals in a tourism context. Therefore, companies should follow the three major steps of target marketing in order to execute an effective target marketing strategy.

Target marketing, as set out by Kotler (2000), coincides with the model of Rudra (2008). Rudra (2008) explains that the first step, market segmentation, involves: (1) dividing a market into distinct groups of consumers with different needs, characteristics, or behaviors who might require separate products/services or marketing mixes (segmentation bases), as well as identifying different bases to segment the market, and (2) developing profiles of the resulting market segments. The *second* step, market targeting, involves: (3) developing measures for every market segment's attractiveness and (4) selecting one or more of the market segments to enter. The *third* step, market positioning, involves: (5) developing the competitive positioning for the product/service and (6) developing a detailed marketing mix for every segment.

As comparing significant demographic descriptors with essential psychographic preferences requires dividing a market into distinct groups of consumers and identifying demographic and psychographic bases to segment the market, the following section will focus on the bases of segmentation as well as how these elements contribute to developing a demographic and psychographic profile of adventure tourists to facilitate the comparison.

Market segmentation bases

Markets consist of consumers, and consumers, according to Waldfogel (2008), may differ in their wants, resources, locations, buying attitudes, and buying practices. Ideally, every consumer can be viewed as a potentially separate market because consumers have unique needs and wants.

The role of market segmentation, according to Kurtz (2008), is to divide the total market into smaller, relatively homogenous groups. This is necessary in today's business world because there are too many variables in consumer needs, preferences, and purchasing power to attract all consumers with a single marketing mix. This does not necessarily mean that adventure tourism companies should change their products/services in order to meet the needs of different market segments, but it does suggest that adventure tourism companies should: attempt to identify the factors that affect consumers' purchase decisions; group consumers according to the presence or absence of these factors; and then adjust their marketing strategies in order to meet the needs of every selected group(s) of consumers.

According to Lee *et al.* (2006), researchers and/or companies make extensive use of a priori segmentation approach (such as geographic and demographic segmentation), and/or a posteriori segmentation approach (including psychographic and behavioral segmentation). As this study propose to compare significant demographic descriptors of adventure tourists in Pretoria, South Africa, with essential psychographic preferences, the geographic and behavioral segmentation bases fall outside the scope of this study but could form part of future research.

Demographic segmentation

Demographic segmentation entails dividing the market into groups based on population descriptors such as gender, age, ethnic group, family life-cycle stages, household type, income, and expenditure rates. This approach, according to Kurtz (2008), is also known as socio-economic segmentation, as vast quantities of available socio-economic data are required to complete a plan for demographic segmentation.

Demographic segmentation is a popular way of segmenting the market because consumer preferences and user rates often vary closely with demographic variables and demographic variables are easy to measure. Even when market segments are first defined using other bases (such as personality or behavior), demographic characteristics should be known to assess the size of the market and to reach it effectively (Kotler *et al.*, 2006). The variables that could assist adventure tourism companies to segment their markets demographically will now be further explored.

Gender is a variable that helps define markets for certain products/services; yet, segmenting by gender can be tricky. Gender segmentation is in some cases obvious, according to Kurtz (2008). However, adventure tourism companies may have to segment their markets differently if a "typical" male or female product/ service is not clearly identifiable. Kotler *et al.* (2006) suggest that companies' marketing strategies should rather be aimed at consumer interests rather than gender as gender marketing is more effective when combined with lifestyle and/ or demographics.

Biological differences among men and women are well researched and the results have been translated into popular mass-markets books (Pease and Pease, 2001). Marketing researchers have also examined gender differences in terms of message processing (Meyers-Levy and Sternthal, 1991); impulse purchases (Dittmar *et al.*, 1995); price promotions (Mazumdar and Papatla, 1995); attitudes towards shopping forms (Alreck and Settle, 2002; Dholakia and Uusitalo, 2002; Chang and Samuel, 2004; Dittmar *et al.*, 2004; and Garbarino and Strahilevitz, 2004); and advertising (Martin, 2003). This stream of research has substantiated differences between men and women regarding the manner in which they process cues, evaluate marketing products/services, develop attitudes, and respond behaviorally.

Age is another variable that adventure tourism companies could use to segment their markets. However, as with gender, age distinctions have become blurred as consumers' roles and needs change, as age distribution shifts, and as studied changes take place in every group. It appears that only Chon and Singh (1995) and Jang and Ham (2009) have researched age segmentation in the tourism field.

Moreover, adventure tourism companies can benefit from taking into consideration the sociological concept called the cohort effect. Kurtz (2008: 288) describes this concept as "the tendency of members of a generation to be influenced and bound together by significant events occurring during their key formative years." The cohort effect helps to define the core values of the age group that eventually shape consumer preferences and behavior.

The significance of the cohort effect for adventure tourism companies lies in understanding the general characteristics of every group as it responds to its defining of life events. According to Jang and Ham (2009), the social and economic influences that every group experiences helps to form their long-term beliefs and goals in life because these can have a lasting effect on their buying habits and the product/service choices they make. Therefore, for adventure tourism companies to be effective they need to understand some basic characteristics of the cyber generation, generation Y, generation X, baby boomers, and the silent generation.

In addition, companies are increasingly segmenting the market according to ethnic groups with a view to increasing their market share. Companies tend to target the largest and fastest growing ethnic groups (Kurtz, 2008), as well as ethnic groups with the most disposable income. The focus then is to inform and attract these groups as spending by these groups is rising at a faster pace than is the case for general households.

Another form of demographic segmentation focuses on the stages of the family life-cycle that, according to Kurtz (2008), is the process of family formation and dissolution. The underlying theme of this segmentation approach is that life-cycle stage, not age, is the primary determinant of many consumer purchases.

As people move from one life-cycle stage to another, they become potential consumers of different types of goods and services (Frash *et al.*, 2008). Therefore, adventure tourism companies should consider whether a consumer is a young single person, a young couple, a full nester, an empty nester, a single parent, a blended couple or an older single person when developing their marketing approaches.

Furthermore, the average household size in South Africa, as indicated by the Health Systems Trust (2007), has decreased from 4.5 in 1995 to 3.9 in 2007. Hayami and Okada (2005) explain that the trend towards smaller households could result from lower fertility rates, young people's tendency to postpone marriage, the frequency of divorce, and the ability and desire of many people to live alone. Today's households represent a wide range of diversity.

Households, according to Kurtz (2008), could include: a household with a married couple and their children; a household that is blended through divorce, or the loss of a spouse and remarriage; a household with a single parent, same-sex parents, or grandparents; couples without children; groups of friends; and single-person households. It is important for adventure tourism companies to identify household trends, should these be applicable, in order to modify their marketing approach, so that they will be able to meet the needs of different groups.

Lastly, a market consists of people with purchasing power, and Kurtz (2008) indicates that a common basis for segmenting the consumer market is income. Companies often target geographic areas known for the high incomes of their residents, and/or they might consider age or household types when determining potential buying power. In order to identify how expenditure patterns vary with income, adventure tourism companies could utilize Engel's Law.

Ernst Engel, a German statistician, published what is known as the Engel Curve, or Engel's Law. This states that the higher a family's income the smaller the proportion of it is spent on food; the percentage spent on housing, household operations and clothing remain constant; and the percentage spent on other items (education and recreation) increases (Engel, 2009). Engel's conclusion was based on a budget study of 153 Belgian families and was later verified by a number of other statistical inquiries into consumer behaviour. It is evident that adventure tourism companies could utilize Engel's Law when segmenting their markets.

Tourism literature includes several studies that use expenditure rates as segmentation bases, although mixed results are yielded. Earlier studies were not able to distinguish heavy users from light users in terms of socio-economic characteristics (LaPage, 1969; Stynes and Mahoney, 1980) but more recent studies found significant differences (Pizam and Reichel, 1979; Woodside *et al.*, 1987; Spotts and Mahoney, 1991; Legoherel, 1998). Based on these results, it appears that segmenting visitors based on travel expenditures may be a useful alternative to the more common approach of segmenting them based on travel activities. Spotts and Mahoney (1991) propose that expenditure rates might be superior to activity measures as a segmentation basis because expenditure rates for a given unit of travel activity can vary significantly from one travel party to another.

It is important to keep in mind that demographic segmentation as a basis can be helpful, but it can also lead to stereotyping, as indicated by Kurtz (2008). Furthermore, it can alienate a potential market or cause adventure tourism companies to miss a potential market altogether. The idea is to use demographic segmentation as a starting point and not as an only alternative.

Psychographic segmentation

Companies traditionally referred to geographic and demographic characteristics as the primary bases for dividing consumers into fairly homogenous market segments. Still, they have long recognized the need for lifelike profiles of consumers in developing their marketing programs.

It was already suggested in the 1990s by File and Prince (1996) that psychographic segmentation could be a useful base for gaining insight into consumer purchasing behavior. This type of segmentation refers to dividing a population into groups that have similar psychological dimensions (George, 2008). It is believed that common values can be found among groups of consumers and these values tend to determine their purchasing patterns. Adventure tourism companies could therefore use psychological characteristics (such as personality, social class and lifestyle) as a base for segmenting the market.

Markets can be divided in accordance with the personality of consumers. This type of segmentation, as said by George (2008), has been used to distinguish different types of tourists. As stated by Lin (2002), personality variables can be used to segment markets and to give products/services personalities that correspond with consumers' personalities.

Moreover, consumers are strongly influenced by the class to which they belong or aspire to belong. Social classes are relatively permanent and consist of ordered divisions in a society whose members share similar values, interests, and behaviors (Kotler *et al.*, 2006). Consumers, according to Kotler *et al.* (2006), can be divided into upper-uppers, lower-uppers, upper-middles, middle, working, upper-lowers, and lower-lowers. These social classes have a strong effect on consumer preferences and adventure tourism companies should build features into their marketing strategies that appeal to these different classes.

Lastly, lifestyle, according to Kurtz (2008), refers to a person's mode of living; it describes how an individual operates on a daily basis. Consumers' lifestyles are composites of their individual psychological profiles – including their needs, motives, perceptions, and attitudes. A lifestyle also bears the mark of many other influences, such as family, job, social activities, and culture.

Adventure tourism companies could utilize various psychographic profile systems to identify market segments according to their lifestyles. Lifestyle profiles of consumers, according to Berkowitz (2006), are often developed using attitudes, interests, and opinions (AIO) of consumers. This could assist adventure tourism companies to identify what consumers in various demographic and geographic segments want and need.

Adventure tourism companies could also utilize VALS™, which according to Strategic Business Insights (2012) is a marketing and consulting tool that helps businesses worldwide to develop and execute strategies that are more effective. This tool, according to Wilson and Gilligan (2005), uses psychology to analyze the dynamics underlying consumer preferences and choices. It does not only distinguish differences in motivation, but also captures the psychological and material constraints on consumer behavior.

Other tools available to adventure tourism companies include LifeMatrix, which according to Kurtz (2008), crunches the numbers of hundreds of personal variables that include political views, religious affiliation, and social attitudes, and comes up with ten psychographic categories that reflect today's lifestyles. These systems could assist adventure tourism companies to create a much richer description of potential target markets, which would allow adventure tourism companies to match their image and product/service with the type of consumers who use their products and services.

To conclude, psychographic segmentation is not an exact science but it would enable adventure tourism companies to quantify aspects of their consumers' personalities and lifestyles so that they can create activities and services specifically applicable to their selected target market. Studies by Mykletun *et al.* (2001) and Sedmak and Mihalič (2008) suggest that psychographic segmentation is a good supplement to demographic or geographic segmentation as it refines the picture of a market segment's characteristics, thereby providing a more elaborate lifestyle profile.

Based on the above discussion, it is evident that segmentation is a tool that can help adventure tourism companies to increase their effectiveness in reaching the right markets (Kurtz, 2008). Similar to other marketing tools, segmentation is best used in a flexible manner, for example by combining segmentation techniques or dovetailing certain segments. Segmentation is a tool that will assist adventure tourism companies to be knowledgeable about their potential consumers and ultimately satisfy their needs with the appropriate products and services. The discussion on market segmentation addressed the first step of the market segmentation process; the next section will elaborate on how to develop profiles of the resulting market segments.

Developing profiles of the resulting market segments

Before a marketing program aimed at a specific market segment can be developed, adventure tourism companies should understand the typical consumer in that market. According to Cravens *et al.* (1987), a profile should identify those characteristics that both explain the similarities and differences among consumers within every segment.

A profile, according to Hanson *et al.* (1994), should paint a clear picture of the typical consumer by using applicable segmentation variables discussed previously – demographic and psychographic. This will assist adventure tourism companies to identify relationships among segmentation bases that can support the inclusion of descriptive characteristics in the profile. Although this profile is a generalized average of the typical consumer in the segment (Mostafa, 2009), consumer profiling is very important because the usefulness of market segmentation is predicated upon accurate profiling. However, relatively low accuracy in forecasting segment membership will result in ineffective marketing programs and may have a potential negative impact due to targeting inadvertent segment members.

As the primary research purpose of this study is to compare significant demographic descriptors with essential psychographic preferences, step one and two of the market segmentation and overall target marketing process will form the basis of this study. The resulting information gained through implementing this process will address the research problem of this study. Nevertheless, in order to identify how this study's resulting information can be utilized by adventure tourism companies in the future, companies should implement market targeting and market positioning strategies. These strategies fall outside the scope of this study, but could form part of future research.

Methodology

This study was based on applied research, descriptive research and a quantitative methodology due to it being grounded in the positivist social sciences paradigm. The target population consisted of adventure tourists, and the sample consisted of adventure tourists making use of the products/services offered by adventure tourism companies within Pretoria, South Africa.

Non-probability sampling in the form of quota and convenience sampling was used to select the sample members. The sample consisted of 250 adventure tourists of whom 50 percent were male and 50 percent female. However, because of incomplete questionnaires that could affect the outcome of this study, the sample that actually realized was 234, providing a 93.6 percent response rate.

This study used quantitative research in the form of a self-completing questionnaire. This questionnaire followed a positivistic approach and consisted of closed-ended, dichotomous, and multi-choice questions. The raw data obtained from the questionnaire were turned into numerical representations to enable statistical analyses on the aggregated data. The raw data were captured onto a database in Microsoft Access that was imported into the SAS (Statistical Analyses Software) format through the SAS Access module. The data were then analyzed according to a bivariate analysis (cross-tabulation and the Pearson correlation coefficient) to determine whether there were any relationship(s) between variables.

Findings

The primary objective of this study was to compare significant demographic descriptors of adventure tourists in Pretoria, South Africa, with essential psychographic preferences. Demographic descriptors are those innate economic, geographical, and social attributes that constitute an individual and describe the location of that individual in his or her social environment. Demographic characteristics provide the impetus for both tangible and intangible variations among the ways consumers think, feel, and act. Moreover, psychographic descriptors refer to detailed information regarding consumers' activities, interests, and opinions as well as their attitudes, values, and needs.

A bivariate analysis in the form of cross-tabulation was used to present the information of demographic and psychographic variables simultaneously and to determine whether any relationship exists between these variables. Furthermore, while the variables were tested, inferential statistics in the form of the Pearson's Chi-square were performed. These statistics are important, as statements will be made about the respondents in relation to the population being studied.

It is important to note that all the demographic and psychographic variables that were considered previously were tested, however only statistically significant results will be discussed.

Age

The age descriptors were divided into the sociological concept of the cohort effect because the core values of these age groups will eventually shape consumer preferences and behavior that could influence adventure tourism companies' marketing approaches. Significant statistical differences were identified in terms of the type of activity they prefer when they are with their families as well as the type of activity they themselves prefer. It is important to note that the silent generation (born 1925–1942) was omitted from the findings as there was only one respondent for the group.

Based on the findings, 88.1 percent of the respondents from the generation X age group (born 1960–1981), 87.0 percent from the baby boomers age group (born 1943–1960) and 70.7 percent of the generation Y age group (born 1982–2001) indicated that they prefer soft adventure activities (for example hiking and snorkeling) when they are with their families. However, there are statistically significantly more respondents from the generation Y age group that prefer hard adventure activities (for example skydiving, abseiling, scuba diving) when they are with their families.

Furthermore, when sorting activities from the most to least preferred, it was noticeable that the minority of the respondents preferred air-based activities compared to land-based and water-based activities. However, 53.33 percent of the generation Y age group preferred air-based activities in comparison to the generation X (28.4 percent) and baby boomers (8.7 percent) age groups.

Family life-cycle stage

Family life-cycles are one of the primary determinants of many consumer purchases and it is therefore important that adventure tourism companies are knowledgeable about their target markets' family life-cycles as this will enable adventure tourism companies to develop adventure tourism packages applicable to selected target markets.

Marital status

In terms of the respondents' marital status, significant statistical differences were identified in terms of the type of transport they prefer when they are within destinations as well as the type of activity they prefer. It is important to note that the widowed group was omitted from the findings as there were only six respondents for the group.

Divorcees (84.0 percent), married couples (82.6 percent), cohabiting partners (64.3 percent) and single people (59.2 percent) prefer to travel within a destination by means of their personal vehicles. However, cohabiting partners have a higher tendency to hire a vehicle, single people have a higher tendency to use a bus or non-motorized transport, whereas divorcees have a higher tendency to utilize a taxi.

Moreover, in terms of the type of activity they prefer, cohabiting partners (57.1 percent) and single people (48.6 percent) mostly prefer air-based activities in comparison to divorcees (38.5 percent) and married couples (23.3 percent). This coincides with the results that the majority of the generation Y age group prefer air-based activities.

Life stage

In terms of the respondents' life stage, significant statistical differences were identified in terms of the type of accommodation they prefer, the type of transport they prefer to a destination, as well as the type of activity they prefer. All the life-stage groups mainly prefer to stay at self-catering establishments (27.3 percent) or camping/caravaning sites (18.2 percent) when they are on holiday. However, if self-catering or camping/caravaning was not an option, families (parents with at least one dependent child) would prefer to stay with their family and friends, pre-families (own household with no children) would prefer to stay at a lodge, dependent individuals (living with parents/dependent on parents) would prefer to stay at family and friends, a guest house or a lodge, whereas, late families (parents with children that have left home or older childless couples) would prefer to stay at a guest house. It would appear that resorts (6.1 percent), private homes (3.9 percent) and backpacker hostels (3.9 percent) are the least preferred accommodation type.

In terms of transport to a destination, late families (79.2 percent), pre-families (74.6 percent), families (71.4 percent) and dependent individuals (40.0 percent) prefer to travel by means of their personal vehicles. In addition, 31.1 percent of dependent individuals, 23.5 percent of pre-families, 20.5 percent of late families and 17.2 percent of families prefer to travel by airplane. However, it seems only to be dependent individuals and families that would consider taking the bus or taxi. Vehicle hire (1.7 percent) is the least favourite method of transport to a destination.

Lastly, in terms of the preferred activity type, late families (76.9 percent) and families (76.5 percent) do not prefer air-based activities. This coincides with the results that the majority of the generation Y age group, cohabiting partners and single people prefer air-based activities as these groups are most likely to be a pre-family or dependent individuals.

Discussion

The primary objective of this study was to compare significant demographic descriptors of adventure tourists in Pretoria, South Africa, with essential psychographic preferences in order to assist adventure tourism companies to promote and sell specific activities and experiences that will meet the specific needs and wants of their identified niche target markets.

Summary of findings and managerial implications

The exact size of the adventure tourism market is still debatable due to the non-existence of a standard definition of adventure tourism. The phenomenon of adventure tourism is both new and complex and the majority of available research on adventure tourism is kept confidential as it is conducted for individual companies' marketing purposes. Government and industry awareness of adventure tourism is not equally developed worldwide and available data on adventure tourism are difficult to use because of the problem of comparability. This exemplifies a need for a tourism classification that can evolve and accommodate more complex forms of tourism, such as adventure tourism. According to Page and Connell (2006), a robust system is required to classify and measure tourism-related terms.

The importance of implementing target-marketing strategies when developing consumer profiles was identified. This study's empirical research identified that market segmentation is one of the most important strategic tools that an adventure tourism company can use in order to match their marketing efforts with consumer preferences.

According to Cravens *et al.* (1987), the segmentation concept is so logical and straightforward that it is easy to overlook the difficulty and expense of implementing it. Segmentation is more likely to be successful if a systematic approach is followed because segmentation strategies do not simply happen; these are the result of applying a systematic analytical and decision-making process.

The first step of target marketing, namely market segmentation, is the act of dividing the market into distinct consumer groups, which might merit separate products/services, or marketing mixes. Markets can be segmented using different bases, and adventure tourism companies should try several approaches, and even combinations of these, in order to determine which will yield the best opportunities. In order for adventure tourism companies to utilize the profile, the last two steps of the target-marketing strategy (market targeting and positioning) should also be implemented.

The steps of this process are reliant on the success of each other; in other words, every step needs to be implemented effectively in order to proceed and successfully complete the systematic process. Therefore, adventure tourism companies should consistently analyze, plan, develop, deliver, evaluate, and update their marketing campaigns to meet their marketing objectives whilst meeting the demands and/or preferences of their target markets.

Lastly, the findings of the study suggests that the baby boomer generation age group (born 1943–1960) is married or divorced and consequently forms part of the family or late family life-stage. These respondents prefer soft adventure activities, for example hiking and snorkeling, when they are with their families. These respondents are not interested in taking part in hard adventure activities, for example skydiving, abseiling and/or scuba diving. This notion is confirmed as they do not prefer air-based activities. Furthermore, this group of respondents prefers to travel to and within a destination by means of their own vehicles and they do not prefer to utilize any other means of transport. Lastly, this group of respondents prefers to stay in self-catering establishments, camping/caravaning sites, with family and friends, or guest houses. They do not prefer unconventional forms of accommodation.

On the contrary, the findings of the study suggests that the generation Y age group (born 1982–2001) is single and consequently forms part of the dependent individuals life-stage. These respondents prefer hard adventure activities when they are with their family, they have a higher tendency to travel to and within destinations with unconventional forms of transport and are most likely to seek eccentric types of accommodation.

This reinstates the fact that segmentation is best used in a flexible manner, for example by combining segmentation techniques or dovetailing certain segments, as adventure tourism companies can now identify sections of the market they can serve best.

Limitations and directions for future research

The structural limitations of this study include the inadequate amount of literature associated with adventure tourism. Adventure tourism has been industry driven; therefore, the significance of theoretical constructs might not have been completely documented as greater attention was paid to empirical applications. Adventure tourism studies are usually carried out from a social-science perspective, therefore substituting research terms or application practices may violate assumptions across these two fields.

In terms of the research methodology, the sample might raise concerns in terms of representativeness and the reality that this study cannot be generalized. *Firstly*, due to incomplete questionnaires that could influence the outcome of this study, the sample that realized was smaller than the expected sample; *lastly*, due to a lack of assistance from some adventure tourism companies, all the adventure tourism companies based in Pretoria could not be included in this study.

Nevertheless, the target population of this study was not the general public in Pretoria; rather, it comprised adventure tourists making use of the products/services of adventure tourism companies within Pretoria. Therefore, the generalization of the study findings to the general public should be treated with a degree of caution. Moreover, due to time and financial constraints this study could not be extended to include more or all provinces in South Africa, nor a bigger sample.

Future research could include consumer behavior patterns focusing on the generation X age group (born 1960–1981), because this study was unable to identify a specific pattern for this age group and they did not fall within the general profile of the baby boomers or generation Y age group. Furthermore, future research could include developing adventure tourist profiles with more behavioral components and/or psychographics such as needs, motivations, or benefits to provide reliable and useful information about adventure tourists' consumer behavior that is specific to their particular adventure travel participation. More research is needed in terms of adventure tourism marketing because the full effect of this type of marketing will be beneficial to the entire adventure tourism industry.

Conclusion

Tourism influences most regions of the world in one way or another. The increase in adventure tourism has precipitated a corresponding need for growth in adventure tourism information. As a result, it is imperative to use a suitable research methodology to retrieve accurate and useful information, as research has become an important instrument for the adventure tourism industry to collect data on a variety of aspects. This study aimed towards contributing to a better understanding of adventure tourists by comparing significant demographic descriptors with essential psychographic preferences of such tourists. This information could aid adventure tourism companies to identify and develop effectual marketing strategies to attract or enter the adventure tourism niche market.

8 How was it for you?

Assessing the quality of the adventure experience

Antonie Bauer

Introduction

What makes an adventure good or even outstanding? This is more than an academic question for companies seeking to optimise their offerings and provide tourists with the best possible experience. Unfortunately, much of the adventure experience is about thrills, excitement, rush (Buckley 2012) or flow (Csikszentmihalyi 1990) – in other words, subjective states of mind largely influenced by individual skills and personality (Wu and Liang 2011). They are only to a very limited extent under the control of the adventure providers and destinations. Nevertheless, the quality of the service also has a big impact on the overall quality of the experience. This chapter explores different ways of measuring service quality, especially in tourism; it then takes a closer look at previous applications in the adventure industry and the most important conclusions from them. In the third section, the results of a research project on the quality of soft adventure in the Irish South-West are presented.

Measuring the quality of services

Of the many definitions of quality available, the one used in ISO 8402 provides a good starting point. According to the International Organization for Standardization (cited in OECD 2006), quality is 'the totality of features and characteristics of a product or service that bear on its ability to satisfy stated or implied needs'. More specifically, the UNWTO defines quality in tourism as:

> the result of a process which implies the satisfaction of all the legitimate product and service needs, requirements and expectations of the consumer, at an acceptable price, in conformity with mutually accepted contractual conditions and the underlying quality determinants such as safety and security, hygiene, accessibility, transparency, authenticity and harmony of the tourism activity concerned with its human and natural environment.
>
> (UNWTO 2003)

Though this definition is quite clear, it is far less clear how the quality of an experience should be measured and what the consequences of different quality levels are. This has inspired an impressive amount of research into the basic relationships between service quality and customer satisfaction, behavioural intentions, i.e. the wish to revisit and word of mouth, and, ultimately, economic performance. Though these relationships are far from undisputed, the majority of publications support the view that product quality impacts on customer satisfaction, and this in turn stimulates behavioural intentions (Cronin and Taylor 1994; Williams and Soutar 2009; Murray and Howat 2002).

Methods for assessing quality and customer satisfaction

Much of the research into service quality, theoretical as well as applied, is based on the SERVQUAL model, which uses a gap method, measuring customers' perceptions of attributes against their expectations (Parasuraman *et al.* 1988, 1991). The original model groups 22 items ('XYZ has up-to-date equipment', 'You can trust employees of XYZ') into five dimensions: tangibles, reliability, responsiveness, assurance and empathy. Assurance, which has come up as the most important category in several adventure tourism surveys, is defined by Parasuraman *et al.* (1988: 23) as 'knowledge and courtesy of employees and their ability to inspire trust and confidence'. SERVQUAL has proved very popular and has been used frequently in tourism contexts even though it has drawn a lot of criticism, both on a theoretical and empirical level (Kozak 2001; Fallon and Schofield 2003). While some of it is directed at the way SERVQUAL is applied, much of it is more fundamental: many researchers object to the gap method and the use of expectations per se, especially for the tourism industry where lack of previous experience with the product makes expectation formation difficult (Crompton and Love 1995; Cronin and Taylor 1992; Kozak 2001; Yüksel and Rimmington 1998; Carman 1990; Ekinci 2003) Nonetheless, SERVQUAL has been widely used and adapted to the needs of several sectors of the tourism industry. There is even a version for adventure, ADVENTUREQUAL; however, it is rather specialised as it focuses on 'young people's outdoor adventure watersports' (Donne 2009).

On the customer-oriented side of quality assessment, related concepts that often use the same dimensions are SERVPERF and Importance-Performance Analysis (IPA). SERVPERF, proposed by Cronin and Taylor (1992, 1994) is based on performance only. Importance-performance analysis assesses customer satisfaction directly, too; in addition, it explores to what extent attributes matter to the client (Martilla and James 1977). Whereas these three methods, known as the American school, are related in their descriptive approach, an alternative concept, known as the Nordic school, considers 'overall categories' (Brady and Cronin 2001: 44): technical quality, i.e. the outcome, and functional quality (Grönroos 1984). Some authors also add value to the relationships examined (Oh 1999; McDougall and Levesque 2000; Murray and Howat 2002).

In empirical tests of the different models, the evidence is mixed, but tends to be in favour of performance only rather than gap models (Taplin 2012a, 2012b; Hudson *et al.* 2004; Yüksel and Rimmington 1998; Baker and Crompton 2000; Crompton and Love 1995; Burns *et al.* 2003).

While the academic literature has a strong focus on capturing the customer's judgement and satisfaction, official assessments of service quality tend to come from a different angle: they usually seek to rate a high number of providers based on a set of 'objective' criteria that allow for standardisation, i.e. they focus on the supply-side. While these criteria would ideally reflect those dimensions of service quality that affect the customer experience most, this is not necessarily the case as the softer factors are hard to measure. Thus, Su and Sun (2007) found that a proposed hotel rating scheme for Taiwan relied heavily on criteria related to assurance and tangibility, whereas empathy, reliability and responsiveness were under-represented.

The QUALITEST framework developed for the EU (European Communities 2003) offers a combination of both the customer-oriented and the supply-side approaches. It was designed to evaluate destinations by combining the subjective measure of visitor satisfaction with quality management and 'objective' quality performance indicators. The latter are based on data from industry surveys and information available to destination managers. In the surveys, companies are asked questions like whether they have been certified according to quality management standards or whether they cater for the needs of tourists with impaired mobility.

Applications in adventure tourism

There has been a fair amount of work applying and adapting the models discussed above to leisure, activity and the outdoors, including studies on national parks (e.g. Tonge and Moore 2007; Akama and Kieti 2003; Arabatzis and Grigoroudis 2010), fitness, sports and leisure centres (e.g. Murray and Howat 2002; Papadimitriou and Karteroliotis 2000) and wildlife refuges (Tian-Cole *et al.* 2002). Equally, some researchers have focused on specific adventure activities such as white-water boating and rafting (e.g. Whisman and Hollenhorst 1998). However, with the possible exception of Aggarwal *et al.* (2011) and Jennings *et al.* (2008) in a purely qualitative analysis, there is very little research on the quality of the adventure sector as such.

At destination level there has been considerable interest in ski resorts, some of it sparked by the alpine region's struggle for market share, e.g. Weiermair and Fuchs (1999). They found that shopping, other sports and food/accommodation affected tourists' quality judgements in 11 winter resorts in Northern Italy and Austria more than the actual skiing; among the 'quality domains', variety/fun came out on top, whereas safety and aesthetics/appearance played a minor role. Fick and Brent Ritchie (1991) identified assurance and reliability as the most important expectations in ski services areas, whereas in the perception of the customers tangibles fared best. In a Greek resort investigated by Alexandris *et al.* (2006), interaction with the employees and the quality of the physical environment (up-to-date equipment, good maintenance of slopes and supportive services, etc.) contributed most to place attachment and customer loyalty. A survey of over ten alpine ski destinations confirmed the link between customer satisfaction and customer loyalty; image became relatively more important for customer loyalty the more often participants had already visited (Faullant *et al.* 2008).

Skills levels apparently also play a role in determining what is most important to adventure tourists. While skilled skiers are predominantly concerned with the quality of the snow, the runs and the terrains, beginners put almost equal emphasis on facilities and care more about price than advanced skiers (Richards 1996). The impact of skills is confirmed by Fluker and Turner (2000), who explored the expectations and motivations of white-water rafting tourists and found significant differences in motivation between the experienced and the inexperienced participants. At a destination level, motivations and expectations are even more diverse, leading to different evaluations depending on what tourists have originally come for (Devesa *et al.* 2010). Consequently, an adventure that is perfect in every respect would rank at the top irrespective of the skills and motivations of the clients, but if the performance is mixed across different dimensions, the perceived quality can vary substantially depending on the customer mix.

Applications of modified SERVQUAL models include ecotourism (Khan 2003) and a Greek outdoor programme (Kouthouris and Alexandris 2005). In Khan's survey eco-tangibles (environmentally friendly equipment and facilities) proved to be the most important service dimension in eco/adventure tourism, followed by assurance. Kouthouris and Alexandris, who looked at participants of a Greek outdoor programme with activities like canoeing, kayaking and orienteering, also identified assurance as the most important expectation. However, the authors concluded that the model was inadequate for an outdoor setting as it failed to predict customer satisfaction and customers' intention to participate in a similar programme again, which in their view was because it did not account for important factors like the physical environment and the outcome (e.g. achievement or enjoyment). Yet the relevance of outcome was limited in another study on aquatic centres by Howat *et al.* (2008). One outcome dimension, 'relaxation benefits', contributed to overall satisfaction, but it was less important than two process dimensions: personnel and facility presentation had the highest impact.

The physical environment played a role in the study of a Greek resort by Alexandris *et al.* (2006) discussed above and in a recent analysis of India as an adventure destination (Aggarwal *et al.* 2011). The latter was based on a simple performance-oriented questionnaire which included the physical environment in a category called 'aesthetic appeal'. Tourists turned out to derive by far the highest satisfaction from this dimension, which contained the beauty of the scenery as well as environmental attributes, whereas they rated accommodation, information, food and safety and security as rather poor. Interestingly, tour operators and government officials, who had also been given the questionnaire, overestimated India's performance in all respects except aesthetic appeal.

Several authors prefer importance–performance analysis for evaluating the quality of the adventure experience, not least because it offers a straightforward management tool that tells a company's or a destination's decision makers on which area to put most emphasis. One example is Tarrant and Smith (2002) in a fairly comprehensive analysis of outdoor recreation across the United States. Serious deficits were only found for 'information on conditions and hazards' (p. 77), where performance was low, but the importance visitors attached to the item was high. The standard recommendation for such a constellation in an IPA is for management to 'concentrate here'. Visitors tended to be quite happy with all other attributes that mattered in their opinions and some others that did not, such as shower facilities or the availability of equipment rental, resulting in the risk of 'overkill'. Ziegler *et al.* (2012) used IPA for the whale-shark tourism experience on the Mexican Isla Holbox. The most important motivations of the tourists they surveyed were proximity to the sharks, the environmental commitment of the boat crew, the quality of the marine transportation services and the information provided by the boat crew. Safety and crowding emerged as areas of concern. O'Neill *et al.* (2000) adapted IPA to the diving sector (DIVEPERF) to assess the quality of dive tour operations in Western Australia. Again, and not surprisingly in an adventure context, assurance came out as the most important dimension both in the quantitative analysis and in interviews with divers, who had paid great attention to safety when choosing the operator. Importance and perform-ance were mostly in line: the quality of the facilities and the suitability of the boat for diving played a fairly big role and received comparatively high scores, whereas the appearance of premises and staff performed less well, but also mat-tered less to the tourists.

Williams and Soutar (2009) chose a value-based framework (PERVAL) for their analysis of two companies' one-day trips to the Pinnacles in Western Aus-tralia in four-wheel drive vehicles. Novelty value and value for money, espe-cially, but also functional and emotional value, had a positive impact on customer satisfaction. In addition, there was a clear link between satisfaction and future intentions for three categories (value for money, emotional value and novelty).

To sum up, in most studies on the adventure sector the participants attached a lot of importance to assurance and the related field of safety, and in some cases the actual performance on safety fell short of the requirements. Crowding also emerged as an area of concern. Tangibles like facilities and equipment played an important role in some of the surveys, but mainly with respect to functionality; most adventure tourists did not care too much about appearance and aesthetics of the facilities. There is some evidence that the physical environment also matters to customers, from the quality of ski slopes to environmentally friendly practices of operators. Finally, according to some of the studies, tourists also care for the availability of information and value for money. Categories like responsiveness, empathy and reliability rarely stood out, but tended to be quite significant nonetheless.

Assessing adventure tourism in the Irish South-West

Much of the Irish South-West – the counties of Cork and Kerry – is sparsely populated and predominantly rural with largely untouched nature, a long coastline, lakes and Ireland's highest mountain range. Not surprisingly, adventure tourism in a broad sense is a mainstay of the local economy. According to O'Brien (2010: 6), activity tourism accounts for 36 per cent of all tourism revenue in Kerry. Tourism in turn is one of the most important industries in the region, employing 15 per cent of Kerry's workforce in 2006 (Kerry County Council 2009: para. 6.1.1). The adventure providers in Cork and Kerry offer a broad range of water- and land-based activities, most of them at the softer end of the spectrum; the majority of the companies are owner-run micro-businesses. The survey presented in this section was conducted in the context of a product, environmental and marketing audit of soft adventure providers in Kerry and West Cork commissioned by the Irish tourist board Fáilte Ireland. Seventy companies, representing over 90 per cent of the major adventure providers in the region identified by Fáilte Ireland, participated.

The approach of this analysis is strictly supply-side, i.e. evaluating attributes directly, not through the eyes of the customers. The other main difference to the surveys discussed above is the comprehensiveness of the approach: almost all adventure companies of the region and all types of activities in the adventure sector were covered, giving a precise picture of the state of the industry both at company and destination level.

The service quality evaluation served a dual purpose. Adventure tourism is high on the tourism authorities' agenda (Fáilte Ireland 2007) as they see huge potential for growth in this area. In order to further develop and market the product, Fáilte wanted to find out more about the current quality of the services offered; in addition, it wanted to obtain a rating of adventure providers. Unlike hotel star ratings this was intended only for internal use, to help the tourism board to better target its support. As part of the rating scheme, the providers were also given their report cards with the information on where they did well and where their businesses underperformed.

Method

In most cases, the survey consisted of a visit to the provider's premises and a structured interview with senior managers, usually the owners of the companies. Most of the answers were provided by the companies; some information was gathered by inspection of the premises or online. In the original questionnaire, there were 12 dimensions that applied to all companies plus activity-specific attributes whose number depended on the nature of the activity. Depending on the nature of the business, there were up to 53 attributes. For this analysis, the product-specific categories and those items that did not provide any meaningful results were left out; 45 items remained.

The approach chosen for the assessing quality was purely digital: if a relevant attribute was present, the company was awarded one point; if it was missing, zero points were given. One of the objectives of the survey was to keep the results as objective and unbiased as possible, with the auditor's judgement playing a very small role. As a consequence, in most cases only the availability of a feature, e.g. parking, was checked; the quality of the feature only came into play when it was clearly substandard, which led to the loss of half a point. Exceptions were made in the category 'appearance of place', which had 'clean and tidy' as well as 'well-maintained' as attributes.

The limitations of the approach are obvious. First, it cannot measure the outcome – the rush, flow or excitement generated by the adventure. However, in light of the literature review above, this may be a minor problem as service quality indicators seem to be rather closely related to overall satisfaction. Second, unlike, e.g. the European hotel grading system (Hotelstars Union 2009) and unlike some of the methods above that assess importance either directly or indirectly, this method does not weigh attributes according to their importance to the customer. Skilled staff has the same value in the rating system as the availability of storage facilities. However, without further research into the importance of every single attribute, any weighting would be just as random as a unit weight for every attribute. And third, the focus on easy to observe and easy to measure criteria neglects the less tangible dimensions that have been shown to play an important role in customer satisfaction. In terms of the original SERVQUAL scale, no categories are identical, but tangibility and responsiveness are covered in a reasonably similar way; assurance is represented by the safety and staff training questions; empathy is captured somewhat by opening times and client–instructor ratios and reliability in one question on whether clients can be sure that activities will go ahead as planned.

On the upside, the survey is very comprehensive. Unlike most other studies, it covers the customer experience from the first contact. Thus, features like an easy to navigate website that has all the necessary information, the time it takes the company to reply to an email inquiry or how many hours a day the telephone is manned are included.

Results

The results of the survey showed considerable variation both in the overall scores for some of the categories and in the scores of the different providers. Dimension ratings for the set of attributes used in this survey ranged from 38 per cent of all possible points to 93 per cent. The worst-performing company scored 51 per cent of all possible points for the 45 items in this overview, whereas the best one reached 93 per cent. Sixty out of the 70 companies fell into the bracket between 63 and 87 per cent that meant a three- or four-star rating. Only three had higher scores, which is the requirement for five stars.

Strengths

Overall, the Irish adventure businesses did best in the tangibles and safety/assurance categories. The highest percentages were reached for 'equipment' (93 per cent of all possible points) and 'appearance of place' (91 per cent). Whereas the former category looked purely at functionality, i.e. the availability of adequate

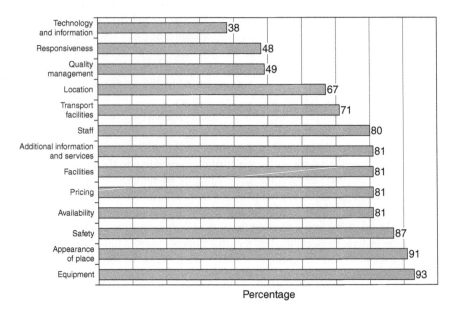

Figure 8.1 Quality scores by category.

equipment like kayaks or a boat for diving operations, the latter factored in more aesthetic considerations: the attributes were 'clean and tidy' and 'well-maintained'. These points were given as long as a certain minimum standard was reached, so they do not reflect the huge differences in the quality and presentation of the premises. Some of them were new, upscale, very well equipped and visually appealing whereas others were rather basic, only just clean enough and only just not too run-down to clear the hurdle.

With a score of 87 per cent, safety was the third best-performing dimension. As the nature of adventure and the findings from the literature survey, especially the prominence of the category 'assurance', suggest, this is probably one of the most important, if not the most important category, in the eyes of the adventure tourist. Nearly all companies had joined the relevant associations, thus subscribing to their regulation and safety standards of associations like AIRE for horse-riding, the ISA for sailing or PADI for diving. In addition, the vast majority of the adventure providers had clear and practiced emergency procedures as well as clear health and safety instructions for their clients; safety equipment was up to date and checked regularly, and all companies claimed to subscribe to best practice standards in safety. One major weakness emerged, however: few Irish companies are able to give international visitors, who do not always speak English all that well, safety instructions in any other language, not even in writing.

Value for money, i.e. 'good' or fair prices, has been shown to impact on customer satisfaction. However, as the fairness of a price is largely in the eyes of the beholder, it was not investigated as such in the context of this survey. What it did take into account were some elements that contribute to the perception of fair pricing. Thus, companies were awarded points if they had a clear price structure and price information was easily available; if they offered special rates to certain demographics such as families, children, the unemployed, pensioners etc.; and if they had a fair cancellation policy. Most Irish adventure providers grant discounts, and almost all of them turned out to be very generous when clients cancel, often not even charging them when they fail to turn up for a booked activity without notice. The reason sometimes is simply that they do not know how to get hold of the person that has cancelled on them or are reluctant to ask for credit card numbers. This somewhat informal attitude towards business is also often reflected in pricing, where a considerable number of adventure providers do not have a clear structure, but tend to 'knock off a few euros' when they feel like it, making the cost of the experience less predictable for the customer. The overall score in the pricing and conditions category was 81 per cent.

The same percentage was reached for facilities, for availability and the dimension additional services and information. 'Facilities' simply looked at the availability, but not the quality, of five items: parking, toilets, changing rooms, storage facilities and eating facilities. While parking does not seem to be a major problem in the Irish countryside – 92 per cent of the providers offer it – only 58 per cent had eating facilities. A more pressing problem from the point of view of the visitor may be the lack of toilets: the score for access to toilets was only 87 per cent. The additional services under review included the availability of packed lunches for full-day activities and information on local activities, entertainment and dining.

'Availability' comprised several aspects, from daily and seasonal opening times (which correspond to one of the empathy items in the SERVQUAL model) to sufficient capacity to accommodate all tourists that want to participate in activities. The industry performed very well in terms of inclusiveness – activities are usually offered for all skills levels, children as well as adults and people with disabilities – and the reliability of service, which means that activities usually go ahead as booked, even if there are only a couple of participants. Capacity is a problem, however, due to the extreme seasonality of the business: nearly half of the providers have to turn away prospective customers fairly often.

In spite of the importance of the way staff interact with the tourists for the customer experience, these 'soft' attributes are hard to measure objectively and without surveying the customers themselves. The approach taken here was to look at skills and customer–instructor ratios. Four skills attributes were considered: skills and qualifications in the activity provided (e.g. instructor licences), the provision of in-house training for local and product knowledge, safety procedure training and foreign language skills. Overall, the instructors employed in the Irish adventure sector scored highly in the skills categories, with one notable exception: tourists can expect to deal with someone who speaks any foreign languages in less than half of the companies. Crowding, which was identified as a major problem in some of the other surveys, does not seem to be a huge problem in the Irish South-West: maximum staff–client ratios were good in 91 per cent of the companies. The overall score for the staff dimension was 80 per cent.

Weaknesses

Performance was somewhat less good in the two dimensions that dealt with the setting of the adventure (67 per cent) and getting there (71 per cent). Rural Cork and Kerry have practically no public transportation to speak of, making it a challenge to travel to most of the places where the adventures take place. Consequently, firms were awarded points for providing pickup services from the tourists' accommodation (56 per cent) or the next bus stop or train station (62 per cent). For those adventures that take place in more than one location, nearly all providers offered transport from one place to the other. The dimension location reflects much of the bureaucratic and legal restrictions adventure providers in Ireland have to live with. Only 71 per cent said that their location offered them the necessary infrastructure. The rest are often hampered by access issues as many of the walking paths lead across private farmland. Depending on the negotiating skills of the adventure provider, tourists sometimes find themselves trotting along main roads instead of walking the hills. Boat operations complained about insufficient harbour facilities. Another issue is signposting, which is heavily regulated and very limited, making finding a place very difficult for tourists.

The numbers start to look substantially worse when it comes to quality management. Barely a quarter of the adventure companies in the Irish South-West have set up any system for managing quality, and slightly less than half have a mechanism for capturing customer feedback like questionnaires, comment cards on the counter or email enquiries after the experience.

Responsiveness was also very weak. This category did not evaluate the quality of the companies' responses to the customers' requests, but simply the promptness of the reaction. This was tested by mystery shoppers, who called during business hours and sent an email to each of the providers. To score a point in the phone test, the companies had to answer the phone or at least ring back immediately; the point for email replies was given to everyone that responded within 24 hours. Only 60 per cent of the providers picked up their phone, and only 36 per cent replied to the email inquiry within a day; quite a few never did.

The lowest average score (38 per cent) was reached in the category technology and information, which assessed the user-friendliness of the providers' websites. Forty per cent of the websites were either out of date or had inaccurate information; only 38 per cent contained all the information that was considered essential, i.e. opening times, rates, location and contact details, and only 17 per cent offered online booking. In combination with the low responsiveness to phone calls and emails, this means that just finding out about the offerings of the companies can be a hard job for prospective customers.

Type of activity and company size

A closer look at how providers of different types of adventure performed reveals some differences. For most categories of activities, the overall rating ranged between 72 and 78 per cent; the average score for all-round adventure providers and adventure centres was 76 per cent. With an average of 81 per cent, diving centres came in first; at the bottom of the ranking were the horse-riding operations with an average score of 66 per cent. Only one out of seven stables was awarded more than three stars, which required a score of over 75 per cent. Overall, 46 per cent of the 70 Irish adventure companies were in one of the two top categories.

Quality as measured in this survey is strongly correlated with company size. Though a good handful of the two- and three-star providers reported six-digit turnover per annum, the majority tended to be rather small. The median annual revenue for these two categories was €60000. On the other hand, only seven of the four- and five-star companies reported sales of less than €100000 per year; the median revenue for the firms in the two top categories was €185000.

Discussion

The results of this quality survey reflect the structure of the Irish adventure tourism sector: nearly all companies are micro-businesses with hardly any permanent employed staff, and many of the firms in the sample are run by lifestyle entrepreneurs with little or no business background. Most of them belong to the type of enterprise described by Swarbrooke *et al.* (2003). Forty per cent have no marketing training at all, not even from one of the short workshops the tourism authority Fáilte Ireland provides. The trend towards 'larger and more sophisticated operations' (Cloutier 2003) has still largely evaded Cork and Kerry. Accordingly, most of the effort seems to go into the adventure experience itself, which performs well on almost all of the attributes considered. Conversely, all aspects of customer service that do not have to do with the immediate experience tend to be neglected by the industry, be it for lack of manpower, time or simply awareness and training. This is particularly obvious in the poor scores for quality assurance, responsiveness and the online availability of information.

The bigger firms performed much better on the quality criteria, probably because they have more financial resources, allowing them to invest in amenities, and more staff, and enabling them to pay more attention to the managerial side of their business. However, the causality may also be reversed to some extent: though the top performers for quality are considerably bigger than the bottom ten on average, the high-quality firms tend to be younger than those with the lowest scores, indicating far higher growth rates over the years. It does not require a huge stretch of the imagination to conclude that this may also have been due to the higher quality they provide, though different marketing efforts probably also played a role (Bauer 2011).

Equally, the highly rated companies seem to have the necessary managerial skills: nearly all of the top performers' managing directors have a business background, whether it is a degree in leisure management or marketing or many years of experience as a chartered accountant. Conversely, among the bottom ten firms for quality, none of the nine for which this information is available is run by a person with a business background. Business expertise seems to translate into better quality, and it has also led to higher growth in this sample.

The relationship between quality, behaviour and profit

The survey measured quality, but it did not assess customer satisfaction or behavioural intentions. What it did measure to some degree was actual behaviour: the companies stated how many of their customers had been with them before and also gave the main sources of their original business. In contrast to most of the findings on quality and behavioural intentions however, there was no obvious correlation between quality scores and percentage of return customers. Five-star providers and two-star providers, both rather small groups, had 58.3 and 50.6 per cent repeat customers respectively; 41.4 per cent of the clients of the three-star companies and 40.1 per cent of those of four-star firms had already been on an adventure with the same provider previously. This metric is not equivalent to how many of a given number of customers come back, however; it would underestimate the return rate of a fast-growing firm relative to one that grows slowly or stagnates. The main determinants of repeat visits were the nature of the activity and the companies' main target groups. Sailing and surfing draw the highest number of repeat customers whereas providers of once-in-a-lifetime experiences like a boat trip to the Skelligs do not tend to see their clients again, no matter how outstanding the experience was. Proximity to population centres like Cork and a focus on residents, especially on children and schools rather than tourists, also explained a lot of the variation in return visits.

On the other hand, there was some evidence of a correlation between the score and the likelihood of positive recommendations. All companies that had kept track of where their customers came from were asked what were their main sources of new business. Overall, word of mouth was mentioned most, followed by the internet. But there were marked differences between the top-rated and the less-well performing adventure providers: only slightly less than two-thirds of the two- and three-star companies said that word of mouth played an important role in generating business whereas 85 per cent of the firms that were awarded four or five stars did so. Riding stables, which had ranked at the bottom for quality, were the least likely to benefit from recommendations (20 per cent), surfing and sailing schools the most (93 per cent). However, it has to be remembered that the water-sports providers typically cater to a predominantly local clientele, especially schoolchildren, which makes it easier for word of mouth to get around to other prospective clients.

Finally, does better quality translate into higher economic success? Surprisingly little effort has gone into investigating the link between satisfaction and financial performance, but the evidence so far is largely in favour of such a link. Studies confirming it include Yee *et al.* (2011), Anderson *et al.* (1994),

Hallowell (1996) and to some extent Rust *et al.* (1995) and Schneider (1991). On the other hand, Wiley (1991) discovered a negative correlation between customer satisfaction and financial performance in a retail environment, but he cautions that the causality may be the reverse as very busy stores mean long waits and little attention from sales personnel. In tourism-related analyses, Bernhardt *et al.* (2000) discovered a positive link between customer satisfaction and the profits of fast-food restaurants in a longitudinal analysis over 12 months; in Chi and Gursoy's (2009) study of three- and four-star hotels, customer satisfaction also had a significant effect on the companies' performance. Gursoy and Swanger (2007) found no direct link between customer service and financial performance in the hospitality industry; they suggest that this may be because good service is a 'given' in the industry.

As discussed above, highly rated adventure companies tend to have significantly higher revenues than the bottom performers. Though this suggests more success in the marketplace, the ultimate measure of financial success is profitability. The companies in the survey simply reported whether they were profitable or not, but in most cases did not state the volume of their income nor whether they had deducted a salary for management. Of the four- and five-star companies, 59 per cent said they were profitable, but only 50 per cent of the two- and three-star firms. The difference originated mainly at the ends of the scale: all three- to five-star firms were profitable, but just two out of seven two-star providers. This lends a little support to the hypothesis that higher quality is rewarded by higher profits, but numbers are far too small for a final verdict.

Remarkably, the areas where the Irish adventure providers performed worst tend to be those where improvement can be achieved easily and at low cost, which means that addressing those weaknesses is very likely to result in better business performance. Thus, one recommendation would be the introduction of a simple system for managing quality and capturing customer feedback such as visitor questionnaires. Even more importantly, short response times to emails and the fairly low investment needed to make websites user-friendly and informative would not only improve visitors' experience, but also help to attract new clients. From a marketing point of view, a good internet presence and quick replies to inquiries are absolute essentials.

Conclusion

In spite of the extensive body of literature on service quality, there has been fairly little research on the adventure sector as such. A comprehensive supply-side survey of the whole industry in South-West Ireland reveals a number of apparently industry-specific results. Most notably, adventure providers in Cork and Kerry seem to deliver high quality in core aspects of the experience such as safety/assurance, equipment and skilled staff, but perform less well in non-core categories such as responding to inquiries. One possible reason is the tendency for the firms to be run by lifestyle entrepreneurs rather than business managers.

There is a clear link between management expertise, company size and quality as measured by a set of 45 criteria and some evidence of positive effects of quality on recommendations and company success. One potential weakness of the approach is the choice of attributes, whose relevance in the customers' eyes was not tested. To validate the results and examine the usefulness of 'objective' criteria for quality assessment, research into the customer side of the adventure experience in Cork and Kerry would be very useful.

Part III

Adventure learning and education

Peter Varley

This part of the book offers insights into the ways we learn to pursue adventure, and how adventure is used as an educational tool. Specifically, Hardwell investigates British rock-climbing traditions and trends as a way in to a discussion about the 'outdoor apprenticeship'; the gradual process of gaining experience and access to the metanarratives and codes of practice surrounding various outdoor pursuits. He suggests that the acceleration of commodification processes in these pursuits has cut short the hitherto 'natural' journey toward a serious leisure career, where learning occurs as much via mistakes as via successes, over time, with long periods of reflection between episodes. The time-pressed consumer-learner can now circumvent this apprenticeship with some intensive courses.

Vernon, meanwhile, tackles how we give, receive and co-create feedback in adventure learning situations, and calls for a recognition of some important dimensions in this process, such as the importance of time (for reflection); the recognition of the crucial issue of objective and subjective positions in the feedback dynamic and a balance of the statuses within feedback relationships.

Continuing a thread concerned with *time*; for reflection, for the accrual of experience, and now, for the adventurous journey, Stott, Allison and Von Wald's chapter explores the benefits of the expedition, applying new methodologies to interrogate these experiences. Their work suggests ways of harnessing the evaluative powers of the participants themselves in identifying the lessons learned and the benefits to be derived from such experiences.

This last paper, the authors acknowledge, has at its core a phenomenon that bridges the gap between adventure tourism and adventure education, and is a reflection of the crossover between the two over the last 100 years. Clearly, each aspect of controlled, marketed, managed and rationalized adventure offers much to inform our understanding of the other – thus, feedback techniques may be borrowed from educational settings and used for tourist debriefs, and the research into tourism experiences could usefully harness the participants-as-researchers approach adopted by Stott *et. al.* Likewise, experiential educationalists may cautiously observe the Disneyization of adventure centres and consider how best to preserve the unique qualities of their practices, avoiding the rationalizing processes of the marketplace. Taking more time – spending time in the outdoors – might be the key. The thread that may be picked up in most of the chapters in this book shows that the adventure experience is often condensed to fit the convenience needs of the consuming public, but in fact the benefits for generating meaning, improving experiences and enhancing learning are all linked to the passage of time during immersive spells in nature.

9 The demise of the outdoor apprenticeship

Ashley Hardwell

Introduction

Sociologists study the way in which humans interact with each other within societies. In studying the intricacies of human behaviour, greater understanding of society as a whole is possible. Donnelly (1981: 568) posed questions over a quarter of a century ago that may still be important today: 'How is society possible? How and why do people develop the sets of norms, values and sanctions that are manifested as socially acceptable behaviour and, for the most part, conform to them?' He goes on to suggest two reasons for wanting to study smaller units or subcultures of society: they are interesting cultural phenomena but they can also give important insight into society. Sport sociologists have similar concerns albeit focused upon how generic concepts taken from broader societal studies either play out in or are evidenced within microcosms of sport. Therefore, any sport with both a long tradition and a recent history of current innovation and expansion provides a perfect opportunity to explore sociological concepts. This gave purpose to this chapter which is to recognise that recent development in the differentiated nature of rock climbing in the UK has begun to shape this activity and allow wider participation from varied interests and backgrounds.

This chapter has two important aims. The first is to give an overview of UK rock climbing, its practices and subcultural issues. UK rock climbing is briefly described to the reader. In doing this it draws first on traditional rock climbing in the UK as a particular style of climbing and then on more contemporary practices. This is because traditional climbing forms the backdrop to rock climbing in the UK. It is the type of climbing with which the majority of UK participants are familiar. Traditional climbing embodies a style of ascent towards which many rock climbers aspire. It is the most psychologically taxing and risky rather than necessarily the most difficult type of ascent. The essay juxtaposes this rock climbing type with more contemporary rock climbing practices. These 'new ways' of climbing and their effect on subculture and practices are then explored.

Its second aim involves the focus of attention of this book. Adventure tourism in the UK will provide an important context in critically analysing the possible benefits of shifts through contemporary rock climbing practices and how the latter has shaped rock climbing activity in the UK. A line of inquiry will be developed suggesting the appropriation (Marchart 2004) of rock climbing into mainstream society through contemporary climbing practices. It is proposed that focus on technical climbing ability is now occurring to the detriment of traditional rock climbing skills and the 'outdoor apprenticeship' essential to its safe practice. Not only is contemporary climbing shaping the very values of traditional climbing but it is also allowing greater diversity of acceptable rock climbing practices in rock climbing overall. These changes have improved accessibility to many different and diverse user groups providing business opportunities in the outdoors. While this allows rock climbing to be developed as an excellent adventure tourism activity a loss of traditional rock climbing skill and general outdoor awareness has occurred and these tensions form the chapter's content. To this end it is a unique attempt to understand the changes within rock climbing and allow a counter gaze (Lim 2008) from within the activity itself. It therefore asks the reader to go beyond the benefits of the commercial world of adventure tourism products and services and consider the possible consequences of greater rock climbing accessibility through appropriation.

UK rock climbing practices

Rock climbing has captured the imagination of participants for many different reasons over the last two decades. It has become one of the fastest growing outdoor pursuits in the UK during this period (BMC 2003). It now has many coexisting facets all displaying obvious differences. Traditional climbing, sport climbing, bouldering, indoor climbing, deep water soloing and competition climbing are recognisable manifestations of types of rock climbing in the twenty-first century. Ethics, practices and even subcultures of each rock climbing type can be identified but all share the ultimate goal of ascending a climb from the ground to its top using equipment only as a safeguard against falling.

Two types of UK rock climbing practice will be explained: traditional and contemporary. The former represents the historical rock climbing legacy in Britain and alludes to a style of climbing where ascents are made from the ground up with minimal information about the climb always with the 'end game' in mind of only using equipment as a safeguard against a fall. This is known as an 'on sight' or 'flash' ascent and is often seen as one of the most coveted styles of ascent by climbers. All British rock climbing types stem from 'traditional climbing'. Contemporary rock climbing in this chapter alludes to indoor climbing, sport climbing and bouldering all of which focus on technical rock climbing movement (see Hardwell 2009). These 'rock' climbing types focus on the end game already mentioned but worry less about the means to the end due to the highly technical nature of the rock climbing.

Traditional climbing

Traditional climbing usually takes place in pairs. Each person ties onto either end of a rope 50 metres or so long. Using a special locking mechanism on the rope known as a belay device one person can feed the rope out to his partner who begins ascending. Traditional climbing uses removable equipment placed in natural fissures in the rock in order to protect the climber from a fall to the ground. The skills required for traditional climbing include route finding, interpreting and 'reading' the rock, interpreting guidebook information, placing equipment in the rock and constructing belays or anchor points to allow safe passage during high rock climbs. In the UK longer climbs are often found in mountain areas and these draw on general outdoor skills (for a fuller explanation see Lewis 2004; Donnelly 2003: 291–304; and Hardwell 2007: 12–14).

Traditional climbs have many unknowns; route choice, equipment used, route conditions, weather and so on and this often results in a compromise in difficulty, ensuring climbs are commensurate with capabilities and all possible variables. The aim of all climbing is a safe ascent and when traditional climbing this may require retreat with dignity (Mortlock 1984). Traditional climbing is psychologically as well as physically testing because the lead climber may often be at risk of a considerable fall before the rope comes into play and relies on the quality of removable protection placed while climbing to prevent a ground fall.

From traditional climbing recognisable ethical codes or 'canons' have developed across climbing types. Rock climbing has no rule book. Using equipment to gain a hold is not a punishable offence. Each climber ascends knowing they will not be berated for poor style as long as honesty is foremost. Yet, at the same time, they are acutely aware of codes of practice stemming from traditional climbing. It is also worth noting that the technical nature of the most difficult traditional rock climbs in the UK is so high that climbers who attempt these deem it necessary to practise them beforehand, an approach more generally adopted by contemporary climbing types. This has led to an interesting paradox. Those setting traditional rock climbing standards in the UK and admired by other rock climbers have, in many cases, adopted codes and canons of contemporary climbing because of the extreme difficulty of the climb.

Contemporary climbing

Other climbing types have taken the 'end game' of rock climbing (ascending rock climbs only using equipment as a safeguard against falling) and used this as a climbing focus. Their aim is to test physical rock climbing skills through attempting technically difficult climbs or shorter boulder 'problems'. Often these are so difficult the climb has to be practised beforehand for the 'end game' to be achieved. This is the domain of the boulderer and sport climber. In sport climbing regularly spaced permanently fixed protection points take the place of removable chocks. Each climb is identified from below by a line of bolts often placed in seemingly blank rock walls. A different grading system developed in France and referring only to technical difficulty is used. The grade indicates the most technically difficult move on the climb but gives no indication of danger because fixed protection is regularly available often rendering the climb relatively safe.

Donnelly (2003: 292) describes the different approaches adopted by traditional and more contemporary climbing practices, particularly sport climbing, as the 'great divide' and suggests it is the 'most serious rift in the history of the sport'. While this rift is documented and explored in terms of different climbing approaches little understanding of its complexity in British rock climbing exists and investigation into the possible development of a cultural shift away from adventure towards more predictable and known outcomes is occurring (Hardwell 2007). This possible change in emphasis may be a legacy of contemporary approaches to UK rock climbing. Climbing approaches changed significantly from the 1970s (Hankinson 1988). A far more systematic and 'sport-like' approach was adopted (Jones and Milburn 1988) and a relaxation of established ethical codes occurred in favour of a focus on the practices required to complete technically demanding rock climbs safely.

Frame conditions

Such changes require contextualisation to allow more comprehensive understanding. Poon's (1993) broad overview of touristic changes can be used to explore the wider 'frame conditions' associated with traditional and contemporary climbing eras. In any time period various frame conditions outside of rock climbing will assist its development in a particular direction. Those activists at the very core of rock climbing subculture (see Hardwell 2009) will drive the activity forward in accordance with the zeitgeist created through the frame conditions. These influences can be summarised by the classic external environment analysis of political, economic, social and technological aspects and are represented thematically in Figures 9.1 and 9.2. Focusing on climbing practices between 1950 and 1965 allows insight into an era of climbing where equipment, although vastly improved from the pre-Second World War era, was still rudimentary and specific training was rarely deployed. It was an era dominated by strong traditional rock climbing ethics in keeping with the frame conditions of the time. This contrasts greatly with the 1970s and beyond.

Traditional frame conditions

The existence of climbing clubs and the difficulty of accessing these, particularly for women, allowed for an exclusive feel to climbing where gaining access to the activity required antics, behaviours and activities (Perrin 2004; Hankinson 1988). There has always been fierce rivalry at the higher echelons of rock climbing yet the overwhelming feel from the many sources commenting on this era is the importance of camaraderie and the intrinsic worth of being associated with the environment (Lewis 2004; Perrin 2004; Wilson 1998; Drasdo 1996; Gray 1993a, 1993b; Hankinson 1988; Birkett 1983). Importantly, rock climbers had little choice regarding the style of ascent; traditional rock climbing was the only style on offer and mountain crags were particularly popular. An outdoor

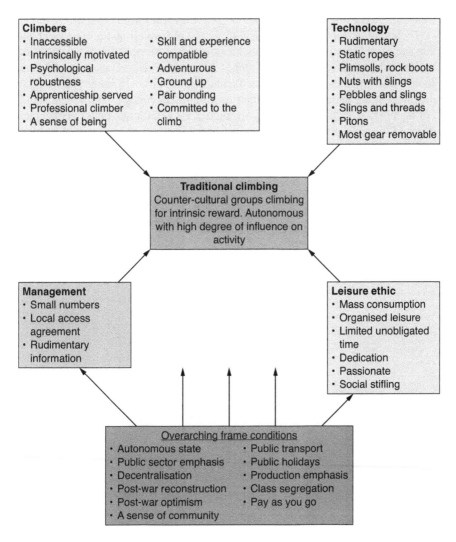

Climbers
- Inaccessible
- Intrinsically motivated
- Psychological robustness
- Apprenticeship served
- Professional climber
- A sense of being
- Skill and experience compatible
- Adventurous
- Ground up
- Pair bonding
- Committed to the climb

Technology
- Rudimentary
- Static ropes
- Plimsolls, rock boots
- Nuts with slings
- Pebbles and slings
- Slings and threads
- Pitons
- Most gear removable

Traditional climbing
Counter-cultural groups climbing for intrinsic reward. Autonomous with high degree of influence on activity

Management
- Small numbers
- Local access agreement
- Rudimentary information

Leisure ethic
- Mass consumption
- Organised leisure
- Limited unobligated time
- Dedication
- Passionate
- Social stifling

Overarching frame conditions
- Autonomous state
- Public sector emphasis
- Decentralisation
- Post-war reconstruction
- Post-war optimism
- A sense of community
- Public transport
- Public holidays
- Production emphasis
- Class segregation
- Pay as you go

Figure 9.1 Historic frame conditions for climbing 1950–1965.

apprenticeship was therefore a prerequisite for safe climbing with longer climbs calling for serious climbing commitment.

Contemporary frame conditions

The marked contrast between the traditional and contemporary climbing eras is that of choice. Heywood (1994: 187) neatly sums this up by commenting that: 'the danger, the unpredictability, the risk, the irrationality of climbing are substantially matters of *choice*; climbers can have their activity raw, medium or well-done according to how they feel or what they want from the sport.'

The attention focus is the physical difficulty of rock climbing movement and this can be achieved indoors or outside. Often physical rock climbing ability far outweighs general outdoor experience. Accessible venues are available and sought after to allow the pursuit of technical difficulty. Different practices are deployed at the expense of traditional rock climbing ethics to allow high stand-ard technical difficulty with safety in mind. Last (1997) has noted higher inci-dents of top rope practices in outdoor venues. Skills associated with traditional

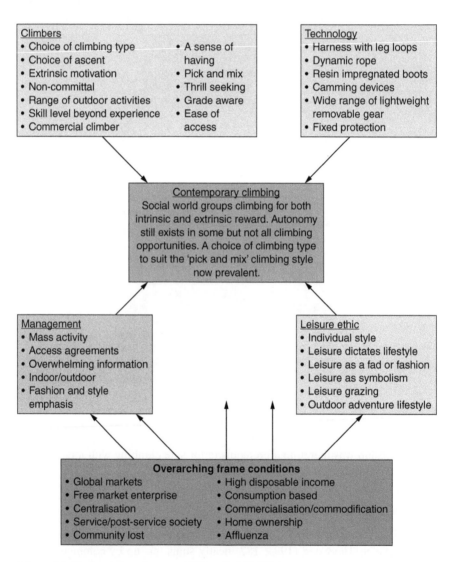

Figure 9.2 Contemporary frame conditions for climbing.

rock climbing have been neglected in favour of technical rock climbing ability. Yet, this style of climbing neatly fits post-modern lifestyles (Jenks 2005). Indoor climbing and bouldering can both be time bound and complement busy lifestyles. They are social activities where public displays of climbing occur. For many they provide important escapes from routine and allow people to experience a different social situation and activity (Hardwell 2009). Contemporary climbing is not an activity solely for outdoor enthusiasts but for anyone wishing to pursue an alternative pastime. For many, indoor climbing is an activity in its own right rather than a progression to other climbing pursuits (ibid.).

The subcultural nature of rock climbing in the UK

Rock climbing has been viewed as a recognisable subculture within society (Lewis 2004; Donnelly 2003; Kiewa 2002; and importantly Donnelly and Young 1988). Subcultural tensions occur inside and outside of rock climbing. According to Gelder and Thornton:

> The defining attributes of 'subcultures', then, lies with the way the accent is put on the distinction between a particular culture/social group and the larger culture/society. The emphasis is on variance from a larger collectivity who are invariably but not unproblematically, positioned as normal, average and dominant.
>
> (1997: 5)

Hebdige (1987: 85) who, through many counter-cultural studies, accepted that subcultures were important contributors to social stability, suggested 'a credible image of social cohesion can only be maintained through the appropriation and redefinition of cultures of resistance'. This he sees as a 'cyclical process leading from opposition to diffusion, from resistance to incorporation and encloses each successive subculture' (ibid.: 100). Beal and Crosset (1997: 75) concluded that 'truly counter-cultural groups do not exist for long'. Donnelly (1993) documented the demise of climbing as a recognisable counter or subculture understanding the outside pressures and inner tensions that would eventually cause its demise.

Contemporary subcultural work (Jenks 2005) and post-subcultural contributions (Macbeth 2005; Marchart 2004; Weinzierl and Muggleton 2004; Kiewa 2002) problematise the heterogeneity of both society and its subcultures. Jenks (2005: 135) observes that 'contemporary society's multiple manifestations are now in such a flux and constant state of proliferation that our real problem resides in attempting to theorize what ... we previously referred to as the "centre".' Macbeth (2005: 5) extends such ideas to subcultures themselves believing two key challenges confront research into sport subcultures:

> At the micro level, analysis of sport subcultures needs to explore heterogeneity amongst its members and reveal the multiple, and sometimes conflicting, identities formed by individuals and groups within subcultures. Internal

tensions and power relations between groups need to be analysed as sites of subcultural production and examined in the context of the subcultures' dynamic relations within the dominant culture at the macro-level.

To view rock climbing as a heterogeneous subculture in opposition to society is too simplistic. Rock climbing as a subculture is complex, not least because of the 'flux and constant state of proliferation' (Jenks 2005: 135) caused through contemporary adapted rock climbing environments and activities. Despite this, rock climbing remains adventurous (Lewis 2004; Donnelly 2003; Heywood 1994) and still differs significantly from wider societal culture (see Varley 2006b; Simmel 1997 [1991] and also Beck 1992 for a general societal overview). But it is the tensions within rock climbing and their effect on rock climbing practice and subculture that is of interest in this chapter.

Subcultural differentiation

Contemporary climbing participants are differentiated. They consist of different types of climbing (bouldering, indoor climbing, sport climbing, deep water soloing). They differ in their approach from traditional climbing and, because their proliferation and accessibility, are being accepted as the way to climb. Luhmann (1996: 60) conceptualises differentiation by suggesting 'a pre-formed' system can be delimited from the environment to form its own environment for new subsystems. Here my interpretation of differentiation is the assumption that traditional climbing is the 'pre-formed' 'delimited' subsystem for contemporary climbing types. The autonomy of these 'new ways' of contemporary climbing requires consideration, not least in order to be developed as products in themselves for adventure tourism operators.

Contemporary climbing practices are becoming more acceptable within traditional climbing and a shift in climbing values towards contemporary forms of climbing may be identified. Luhmann (ibid.) goes on to suggest that eventually a subsystem is able to 'observe its own operations' and 'monitor its own cohesion' as opposed to being reliant on the 'pre-formed system'. In effect, he suggests that new autonomous values and norms are created within the 'pre-formed system'. These new value systems in rock climbing align themselves more readily with societal values giving weight to Hebdige's (1987) subcultural appropriation theory. Figure 9.3 represents this schematically and shows the importance of differentiation in the overall demise of a strong counter or subculture. To provide imagery to help with this explanation Smith (2011) showed aerial film of the breakup of ice shelves in the Antarctic. As a unified whole the ice shelf is protected but once fragmented (or differentiated) each section is subsumed into the southern ocean. Such changes only occur given the right frame (environmental) conditions.

A further way of depicting traditional and contemporary rock climbing approaches in the UK and their alignment with society is to use Young's (1997 [1971]) theory of subterranean values. Its framework will focus solely on the

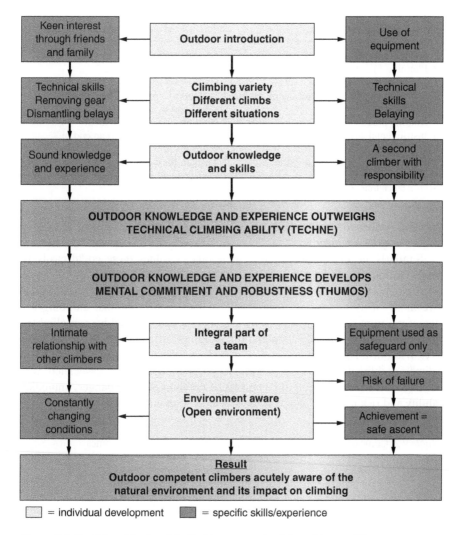

Figure 9.3 Traditional (authentic) climbing apprenticeship and its possible outcomes.

micro-culture of climbing rather than its intended purpose to compare and contrast values of the wider urban society with subculture. Young (1997 [1971]: 73) discussed subterranean values seeing these as more likely to be expressed in alternative leisure settings. Examples might be wind surfing and skate boarding (See Wheaton 2000, 2004; Beal 1995). Table 9.1 depicts these contrasted values.

Using the problematic dualistic approach of contemporary sport and traditional climbing adopted by other academics (Donnelly 2003; Heywood 1994, 2006; Lewis 2000, 2004), Young's typology shows wide disparity of climbing values and manifest practice. 'The formal work values' could easily be attached

Table 9.1 Formal and subterranean values contrasted

Formal work/societal values	Subterranean/alternative leisure values
1 Deferred gratification	1 Short term hedonism
2 Planning future action	2 Spontaneity
3 Conformity to bureaucratic rules	3 Ego-expressivity
4 Fatalism. High control over detail, little over direction	4 Autonomy, control of behaviour in detail and direction
5 Routine predictability	5 New experience, excitement
6 Instrumental attitudes to work	6 Activities performed as an end in themselves
7 Hard productive work is a virtue	7 Disdain for work

Source: taken from Young 1997 [1971]: 73.

to more contemporary approaches adopted by sport climbers. A second table of values may be produced.

Similarly in turning attention to subterranean values these could easily be linked to traditional climbing approaches.

Contemporary forms of the activity (bouldering, indoor and sport climbing) are more easily aligned to macro-social values than traditional climbing and therefore more readily influenced by society and appropriated by non-climbers. The result is institutionalisation and regulation of different aspects of the activity. Without this, adventure tourism would find the natural unpredictability of climbing difficult to manage. While appropriation may be associated with demise of the more subcultural elements of climbing such as danger, unpredictability and risk it allows its use as an adventure tourism activity to develop.

Table 9.2 Comparison of formal work values and sport climbing outcomes

Formal work values	Sport climbing practices
1 Deferred gratification	1 Climbs attempted on a regular basis over a period of time. Immediate success rare
2 Planning future action	2 Working the route/practising the moves – working towards success
3 Conformity to bureaucratic rules	3 One dimensional climbing/move sequence, end product focus, climb equipped by others
4 Fatalism. High control over detail, little over direction	4 A concentration on minutiae of sequences but must follow bolts and work each move
5 Routine predictability	5 Bolt protection/safe outcome/eventual success – certainty
6 Instrumental attitudes to work	6 Goal oriented – methodical/repetitive
7 Hard productive work seen as a virtue	7 Gym training, working out, indoor practice, keeping fit

Source: adapted from Young 1997 [1971]: 73.

Table 9.3 Comparison of subterranean values and traditional outcomes

Subterranean values	Traditional climbing practices
1 Short term hedonism	1 Adventure/the outdoors
2 Spontaneity	2 Unconstrained/free/natural
3 Ego-expressivity	3 Climbing hubris
4 Autonomy, control of behaviour in detail and direction	4 Natural line and form/rockscape experience
5 New experience, excitement	5 Unknown entity, possibility of failure
6 Activities performed as an end in themselves	6 Love of the outdoors, beauty and nature/ part of the landscape
7 Disdain for work	7 Apprenticeship-natural affinity/skills/ ability/no end product

Source: adapted from Young 1997 [1971]: 73.

Outdoor apprenticeships

A further outcome of contemporary climbing practice is the demise of a holistic skill set enabling independent and autonomous enjoyment of rock climbing. The use of specific teaching techniques have grown over the last 20 to 30 years and courses and masterclasses are common. Heywood (1994) argues that all types of climbing are now sanitised and rationalised. In this he includes traditional climbing and suggests it is rationalised through the equipment, information available and training techniques deployed. He also argues that the difference between sport climbing and traditional climbing is becoming less obvious:

> Sport climbing and adventure climbing as it is practised by most people most of the time are not separated by an unbridgeable chasm; they are already closely related, and this suggests, worryingly from the point of view of those who value the 'British approach', that the spread of sport climbing can be seen quite reasonably as a natural development in climbing practice generally.
>
> (Heywood 1994: 191)

This rationalisation is supported by the frame conditions. We are technologically driven: equipment is important both practically and aesthetically, time is precious and there is a need to utilise it wisely favouring contemporary climbing practices. Access to climbing areas has improved and sport climbing crags with easier grades are regularly used by increasing numbers of climbers and groups. Indoor climbing centres continue to be developed showing demand is still buoyant (BMC 2003). There are a growing number of outdoor operators in the UK (ibid.) and guided trips seem to be more commonplace in UK and European mountains.

Contemporary climbers are realising hardship and long outdoor climbing apprenticeships are no longer necessary with the advent of modern facilities.

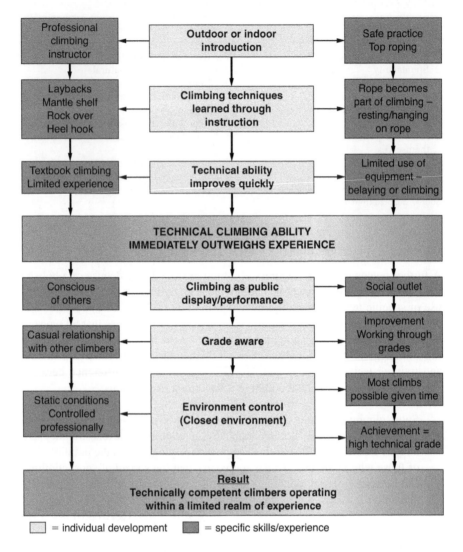

Figure 9.4 The modern (clinical) climbing apprenticeship and its possible outcomes.

Climbers become fit and stay fit indoors. They can learn to belay and lead climb and have sufficient skill to render climbing safe on pre-placed equipment. An outdoor environment offering sport climbing can therefore be the beginnings of outdoor experience. Even climbing outdoors in such circumstances may be seen as a closed environment in that, as much as possible, the crag has been rendered safe. Sport crags tend to be in reasonably accessible; others may frequent the crag and it could be viewed as an extension of indoor practices. The responsibility for safety has shifted to the professionals who develop indoor and outdoor facilities for commercial gain and the love of the sport. Such issues bring into question the place of the traditional outdoor climbing apprenticeship (see Figures 9.3 and 9.4).

There is little need for long outdoor apprenticeships in contemporary climbing types. The outdoor apprenticeship is a realm of holistic outdoor experience where skills of map work, meteorology, geological, geographical and topographical knowledge as well as guidebook interpretation and specialist equipment knowledge all play a part in safe climbing practice and are firmly rooted in traditional climbing. At many traditional climbing venues the environment is less predictable, routes far more committing and specific skills are necessary for safe ascents. Rope work, placing and removing equipment, belaying safely, abseiling, route choice and anticipation of possible problems based upon knowledge and experience may all be prerequisites for traditional climbing. Self-rescue, first aid and emergency protocols are essential. The onus is on a competent pair of climbers with equal skill and experience to deal with situations that may arise. For more contemporary climbing practices participants' fitness and flexibility combined with good technical skill are the only necessary requirements. Outdoor skills and knowledge required are minimal. There is little need for the type of extensive apprenticeship seen in traditional climbing. This is further confirmation of the sanitisation and rationalisation of other climbing forms when compared to traditional climbing (Heywood 1994; Lewis 2000, 2004).

Questions of safety within contemporary climbing types are largely left to the 'professional climber': frequency and quality of fixed protection, configuration of belays and lower off points are all decided beforehand (see Oliver 2006). In some instances even stability of the rock and therefore safety of the climbing venue is the result of extensive cleaning and preparation by local activists. Climbers may even come to expect this level of attentiveness and preparation if their general experience of climbing is indoors. Concern within this outcome is also raised due to the increasingly litigious nature of British society and ensuing blame culture.

Differing levels of knowledge, experience and outdoor skill acts as a segregator between outdoor enthusiasts and those seeking the physical challenge of rock climbing. Representations of the apprenticeship process in traditional and more contemporary climbing practices are depicted in Figures 9.3 and 9.4.

Outcomes of merging styles and frame conditions

Leisure lifestyles are symbols and definers of who we are (Wheaton 2004). The last two decades have seen the outdoors carrying more cultural capital (Bourdieu 2001 [1986]) in Western societies. This is underpinned by a $220 billion spend in the US alone on adventure tourism travel and related products (Adventure Travel Society in Cater 2007: 63). In the UK, Campbell *et al.* (2007) reported a direct spend in 2003 of £631 million on adventure breaks to Scotland alone. Secondary spend is generated from many prestigious events based in Scotland. For example, the UCI Mountain Bike World Cup held annually at Fort William has an estimated associated spend of £2 million (Campbell *et al.* 2007: 7). Scotland has established itself as Europe's adventure capital with numerous outdoor adventure activities well established.

Rock climbing in the UK is considered an important facet of adventure tourism for many adventure tourism operators. Buckley (2007: 1428) gives a product-oriented definition of adventure tourism as 'guided commercial tours, where the principal attraction is an outdoor activity that relies on features of the natural terrain, generally requires specialised equipment, and is exciting for the tour client'. While not considering the popularity of multi-activity adventure holidays now offered by organisations in the UK such as the Youth Hostel Association and the many individual operators, it does emphasise the specialist nature of the adventure tourism industry and the product it offers. Multi-day journeys in the UK are less popular than in other countries where more extensive wilderness travel and settled weather is an attraction. Popular adventure activities in the UK such as scrambling, gill scrambling, canyoning, coasteering, abseiling, caving and mine exploration all use specialist equipment and skills adapted from rock climbing.

Indoor climbing walls and bouldering centres have increased dramatically in the past two decades (BMC 2003) and an increase in visitor numbers obviously accompanies this. 'Indoorisation' (Bottenburg and Salome 2010) of the outdoors allows safe practice of rock climbing in an artificially created environment where with rudimentary skills anyone can participate. This, coupled with a proliferation of glossy magazines, blockbuster films, advertising through climbing, online information and chat rooms has led to more general climbing accessibility. Its status as a counter-cultural activity only for those who have amassed the know-ledge, skill and experience to operate in the vertical environment has diminished considerably and mainstreaming has occurred. Beedie and Hudson (2003) provide examples of this in mountaineering where money will buy a summit almost regardless of climbing experience; see also Bullock (2011). Beedie and Hudson (2003: 625) suggest evidence is available to show 'a dilution of the essential ingredients of "being a mountaineer" as a result of the democratisation process facilitated by the arrival of some urban characteristics in wild mountain areas' is occurring. The outdoors and involvement in lifestyle sports (Wheaton 2004) is an important thread in the weaving of a personal tapestry attractive to others. Ensuring a positive personal profile on web-based social sites such as Facebook is an important objective and the outdoors may help in this process. Such changes will only occur given synergy between rock climbing and its frame conditions.

The following two examples from contemporary climbing practices empha-sise the importance of this synergy in order for significant change to occur. Boul-dering is not a contemporary activity. Guidebooks show photographs of climbers bouldering as early as the beginning of the twentieth century. But it has never captured the imagination of climbers as an activity in its own right until the frame conditions came together that allowed bouldering to appeal to contempor-ary climbers. The style and branding of bouldering as a 'freestyle' activity akin to other outdoor sports such as surfing has occurred (see Barkham 2006; Buckley

2003). It suits the busy, 'quick fix', often fragmented lifestyle of the twenty-first century (Roberts 1999) and offers quality time with friends. It is popular because of dovetailing that occurs with changes experienced in society and the coming together of the right conditions at the right time in order for bouldering to flourish.

The second example concerns issues of globalisation. Climbing no longer has to be an isolated activity involving two people. Global networking ensures a voice can be given to any climbing occurrence. Web forums, chat rooms and personal or shared web pages mean instant access to climbing information and events (Barkham 2006). Global networks also mean a shrinking world where climbers are able to quickly access climbing venues through cheap air travel and a network of services specifically aimed at the climber. Readily available information on climbing conditions allows focused forays into the mountains knowing that routes will be available to climb.

Relationships in climbing have changed not least because of the World Wide Web, but so too has the relationship between climbers and society more generally. The outdoors is cool: it brings with it a positive 'feel good' factor recognised by many through the proliferation of imagery now available. Rock climbing is synonymous with the outdoors and can now be accessed by all. Hardwell's (2007) research reveals the most likely introduction to climbing for many younger participants to be a birthday party. Campbell *et al.* (2007) cite stag and hen parties as being important client groups supporting the adventure tourism market. Donnelly (1993: 127) observed that climbing is a resilient subculture because 'it has existed for so long as an alternative to mainstream sport, an unincorporated and self governing parallel to the dominant sport culture'. However, he also suggested its resilience 'appears to be coming to an end' (ibid.) and such examples underpin these thoughts.

The significance for adventure tourism

The changes documented suggest a loss of traditional climbing. There are more people climbing but less interest in the traditional style of climbing which has been the mainstay of UK rock climbing for a century. But with change and new ways of practicing rock climbing come opportunities. Commercially oriented activity in the outdoors relies on identifying and then minimising the actual risks involved while recognising client risk perceptions may be high (Priest 1990; Mortlock 1984). Capitalising on perceived risk allows for high customer satisfaction and possible repeat business (Campbell *et al.* 2007). INSIGHTS (2003) provided four categorisations of adventure tourists allowing for client differentiation. Samplers, learners and dabblers may all be more easily catered for using perceived rather than actual risk situations. Here contemporary rock climbing practices may be used to develop personal rock climbing skills safely. However, the fourth client group category, the enthusiasts, require careful consideration as experience often brings with it a requirement for more demanding activities (Buckley 2012).

Understanding client differentiation and their motivations is important in developing an adventure tourism package that meets the expectations of the client. This may be more important in adventure tourism than any other tourism service offered and, because of the open environment in which services are offered, may be more difficult to fulfil. Buckley's (2012) table of adventure activity motivations is adapted in Table 9.4 to show how a common contemporary climbing practice of top roping climbs in the outdoors may be fulfilling for samplers, learners and dabblers but leave the enthusiast wanting a more challenging (authentic) experience (Hardwell 2009). Applying this model can further highlight how changes in rock climbing practices and accessibility may aid the provision of meaningful experiences for some but not all client groups in adventure tourism. Importantly, the enthusiasts are less likely to require direct service provision from outdoor centres and professionals because they may already own the equipment and have acquired some skills in the activity (Campbell *et al.* 2007). It is the samplers, learners and dabblers who may be directly introduced to rock climbing through outdoor centres and professionals. An introduction using any of the contemporary methods highlighted (bouldering, indoor climbing [to a lesser extent], top rope climbing on accessible climbing venues) will provide a meaningful experience for the samplers and dabblers and build essential skills for the learners. Accessibility of these venues and introductory options has increased dramatically in the last two decades.

The uniqueness of rock climbing as an adventure activity (and outdoor activities more generally) stems from providing challenge regardless of ability or skill. Most people recognise the inherent risk of heights and to defy gravity trusting only a single rope and a climbing partner provides a thrilling experience. Risks can be minimised, perhaps negated when using indoor venues and the activity can be developed as a meaningful adventure tourism experience, particularly for less experienced outdoor participants.

Physical accessibility is important for adventure tourism operators but so too is social accessibility. Climbing now has a much broader following and fewer are taking Scott's (1994) stance of the importance of an apprenticeship in the mountains. The fast-tracking nature of gaining access to the high mountains is never more prevalent than in the Himalayas (Beedie and Hudson 2003). To an extent this has demystified climbing and mountaineering as an activity and ensured access to far wider participants. The older traditional climber is seen next to the sampler during the dark winter months as each participant meets their motivations at the indoor climbing wall. Marchart (2004) discusses appropriation and this is particularly important to UK rock climbing in the twenty-first century. Rock climbing subculture is becoming far more penetrable and fluid around its fringes allowing more people to be involved in the activity and enjoy movement on rock in safe yet absorbing situations (see Hardwell 2009).

Adventure tourism in the UK seems characterised more by short-term multi-activity breaks fitting into Rubens (1999) 'narrow' view of adventurous activities. For example, registered multi-activity break providers make up 16 per cent of registered provision providing direct adventure services to clients in Scotland

Table 9.4 Comparing the contemporary climbing practice of an outdoor bottom rope experience for different participants

Internal, performance of activity	Description	Contemporary climbing	
		Dabblers, learners and samplers	*Enthusiasts*
Thrill	Adrenaline, Excitement	•	
Fear	Overcoming fear	•	
Control	Maintain physical and mental control of body	•	•
Skills	Using expertise to perform very difficult tasks	•	•
Achievement	Overcoming challenges to meet difficult goals	•	
Fitness	Activity simply as a way to keep physically fit	•	
Risk	Danger as a direct motivation	•	
Internal/external, place in nature	*Description*		
Nature	Appreciation of beauty	•	•
Art	Perception of activity as artistic	•	
Spirit	Activity as spiritual experience	•	
External social position	*Description*		
Friends	Enjoyment in sharing an activity with others	•	•
Image	Enhancing how one is seen by others	•	
Escape	A change from routine of home and work	•	
Compete	Competition against others	•	•

Source: An adaptation of Buckley's table of Motivations for Adventure Activities (2011: 2).

Notes
1 All motivations taken directly from Buckley (2011).
2 The dots indicate a met motivation.

(Campbell *et al.* 2007: 3). But more research is required into the independent adventure enthusiasts who constitute up to 72 per cent of the adventure tourism market (ibid.: 11). What is changing markedly are the client groups enjoying adventure tourism. 'There are signs that activity holidays are no longer just the preserve of young adrenaline junkies, but are becoming more 'mainstream', attracting more women, more over-50s and more families' (Mintel 2010: 1). A more European feel to rock climbing as a social activity for all family members would allow even greater accessibility and such an approach is already being seen in many indoor climbing venues and mountain biking areas where cafes and auxiliary services are increasingly available.

Conclusion

Understanding rock climbing as a multifaceted activity serves two purposes in this chapter. Subcultural theory has allowed a critical evaluation of how this process has occurred but, more pragmatically, the importance of understanding the array of market and business opportunities available through the process of differentiation has been highlighted. These changes in rock climbing are a result of wider societal changes or frame conditions that shape any activity (Hargreaves 1986). Maffesoli (2000: 73) states that 'in each era, a type of sensibility predominates; a style which specifies the relationships we forge with others'. This sensibility predominates within subcultures and between society and subcultural groups. Rock climbing as an activity is becoming more widely accepted through the process of appropriation (Hardwell 2007) and this opens up commercial opportunity and while the samplers, learners and dabblers may enjoy the appropriated forms of rock climbing and satisfy their motivations for involvement in adventure tourism, the enthusiasts will want a climbing experience more close to the core function of rock climbing.

For the seasoned climber the purpose of rock climbing will remain unchanged. There will always be opportunity for traditional climbing practices, with the UK still remaining the bastion of traditional climbing style worldwide. But there is also a requirement to let go, to embrace change, to decide what can be given over to those who wish to experience similar thrills and excitement that have kept many involved in rock climbing for a lifetime. This is already happening thoughtfully and successfully in many indoor climbing centres. Different user groups with very different agendas coexist quite happily. The changes have brought more employment opportunities for those dedicated to the outdoors and adventure tourism continues to thrive despite the global recession (Mintel 2010). The change in rock climbing practice over the past three decades and the dedication of local activists in overseeing sensible venue development will ensure rock climbing remains an important inclusion in the suite of activities offered by adventure tour operators without compromising its traditional roots. In embracing the inevitable changes occurring in many leisure pursuits it is worth considering the balance between the new and the traditional. Such thoughts are neatly captured in the following passage by Beck.

We need ideas and theories that will allow us to conceive the new which is rolling over us in a new way, and allow us to live and act with it. At the same time we must retain good relations with the treasures of tradition.

(Beck 1992: 12)

Present frame conditions now, more than any other time, favour the outdoors as a place for recreation, enjoyment, escape and excitement and because of this there is more opportunity for outdoor apprenticeships. Adventure tourism has quickly capitalised on contemporary climbing practices, not least through indoor climbing centres. But I see few reasons why we need to forge ahead with the new while neglecting the traditions that have been instrumental in bringing us to where we are now. There is no reason why we cannot develop the best of both worlds. We can provide opportunity for growth in the new yet still underpin traditions of the past. As potential providers of adventure tourism experiences we *do* have a responsibility to our clients, employees and the environment. There has to be a respect for how others before us have used and developed the activities in our portfolio. Simple ways of developing a culture of respect for traditional practices can make a difference to both the staff and client experience. For example, the dates of a recent adventure tourism conference in Fort William purposefully coincided with the Fort William Mountain Film Festival and delegates were encouraged to access films of traditional climbing action spliced with contemporary forms of climbing practice.

Many of us working in the outdoors have not decided to do so for fame and fortune. Instead, we have an intrinsic love of the outdoors coupled with our own outdoor apprenticeships built through history and embracing tradition. Ensuring we share our experiences and practices regularly will enrich our own lives, the lives of participants and the programmes we develop. This heady mixture of appreciation of the outdoors through traditions, practical experience and skill development will see to it that all participants take something meaningful from their adventure tourism experience.

10 Structured feedback in outdoor adventure education

What are we accomplishing?

Frank Vernon

Introduction

Experiential approaches to education, despite popularity amongst stalwarts (e.g. Kolb, 1984; Warren *et al.*, 2008) and budding supporters (e.g. Eyler, 2009; Rudolph *et al.*, 2007), have been suffering a recent identity crisis. Oft-cited theoretical and practical influences grounded in cognitive epistemologies (e.g. Kolb, 1984) and moral psychology (e.g. Hahn, 1934) are being openly critiqued as inadequate and naïve, aristocratic and militaristic (Brookes, 2003a, 2003b; Brown, 2009, 2010; Delandshere, 2002; Fenwick, 2001; Quay, 2003; Roberts, 2008; Seaman, 2007, 2008; Seaman and Coppens, 2006; Seaman and Nelson, 2011; Worsley, 1985). Further, oversimplified translations misconstrue influential scholars' work as compatible, if not mutually informative (e.g. Joplin, 2008; Panicucci, 2007), adding to the already murky waters through which educators must identify educative practices. While early views of experiential learning founded on individual, cognitivist epistemologies were undoubtedly helpful in shaping a distinguishable field of practice, the growing chorus advocating a paradigm shift warrants discussion.

It may be, appropriating a potential alternative framework highlighted by Seaman (2007) that members of the experiential education field have identified a structural contradiction (Engeström, 2001) impeding, if not derailing, our purposeful, cultural–historical activities as educators and scholars. If this is the case, a readjustment of habit (Dewey, 1922) may yield what Engeström (2001: 137) refers to as 'expansive learning', 'accomplished when the object and motive of the activity are reconceptualised to embrace a radically wider horizon of possibilities than the previous mode of the activity'. Or, to put it another way, individual–cognitivist orientations to learning, such as Kolb's (1984) interpretation of others' learning theories as cycles and the educational structures these objectifications then informed, are in tension with stated goals of negotiating and maintaining educational experiences of lasting and identifiable value. As alternatives, these authors advocate adopting socio-cultural theories of learning historically rooted in the work of John Dewey and Lev Vygotsky, as well as scholars who have furthered this work (e.g. Engeström, 2001; Lave and Wenger, 1991; Rogoff, 1993).

Others have written in greater detail than I will go into here concerning the limitations of assigning goal-oriented cognitivist models of learning with universal applicability (e.g. Fenwick, 2001; Seaman, 2008). I am in agreement, however, with the 'individual participants [beginning] to question and deviate from [experiential education's] established norms' (Engeström, 2001: 137), in that generating context-free and individually bound 'knowledge', discovered out of immediate, temporal 'experiences', impedes our educational practices by rooting learning in deterministic, behavioural 'input–process–output' empiricism (Delandshere, 2002). This is not because learning cannot be treated thus (although, as I will discuss later, this tactic misses the expansive potential learning of experience), but because such a view of learning – and, in turn, education – is hostile toward the individual and collective horizon of possibilities in a world always in the process of becoming.

Separating and objectifying experience, reflection and future action as static and individually purposeful cognitive interactions with the external world has a number of unintended outcomes and internal contradictions worth discussing. Indeed, although not explicitly stated by many of the authors advocating the appropriateness of socio-cultural learning theories in grounding experiential education's scholarship and practice, such a shift from individual–cognitivist epistemology to pragmatic – and, in my mind, critically pragmatic (Biesta, 1994; Kaldec, 2007) – epistemology demands readjustment in our ways of acting as educators. It is to this end that I will orient my chapter. My intention here is to start from the assumption that much of the experiential education field's practices have been shaped by the ideas of Kolb (1984), and that if we were to move beyond his interpretation – and our superficial appropriation, which I argue, while influential, has run its course – of the work of Dewey and others in favour of a more nuanced understanding, then this is not merely semantics, nor regulated to abstract discourse, but rather a dynamic reconstruction of practice, which I define as the purposeful use of experience for potential learning.

To accomplish this I will focus on the use of *feedback* in experiential education programming. I have chosen feedback for three reasons. First, the specific use of feedback appears shaped by beliefs about the nature of experience, reflection and action that are called into question by the aforementioned authors. Second, the structured practice of feedback shapes a learning environment felt unproblematic, if not enabled, within a 'learning cycles' perspective, and I find this particularly troubling. Third, I am of the belief that a discussion of feedback has the possibility of showcasing the extent to which a reconstruction aligned with socio-cultural, critically pragmatic theories of learning will alter our use of lived experience for educational benefit.

Locating feedback as current practice

With dinner finished and dishes cleaned, headlamps bob among backpacks and tarps in the growing darkness, disappearing briefly and reappearing as warm layers are pulled on. The two co-instructors already sit patiently with mugs of hot tea as students begin to join near where everyone had eaten. Within minutes and without explicit direction a circle is formed, and the ideoculture (Fine, 1979) begins their night-time ritual of 'evening meeting'. This is familiar to them; common themes are touched upon each night. One topic of the meeting, the topic pertinent to this chapter, is that of the structured time for 'feedback'.

When it becomes time for feedback to occur, the group follows a pattern born of common social practice over the previous two weeks. First, a student who had been assigned the role of 'leader of the day' (LOD) recounts her experience; addressing aspects of her performance she feels were both well- and ill-received. After she finishes her monologue, her peers begin to critique her actions. They attempt to tie her specific behaviours with their personal resultant reactions as well as recommendations for future action. If a peer does not tie a felt success or failure with a specific act, she is able to ask for clarification – outside of thanking her peers for their feedback, this is the only voice afforded her during this discussion. While at one point in time she may have attempted to construct a dialogue to share meaning with her peers in an attempt at coming to a mutual understanding of intentions and responses, she has learnt not to 'get defensive' and subsequently be labelled as someone who is 'bad at receiving feedback' through the course. Instead, she listens and is left to discern how she can appropriate new acts or ways of thinking which yield laudable growth as a leader within this group, and purportedly beyond. After her peers and the co-instructors have finished highlighting her actions and inactions that they felt either helped or hampered her performance as the LOD, the co-instructors push for a transition to a new topic of discussion. The group assents, and as suddenly as the spotlight was on the individual who occupied the role of LOD, it is off and onto a description of the next day's activities.

The above description is not a verbatim account of a feedback session, but rather is a prototypical example built from research (e.g. Gondek, 2008; Vernon, 2011a), practical guides (Outward Bound USA, 2008), and my own lived experiences as an experiential educator for the last 14 years. Indeed, I have used or been witness to feedback as an aspect of adventure and experiential education curriculum among every programme and population I have worked with. In addition the practice in every classroom I have taught or been a student in; is so commonplace as to appear ubiquitous. That it appears commonplace is, in my mind, cause for concern. Evening meetings, after student-led lessons or activities, between co-instructors at the end of the day or course, and on student and staff course-end evaluations are some of the places where feedback is commonly used to enhance learning opportunities, and it is my goal here to specifically call into question the assumedly unproblematic structure and use of feedback as a cultural–historical practice in experiential education.

This critique will be arranged as follows. First, I will orient 'feedback' within a pragmatic conceptualization of learning and knowledge (Dewey, 1922, 1938), as well as flesh out how feedback has been constructed as a cultural tool within the adventure and experiential education fields (e.g. Chase and Priest, 1990; Crosby, 1981). After identifying the purposeful structure of feedback in our educational system, I will critically inquire as to the unintended and problematic aspects of this structure. Lastly, I will relocate our use of feedback within a critically pragmatic (Kaldec, 2007) educational framework in a manner I feel many of our curricular practices call for as we transition away from tired educational models (cf. Fenwick, 2001; Seaman, 2008; Quay, 2003).

In what became the method de rigueur among experiential educators, Kolb (1984) drew out a synopsis of learning theory borne of Lewin's action research. His attempt at visualizing Lewin's findings as a cycle of concrete experience, observations and reflections, formations of abstract concepts and generalization, and testing implications of concepts in new situations translated into what is now thought of as 'Kolb's experiential learning cycle' (Eyler, 2009; Panicucci, 2007), although in its earliest form was referred to by Kolb (1984: 21) as 'The Lewinian Experiential Learning Model'. This early model for learning was generated to explain behaviour modifications that occur after 'here-and-now experience'; feedback was thought of as crucial after-the-fact representations of the consequences of action and its connection with pre-action desired goals. Whether it is fair to assume Lewin's perspective on learning, who was a social psychologist influenced heavily by symbolic interaction, gestalt psychology, and critical democratic action research (Burnes, 2004; Dickens and Watkins, 1999), was adequately captured in three short paragraphs and a simple cycle metaphor is for another discussion entirely. It could be noted, though, that much of the experiential education field's history is pockmarked with attempts to 'get the gist' of complex concepts as readily applicable models.

Kolb's (1984) conceptualization, which appears to be the wellspring for early practical application (Crosby, 1981; Joplin, 2008; Panicucci, 2007; Wurdinger, 1996), provides a metaphor of learning as empirical testing; an individual carries out an action (experience), after which data is collected regarding the effectiveness of the action in obtaining desired goals (feedback), which is then reflected on to assess potential new ways of acting in the future. Such an idea of feedback is parallel to, yet divergent from, traditional views of feedback in education literature. Whereas feedback is thought by both traditionalists and within Kolb's cognitivist orientation as information accessible after an act, some traditional educators also view feedback as an evaluation of an act when compared to an objective standard for the act (Passier and Jeuring, 2004). Mory (2004) describes feedback in education as a system for communicating multiple educational messages, such as timeliness, motivation or guidance; feedback is structured to allow an educator to provide a student with information that purportedly supports her or his learning. Within the experiential education field of practice, feedback appears to take on qualities of both Kolb's organic reflected consequence and traditional education's direct evaluation of performance while implicitly drawing from an external standard.

The ideological foundation of feedback

I must return momentarily to the earlier description of feedback occurring during the evening meeting of a hypothetical wilderness expedition. The members of this community, who at this moment in time occupy the roles of *co-instructors*, *participants* (all of whom also take on the role of *givers*), and *LOD* (who in this episode also takes on the role of *receiver*), are using the space to construct feedback. Throughout the day, the LOD performed actions she felt supported the group and showcased her abilities as a peer leader, and during this time the other members of the community observed her actions and took note of their own positive or negative reactions or, failing that, attempt now to recollect their reactions and bring to bear useful commentary. The episode of feedback has been taught, and all members of the community recognize norms regarding how both giver and receiver are to act if feedback will be labelled appropriate. As an example, the *Outward Bound Instructor Manual* (2008) provides guidelines for giving and receiving feedback, including givers using 'I' statements, describing specific observed behaviours, separating the feedback from the event, making sure the receiver understood you, distinguishing the receiver's behaviour from subjective experience; and, for the receiver, 'listen objectively – without becoming defensive' (Outward Bound USA, 2008: 3.19), ask for specific examples, take time to reflect before responding, and recognize that failing to be a good feedback receiver will result in negative social consequences.

Chase and Priest (1990) are perhaps more direct in prescribing a set of behaviours for experiential educators that they claim 'proves reliable'. The question of how and where they articulate 'proof' notwithstanding, their advice by way of a metaphor of feedback as a 'sandwich' appears rooted in deterministic, cognitivist epistemology:

> feedback is well received and more likely to be accepted if it is delivered in a **'sandwich'** form: two pieces of bread and a slice of meat. The bread in this metaphor represents positive feedback of a complimentary nature, while the meat represents the negative feedback of a critical nature ... although this may be difficult to achieve in all critique situations, the sandwich approach proves reliable, where good points tend to soften the impact of the bad, yet permit the bad to be assimilated and acted upon.
>
> (Chase and Priest, 1990: 11)

Much time may be spent analysing such a statement, so suffice to indicate the manner in which the authors advocate manipulating communicative acts to obscure, rather than open, the learning environment (for an example in practice, see Brown, 2002).

As an immediate back-and-forth, then, 'feedback', in an idealized state, operates thus. An individual member of a group carries out an act (or fails to act when felt necessary by an observer) and the observed behaviour has felt consequences among other members. At some later point in time, when deemed appropriate, someone bids for a feedback episode (Carspecken, 1996), typically by addressing the individual and letting them know that they 'have a piece of feedback for them'. Both individuals enter into a communicative sequence that is intersubjective, that is, both implicitly understand the norms and ways of acting required for feedback to operate, and thus adopt the roles of 'giver' and 'receiver' and the normalized behaviours associated with each role. The giver addresses the receiver's previous act, evaluating the effectiveness of it based on his or her own internal state, while the receiver listens and independently assigns meaning to the giver's remarks. Deviations from the typification, such as the giver attempting to speak for others' experiences or the receiver attempting to explain their intentionality for the act, result in sanctions on either transgressor for failing to give or receive 'good' feedback. These episodes are typically carried out as group ritual, as this is felt to maximize the opportunity to simulta- neously maintain the typified structure and support learning. I hope to show, given the discussion that follows, that the feedback ritual is assented to despite marginalizing and devaluing the community members and their learning poten- tial, and thus fits within a critically pragmatic conceptualization of 'ideology' (cf. Habermas, 1991).

The above interactive sequence, informed by the 'ground rules [allowing] feedback to be useful for both giver and receiver' (Outward Bound USA, 2008: 3.18) and constructed as a legitimate, purposeful activity (Lave and Wenger, 1991) in the experiential education community, is based on a system of beliefs about education and educative experiences worth investigation. Of the constella- tion of backgrounded beliefs enabling such an activity I will highlight here *time and reflection, objectivity and subjectivity*, and *privilege of voice*. Each of these, which I will explain in depth, is indelibly interdependent and mutually informa- tive with one another in the culture's concerted attempt at maintaining a struc- ture that appears coherent.

Time and reflection

A 'cycle' model of learning bounds experience as sequential steps leading to observable 'learning', i.e. behavioural changes that increase the effectiveness of a set of actions at achieving a desired goal. In such a scenario, an individual must carry out an imagined purpose temporally; it is after the 'experience', or in other words, once this episode within her lived experience has reached a point of transition, that she 'steps back' and recognizes consequences. This feedback, which is the echoes of our actions through which we orient our purpose in inter- subjective meaning-making, is now available to re-evaluate and re-construct a purpose in the imaginary, purportedly to be enacted as purposeful action at an unknown point in the future.

The issue of *reflection*, or understanding, as a function of *time* is interesting. Setting up a differentiation between 'experience' and 'reflection' allows us to use episodes for different ends; sometimes we are acting, and other times we are reflecting on the consequences of those actions. The ability to simultaneously act and assign meaning to those actions based on a variety of available sources of information, and even still to readjust action in a continuous and ongoing manner is outside the realm of learning when thought of as a 'cycle'. Instead, students must be allowed to engage in something referred to as *an* experience, and then afforded the opportunity to reflect as separate episodes. Further, potential information with which the actor could reference their behaviour in a larger realm of meaning is purposeful withheld by other members of the community, allowing him or her to act relatively unobstructed, only to identify those potential obstacles or unintended consequences at a later point in time. Also, as referenced earlier, some students are directed to treat feedback as an experience, and as such must not assign meaning and respond to feedback, but instead must use the time to listen but not understand, as understanding comes at a later point in time when removed from the immediate experience. If understanding were possible in the experience, then response would be acceptable, but instead members of a community are caught in a web that purposefully denies mutual understanding and collective critical discourse.

This brings up a troubling issue: is our understanding of our lived experience always a few hours' or days' lag from the situation through which we originally engaged in the knowledge-providing acts? If this is the case, we live in a never-ending game of catch-up, wherein we are blind to our own trajectory, only stopping to readjust when an obstacle demands it. This is because we are unable to readjust if we are unable to understand, or grasp, the (potential) consequences of our actions while constructing our means–ends. Oft-cited as the grandfather of the educative use of lived experience, Dewey (1922: 190) put forth a similar explanation of how learning occurs, describing the moment of deliberation starting 'from the blocking of efficient overt action'. It is when individuals find their actions blocked, which until that point was action felt efficient in achieving desired goals, that purposeful and imaginary deliberation yields readjustments and new ways of acting. He clearly describes an action–feedback–reflection–change system of intelligence similar to how Kolb (1984) interprets him, but this needs some clarification.

Imagine an individual walking through a forest; while moving in a single direction he can be described as carrying out an efficient action, as he is achieving his purpose of walking through the forest. It is not until he runs smack into a tree that readjustment becomes possible in the above model, because acting and thinking are incompatible, and so his trajectory throughout time becomes a comical pinball-like manoeuvre as trees are hit, new directions are started, and they are again carried out until an obstacle is reached. This is because readjustment due to anticipating feedback or continuously assigning meaning to one's lived experience simultaneous to both purposeful construction and action is not achievable in such a model. Scheffler (1974: 237) makes a similar critique of his interpretation of Dewey, identifying such a model of learning as constructing a situation wherein 'with adoption of a plan or end-in-view … thought should cease, since overt action has resumed; by hypothesis, the original block no longer exists'. This is not what may be referred to as 'thoughtful action' – in fact, the very phrase becomes oxymoronic.

We must be clear, though. Dewey (1922, 1938) explains how we use our lived experiences to achieve educative ends, but this discussion is removed from his intended context when not buttressed by its critical and pragmatic origins

(Kaldec, 2007). Dewey (1922: 102) understood this drawback to such failures of adopting a critical and continuous method of intelligence, describing change to our efficient cultural habits as depending 'upon the clash of war, the stress of revolution, the emergence of heroic individuals, the impact of migrations generated by war and famine, the incoming of barbarians'. We fail to understand Dewey's vision of education if we interpret his description of how we use experience for learning as a static concept (Seaman and Nelson, 2011). We are members of a world always and constantly in the process of becoming, and discussions of how we engage in such a world are threefold; where we have come from, where we are, and how to continue so to expand the horizon of potential. Dewey's treatment of how we learn is not a claim of static truth, and to use it as an anchor misses his claim: it is an orienting point from which we pivot and push off toward an always-expanding goal of collective, deliberative, critically reflective social discourse aimed at continual reconstruction. It is this for which he hoped we would leave our pinball trajectory, purposefully changing the manner in which we currently use experience for growth in favour of imaginatively and continuously reconstructing our purposeful actions as we critically examine our trajectory in an ever-complexifying world which we both shape and are shaped by (Dewey, 1916, 1922).

This is not to say we cannot identify learning achieved through lived experiences in such a differentiated and isolated fashion as our current use of feedback may assume, but this is not because we have stumbled upon a universal knowledge of how learning occurs. It is simply our current, and underwhelming, use of lived experience for educational gain, and it is not our only option. I argue that learning is stymied because experience becomes temporally bounded and usefully separated as life 'episodes' wherein reasonably similar appearance gives rise to new experiments. Learning becomes something of guesswork, of testing out new hypotheses in a search for the 'right' method of behaviour to achieve desired goals, yet all the while displacing the opportunity for readjusting and achieving potential goals now onward to some future, imaginary opportunity. We do this when operating with a 'feedback' mentality by purposefully withholding or removing the consequential information with which immediate readjustment may be achieved so that it can be reflected at some later point in time. If experience was thought of not as segmented – yet, apparently, recirculating – external phenomena, but instead as a continuous engagement of expansive potential usefulness, then the opportunity to develop a habit of critical readjustment so as to continuously reconstruct the nature of means and ends replaces staccato and always-late changes in behaviour. What I mean by all of this is that the experience–feedback cycle, as currently conceptualized, is lacking in educative benefit because we are making lacklustre use of experience; the prevention of continuous growth is an unforeseen and unfortunate effect of purposefully withholding orienting information from actors until the time for action has passed – and, perhaps worse, training ourselves in habits where we recapitulate the same processes.

Of course, it is possible to carry on an action while readjusting means and ends simultaneously and without requiring feedback as either the blockage of immediate action or the post hoc revealing of consequences purposefully with-held by others. To return to the earlier metaphor, one does not walk through a forest in such a manner where thought is absent from action, only stimulated by immediate blockage; indeed, such an act would be considered by an onlooker to be comically inefficient and lacking in a robust method of intelligence. Instead we take in orienting stimuli continuously while readjusting means and ends; the same may be said of engagement in the larger structures of our lived experience – if we choose to use experience in such a manner. Whereas currently the dog-matic separation of experience and reflection leads members of an experiential education group to honour the immediate 'experience' of action by withholding potential orienting information until a later time with the intention of reintroduc-ing an awareness of consequence, aligning our field's activities with pragmatic socio-cultural views of learning would advocate new ways of acting. The poten-tially educative nature of experience lies in developing a habit of a method of intelligence; that is, continuous readjustment built from individual and collective critical reflection (Dewey, 1922; Kaldec, 2007). Members of a community should, therefore, be encouraged to deliberate on the potential lines of action in the *now*, treating experience as a continuous opportunity to increase the com-plexity with which they explore the horizon of possibility. This comes from treating feedback as immediately and openly useful, although some changes to how we understand feedback may be in order.

Objectivity and subjectivity

What limited literature exists concerning the how-to of feedback in current prac-tice forms a fascinating picture of how objective and subjective claims are to be built into knowledge. Prescribed practices such as focusing on another's acts and one's own emotional responses as appropriate to communicate, or listening to the communicative act of the 'giver' with attention to maintaining objectivity (Outward Bound USA, 2008), are notable examples. On the one hand, members of the community are encouraged to be mindful of external stimuli and resultant internal (subjective) responses, and also to bring forth the subjective as socially available and valued information that leads to educative experiences. On the other hand, members are simultaneously led to believe that internal, emotional responses hamper learning, and it would be better to distrust emotion or subjec-tivity in favour of objectivity when they interact with other members' communi-cative acts. Further, there appears, across the literature on feedback, a fetish with using others' behaviours and one's own emotional states to construct a unidirec-tional communicative climate; when providing feedback we assume to 'know' information of value based on others' behaviours (e.g. Chase and Priest, 1990) while maintaining for ourselves the privilege of exploring emotion and intention. The structure of feedback ensures the knowledge claim of the giver, based on this paradox, is unable to be called into question or critically examined in a social sphere, whereas the knowledge claim of the receiver (based on others' assigned meaning to her once-and-future actions) is simultaneously open to – at best – semi-contextual critique, and indefensible. Such an environment fails to construct an openly democratic or collectively critical discourse, and this is where I now turn my attention.

To add nuance to the discussion of objectivity and subjectivity, given the potentially contradictory nature of how such phenomena are currently claimed as knowledge and put to use, I now turn to the critical and pragmatic work of Habermas (1984) and his reconstruction of validity as intersubjective and assumed claims of truth concerning objective, subjective, normative and, with the addition of Carspecken (1996), identity. His voluminous work cannot be exhaustively treated here, so I will briefly highlight a few aspects of his writing that are particularly relevant to this discussion. First, Habermas insightfully identifies objective and subjective (as well as normative) as socio-cultural and historical assumptions subject to change as our use of experience changes. For example, an historical survey of scientific 'knowledge' will identify the manner in which objective claims of truth have failed to remain constant, save when powerful interests benefit from the durability of a belief structure, but instead have remained, and will remain, in flux. Second, Habermas calls into question ontology-first pairings of objective/real and subjective/imaginary or subjective/suspect as misunderstanding the manner in which both, among others, are drawn on simultaneously in understanding and acting. Third, and following the logic of these previous two insights, Habermas and Carspecken identify, within a horizon of foregrounded to backgrounded assumptions justifying the validity of a current act, the simultaneous coexistence of objective, subjective, normative and identity claims.

A further exploration of these terms may be in order, to bring our discussion into line with the assumed belief structure of pragmatism and socio-cultural theories of learning. Objective claims should not be thought of as synonymous with claims of what is 'real' or 'trustworthy', but rather as culturally multiple-access, that is, as resting the partial validity of a statement on knowledge of shared access. Subjective, conversely, rests the partial validity of a statement on knowledge that is of limited access, that is, that the individual communicatively acting reveals, such as an emotional state. Normative relates to the socio-cultural and historical beliefs about what should or ought, and identity relates to the identification of self and others.

As an example, consider a parent communicating the following to a child while preparing a meal: 'Would you set the table?' In this communicative act, we can interpret that the meaning of the statement rests partially on an understanding of 'table', and what is to be set on it – the local cultural tools used to eat and drink with. These are claims of knowledge simultaneously multiple-access and also limited to members of the culture. An outsider may find her or himself confused by unfamiliar tools and customs if the same request was made of him or her in that context. Also within the communicative act are limited-access claims: namely the intersubjective claims made available to members of the culture as to how the parent would feel if the child was to accept or refuse the request, how the parent feels about making the request etc. The statement also rests on assumed claims concerning who should set tables, how parents should act toward their children and vice versa, how tables should be set and so on. The identity claims in the statement relate to statements such as 'I am a parent who asks, not tells, my child', 'I am a parent whose children are involved', and many, many more. The horizon of assumptions upon which a claim rests provides a way to understand and query the knowledge, and therefore validity, of the communicative act, and all exist simultaneously in all communication, although some are certainly more foregrounded or backgrounded depending on the act.

Habermas' (1984) reasoning opens many lines of inquiry, not least of which is the misguided obsession with objectivity in academia and education (cf. Carspecken, 1996; Korth, 2005). The objectivity Outward Bound USA (2008) refers to does not appear to be aligned with Habermas' (1984) discussion, but rather calls for us to listen to others' evaluations from an emotionally detached, third-person perspective. Notice the tie that binds emotional or subjective aspects of interaction with defensive posturing while simultaneously ignoring the multifaceted nature of the givers' communicative act. If we are to attend to one another's complex and concerted communication as portraying objective, subjective, normative and identity-based meaning simultaneously as an objective listener, we run the risk of either glossing over or ignoring important non-objective statements, or assigning the value of 'objective' to non-objective aspects; either way we misunderstand one another in our attempt to streamline the effectiveness of communication within feedback (e.g. Chase and Priest, 1990).

What I mean is this: to attend to the communicative act of an other, when their intention is to evaluate one's own behaviours (and, in extension, oneself), in a manner which privileges objectivity, we assume that objective truths concerning social acts are an established aspect of experiential education fields' repertoires of practice. While attempts at operationalizing 'good' social interaction as sets of timeless – yet situational – skills has certainly been an area of discussion (e.g. Priest and Gass, 1997), such discussions are reinterpreted within a socio-cultural, pragmatic perspective of learning and education. Positive social behaviours, such as 'leadership', are evaluated not on an objective scale, but instead acts pointing toward leadership are informed by an imaginary and intersubjective representation – what Dennis (publishing as Korth, 2007) refers to as the 'emergent ideal type'. Leadership exists as a concept due to the cultural–historical generation of a constellation of beliefs and norms, wherein the imaginary ideal – that is, simultaneously generative and non-objective – informs and is informed by our actions labelled as 'leadership' in type. When we provide evaluations to one another concerning our abilities to act in manners appropriately defined as 'leader-like', we thus evaluate based on an imaginary – the nonexistent 'ideal' leader. Treating such discourse as objective, or the nature of leadership as objective, stymies the potential for critical social inquiry and readjustment of both acts as well as the culturally and historically mediated imaginary ideals which inform such acts. Or, in other words, attending to feedback as objective serves a purpose not as liberating or emancipating, but as a coalescing of members' beliefs around a dominant belief structure with no recourse for querying the relative validity of such beliefs.

Therefore, while *objective* appears to be used to indicate adopting emotional detachment in favour of quiet calculation in the experiential education field, Habermas' (1984) work is still informative within this discussion. First, he correctly points out that we neither communicate nor interpret with pure objectivity. Furthermore, a conversation foregrounding strictly objective information is of very little use when attempting to learn how to successfully interact in society, which is indelibly shaped by non-objective knowledge (Biesta, 1994). Second, and stemming from this, when providing feedback to one another we are not left with a dichotomy of objectivity or subjectivity to compartmentalize, but instead the simultaneous portrayal of objective, subjective, normative and identity claims that interdependently embody meaning. The educational field, therefore, has obscured the nature of learning while constructing a climate built on a specific belief structure concerning the way interaction should be.

One can see the commendable intention in early development of such a communicative climate drawn from beliefs of learning stemming from cognitivist models and early norms concerning appropriate styles of interaction portrayed as objective truths. The unquestionable, objective quality of feedback could be seen as maintaining the autonomy of various members of the communicative act: feedback as an object between – yet not connecting – the giver and receiver, with rules in place to maintain such a structure, appears safe. Were communication to play out thus as both educationally valuable and without negative consequence, such a practice would seem appropriate.

Privilege of voice

The unintended consequences of such a communicative climate, I argue, are too numerous to continue the status quo. I have discussed the manner in which our use of feedback relies on inadequate models of learning that make ill use of time and reflection, and also that we could make better use of pragmatic and critical socio-cultural–historical conceptualizations of communicative meaning as opposed to dichotomizing objectivity and subjectivity as synonymous with real and suspect. Backgrounded in my discussion has been a critically pragmatic aim of furthering the potential of collective critical discourse and continuous readjustment as educative use of experience (Biesta, 1994; Dewey, 1916, 1922; Kaldec, 2007; Seaman and Nelson, 2011). Using feedback as here-and-now information of use in orienting our acts within a larger web of meaning and engaging in inquiry which expands the complexity of this socio-cultural–historical web and our interaction with it moves us toward developing habits of continuous readjustment and critical reflection. Critical collective discourse, however, which is argued to be indispensable in maintaining a growth-oriented democratic society (Dewey, 1916), is where I will now turn my attention. The previous discussion on intersubjective communication and meaning-making as simultaneously – and necessarily –

objective, subjective, normative and identity-based was meant to set a baseline from which to embark.

It should be possible to conceptualize, given the discussion thus far, a nuanced interpretation of feedback to be used as a structured and social educative tool in experiential educative programming when approached from a sociocultural and pragmatic perspective. Members of the experiential education community of practice carry out meaningful social acts while others observe and withhold potential information from which readjustment may emerge. At a later point, the actor's behaviours are reconstructed and tied to knowledge claims from her or his peers in the community. The communicative acts are objectified through the marking of 'giver' and 'receiver' roles and associated norms as well as the actual communicative exchange objectified as the passage of a statement containing neutral, independent and inherently meaningful truth worth attending to with an objective habit of thought. Furthermore, and most perplexing, the normalized structure does not permit each participant in the interaction to query the truth claims of both self and other in collective critical discourse. Instead this structure of feedback as an educational tool allows educators to associate an attempt at critical discourse, that is, questioning the validity of the comments of the 'givers' and opening a dialogue about the episode, as synonymous with acting defensively. Those participants enacting the roles of 'receivers' are therefore encouraged to submit to a defenceless evaluation by peers and educators. To be clear, we do not reflect upon 'an experience' and a neutral truth-claim as potentially fallible, but rather we reflect on a *self-in-experience* and aspects of that person's fallibility. The social norms governing feedback are set up as such, in my interpretation, because the self is rendered vulnerable and devalued in such an environment, and so we naturally choose to defend ourselves, and thus our norms serve to silence and habitualize into an ideological practice.

Traditionally relied-upon views of learning as both individualistic and outcome-focused has constrained discussions of processes or habits of thinking and practice as enacted by both individual and social as within the educational influence of experiential programming. However, attempts at consciousness-raising by some scholars (e.g. Brown, 2010; Fenwick, 2001; Seaman and Nelson, 2011) bring to focus the manners in which social practice and learning are inseparable. That is, learning is achieved through the structured use of feedback, but the learning involved relates primarily to communicative habits among peers and superordinates, such as developing a durable habit of dismissing others' attempts at drawing us into a discussion when we evaluate these behaviours as a failure to listen without becoming defensive or, in learning to enter a discussion of interpersonal conflict not from curiosity or desire for mutual understanding and collectively raised consciousness, but from prioritizing the safety (and, thus, stunted growth) of self by focusing solely on the behaviours of an other and potential modifications to those behaviours which align more closely with our own idealized norms. Feedback is not a neutral instrument supporting learning, then, but rather a process that shapes how we think about learning.

Brown (2010) highlighted the issues concerning the historical desire to mark and confirm transfer within educational programming, advocating for viewing changes in social participation as a viable alternative. I argue, given the above discussion, the habits of social participation through which operationalizable phenomena of learning, such as 'leadership', are formed encourage students to reconstruct quantifiable behaviours according to social influence – the difficulties in recognizing durable behaviour changes should not be surprising, as the more basic habits of learning which shape these behaviours of interest work against, not for, identifying stability among behaviours as objects of measurement, save where the social climate is marked by stable belief structures. Furthermore, the metaphor of 'transfer' describes a discontinuity of lived experience, of a lifeworld in which we jump between episodes of minimal interaction. I am not so sure such a metaphor is adequate in its explanatory power. Experience is continuous and horizontal; instead of envisioning ourselves leaping through and across contexts, we may consider ourselves in a continuous interaction with a lifeworld of constellated complexity and always in the process of becoming (Kaldec, 2007).

Repositioning the discussion of learning as always already culturally and historically shaped, socially interactive and orienting our expansive growth – that is, what Dewey (1922) referred to as a 'method of intelligence' – forces those of us who use experience for educational goals – a field of practitioners sometimes referring to themselves as 'experiential education' – to simultaneously reposition academic discourse and to critically reconstruct curricular practice. I have chosen here to investigate a unique structure of 'feedback' as a curricular piece. Within such a view of learning, I advocate the practice as using the consequences of action to continuously orient and readjust as opposed to being withheld so that a future imaginary episode may be improved upon. Further, I advocate a disruption of the social structure, namely through obscuring the roles of 'giver' and 'receiver' and the norms associated – as I believe this structure introduces an unjust superordinate and subordinate relationship of consequence within the field of practice (cf. Brown, 2002; Vernon, 2011b). Instead, participants in the community should be encouraged and enabled, that is, taught, to collectively and critically examine their shared experience through open democratic discourse in a manner which orients an exploration of the expanding horizon of potential experience. To put it very simply, we should be engaged in dialogue wherein all is open to investigation, and this becomes the habit through which learning's value is located.

11 Learning outcomes of young people on a Greenland expedition

Assessing the educational value of adventure tourism

Tim Stott, Pete Allison and Kris Von Wald

Introduction

Outdoor adventure education has a rich history in the UK (Allison *et al.*, 2011; Allison and Telford, 2005; Cook, 1999; Loynes, 1999a, 1999b). It is a sector of educational provision that has provided challenging experiences as part of and beyond formal schooling with the specific aim of eliciting personal growth in young people in some form for over 100 years. Much adventure-based education is founded on the rich history of expeditions (discussed in further detail below) and on the work of Kurt Hahn (Veevers and Allison, 2011) who was the inspiration for Outward Bound, The Duke of Edinburgh Award, United World Colleges and Round Square Schools. In the USA a parallel and overlapping movement has emerged which draws heavily on experiential learning theory and is often attributed as drawing on the philosophy of American pragmatist and educational philosopher John Dewey (Seaman, 2008). One of the underpinning assumptions of much theory and practice is the premise that humans must encounter their physical and/or psychological limits in order to enhance their capacity to successfully address the challenges of everyday life often associated with developing the virtues (see Csikszentmihalyi and Csikszentmihalyi, 1990; Ewert, 1989; Hunt, 1990; Priest, 1990; Priest and Gass, 1997). This is epitomized by the Hahn quote 'Your disability is your opportunity' (Hahn, 1960: 4).

Despite this 'development-through-challenge' approach being widespread in practice, it is largely uncontested as a foundation for a sector that is characterised primarily by residential experiences and expeditions. In the UK, there is a centuries old tradition of adventure and exploration, which some have argued has laid the foundation for the modern concept of outdoor education (Allison and Telford, 2005; Loynes, 1999b; Williams *et al.*, 1998; Westphal, 2011). The first British overseas youth expedition organisation to identify the potential benefits for youth development through expeditions was the Public Schools Exploring Society founded in 1932 (known today as BSES Expeditions) (for a more detailed history see Allison *et al.*, 2011). This sector of outdoor adventure education has grown significantly in the past half century (Hopkins and Putnam, 1993; Nicol, 2002). In the UK, there are now more organisations providing educational expeditions for young people as school vacation or gap year experiences than ever before (Jones, 2004).

Since the 1990s, several studies have attempted to understand the impact of outdoor experiences on young people and, while being cautious of over-generalisation, positive claims can be found (Hattie *et al.*, 1997; Rickinson *et al.*, 2004). While much research has been conducted in the field of outdoor education programmes in general, a handful of studies which specifically deal with the British youth overseas expeditions include Grey (1984, 1998), Kennedy (1992), Watts *et al.* (1992, 1993a, 1993b, 1994), Allison (2000, 2001, 2002), Allison and Beames (2010), Stott and Hall (2003), Beames (2003, 2004a 2004b, 2005), Pike and Beames (2007), IPPR (2009), Allison and Von Wald (2010). Both anecdotal evidence, and now a growing body of systematic research evidence (Stott *et al.* in review) suggests that expedition experiences can develop knowledge, skills and understanding which can enhance a person's well-being and future employability (e.g. Stott and Hall, 2003).

Perhaps the biggest problems with understanding the influences of adventurous experiences are that both quantitative and qualitative methodologies are each fraught with their own specific problems and their findings are treated with suspicion by different stakeholders. In very general terms, fundraisers and purse-string-holders often demand to see causality or 'direct links' (e.g. statistical significance) between programme attendance and personal and social development (see Allison and Pomeroy, 2000; Seaman, 2009). On the other hand, many academics are critical of using quantitative instruments to measure the highly subjective and individual ways in which participants are influenced by a given experience (Allison and Pomeroy, 2000; Barret and Greenaway, 1995; Greig *et al.*, 2007) with difficulties of timing of any 'measurements' being perennially problematic (Bechhofer and Paterson, 2000).

This debate between approaches to understanding participants' experiences in adventure education programmes is a large part of the rationale for this enquiry. Although we aim to further the body of empirical research that has been conducted on overseas youth expeditions, we are specifically concerned with developing a way of understanding these experiences that starts to overcome the pitfalls associated with previous research. In order to address these aims, we developed a mixed-methods questionnaire that was initially piloted by participants before and after a ten-week Raleigh International expedition to Costa Rica (Beames and Stott, 2008). Recognising the downfalls of experimental research design we supplemented this work with observations during the expedition. We also focused on what participants reported during and at the end of the expedition rather than after the expedition and the associated aspects of longitudinal work which we consider to be a separate project (see Allison *et al.*, 2011).

Methodology

This chapter discusses research carried out on the BSES[1] South-West Greenland 2009 summer expedition to Tasermiut Fjord in July–August 2009. Forty-five young people aged 16–21 participated in this five-week expedition in a wilderness part of South-West Greenland. The participants were divided into four groups (called Fires) of 11–12 young explorers (YEs), each with at least two leaders and each with a different science focus. One of these Fires carried out research to develop insights into the learning by participants of the other three Fires, and aimed to develop a model for measuring the learning for future use on BSES expeditions.

Research design

This enquiry concentrated on understanding participants' experiences on one particular expedition bound by time and place. Therefore, a case study design was most helpful (Silverman, 2010). We were determined to find a way of finding answers with a methodology that appeased stakeholders while addressing critiques. By devising a mixed-methods approach, we developed banks of qualitative and quantitative data that support improved understanding and provide the basis for triangulating the findings.

Pre- v. post-questionnaire

An expedition learning questionnaire (Beames and Stott, 2008) was adapted for the purposes of this expedition. The Expedition Learning Questionnaire (ELQ) designed for this study was inspired by the Life Effectiveness Questionnaire (LEQ) developed by Neill (2000) and Neill *et al.* (2003), and by Stott and Hall's (2003) 105-item questionnaire. The ELQ uses two approaches: (1) 46 questions with a five-point Likert scale to gain data on participants' perceptions of expeditionary learning; and (2) two open-ended questions for participants to expand upon their thoughts without the constraints of the rating scale.

Participant observation study during the expedition by Social Science Fire

Young explorers (YEs) in the Social Science Fire became researchers as they discussed epistemological perspectives; explored quantitative and qualitative methodologies and inductive and deductive reasoning; and debated the concepts of truth, reality and bias. They practiced interviewing, making observations and checking interpretations and identified their interest in the following research question: What can be learned about group dynamics from individual Fire member behaviour?

The focus areas for the investigation were chosen from the BSES personal development model anticipated outcomes.[2] The YEs designed group observation methods to explore the anticipated outcomes which were relevant to group dynamics: leadership, team working, communication and group management.

Sampling, ethics and data collection

There were 32 volunteers to participate in the ELQ and 36 for the group observations, all aware of the usual provisos of their right to withdraw without penalty at any time; their anonymity being preserved; and the data being kept secure and then destroyed once the analysis was complete (Kvale, 1996; British Educational Research Association, 2004). The ELQ was completed by participants in Iceland before they boarded their flight to Greenland and at the airport in Greenland shortly before they returned. The group observations were undertaken with each Fire once at three different times during the five-week expedition.

Data analysis and verification

The Wilcoxon matched-pairs test (Wilcoxon and Wilcox, 1964), was selected for the pre-post ELQ analysis with the null hypothesis (H_o) being that there would be no significant difference between the pre- and post-expedition scores. The alternative (H_1) hypothesis was that there was a real difference between the pre- and post-expedition scores which would have arisen due to the young persons' participation on the expedition. Thus, if the statistical tests showed a significant difference at least at the $p < 0.05$ (or 5 per cent) level we would conclude that the expedition had changed the young persons' opinions and we would accept the H_1 hypothesis.

Qualitative data from the second section of the ELQ was analysed through computer-assisted open-coding. Reading and re-reading of the scripts allowed dominant themes to emerge and be labelled. These themes were then filed under pre-determined categories. The group dynamics investigation involved YE researchers observing each of the other three Fires completing an activity where they were presented with a blue storage barrel and instructions: 'You are stranded on the edge of the fjord with all leaders down and 20 items in the barrel. You have 10 minutes to agree five items that will get you to safety and provide rescue for your leaders.' Each Fire was also observed completing another activity that was normally part of the expedition – either meal time or sorting rations.

In small groups, the YE researchers had a focus on one of the four group skills, using different approaches for each but keeping notes about observations and recording interviews. The observers compared notes with each other and asked questions of the group they were observing. Initial analysis of the data highlighted how the four skills were interrelated, and the data that one group used as indicators for their topic was often data that another group also used as indicators for theirs.

Findings

Questionnaire findings

Thirty-two matched pairs of pre- and post-expedition questionnaires were returned. Table 11.1 shows the results of the Wilcoxon matched-pairs test on the

Figure 11.1 Reviewing 'the blue barrel activity'.

46 Likert scale ELQ items arranged in rank order according to the strength of the Wilcoxon *T* statistic measured by the Wilcoxon matched-pairs test.

The Wilcoxon matched-pairs test identified that 12 of the 46 items showed statistically significant (at least $p<0.05$) pre- to post-expedition changes. This confirms that for those 12 items the H_1 hypothesis can be accepted. Within the 12 items, six were significant at the highest $p<0.005$ level, two at the $p<0.01$ level, two at the $p<0.025$ level and two at the $p<0.05$ level. Thirty-three items showed no significant change (NS) and so supported the *Ho* hypothesis.

Questionnaire: findings from open-ended questions

Analysis of the pre-expedition open-ended questions identified the following important themes:

a   Adventure and physical aspects of the expedition were the main attraction.
b   Making new friends and learning about group work.
c   Becoming independent individuals and being able to look after myself.

The attractions to BSES, rather than to other organisations were:

a   Science work in a remote environment that could otherwise not be visited alone.

Table 11.1 Results of Wilcoxon matched-pairs test on Greenland 2009 pre- v. post-expedition learning questionnaire presented in rank order of statistical significance

Question no.	Statements/questions	Significance level of Wilcoxon statistic
12	I have important responsibilities to my home community	0.005
15	I have the skills to peacefully resolve group conflicts	0.005
17	I speak my mind in group situations	0.005
24	People can always rely on me	0.005
27	I am a confident person	0.005
37	I can see solutions to most situations	0.005
18	I am good at listening to other people's points of view	0.01
33	I am able to set personal goals, make plans to reach them, and achieve them	0.01
5	I am aware of the different ways in which my everyday choices affect the natural environment	0.025
23	I am aware of how my behaviour may be perceived by others	0.025
4	I am very conscious of my own actions in relation to concepts of carbon footprint, food miles, and reducing/reusing/recycling	0.05
9	I understand the ways in which every day consumer choices at home may affect people's lives in other countries	0.05
14	It's important to me to feel that I can make a difference	NS
22	This expedition experience will enable me to interact more effectively with my friends and family back home	NS
10	I am sensitive to the customs and beliefs of those from other cultures	NS
25	I am tolerant of people whose beliefs/opinions contrast with my own	NS
35	I am able to reflect on, and learn from, my experiences	NS
40	Mental and physical hardship is a critical element of the BSES experience	NS
32	I can efficiently manage and organise my life (e.g. time, relationships, work/study, other commitments)	NS
34	I am aware of my mental strengths and weaknesses	NS
1	I have a strong appreciation of landscape and wildlife	NS
16	I am able to plan and lead group projects	NS
19	I am sensitive to the needs of others	NS
31	This expedition will change the direction of my life	NS
36	I am resilient and can motivate myself to succeed even when the 'chips are down'	NS
41	Groups being in remote settings where they need to be self-sufficient is a key part of a BSES expedition	NS
46	The diversity of the participants in each Fire is important	NS
8	Giving my time and resources to those with less is very important	NS
11	I want to influence local decisions in my home neighbourhood	NS
29	This expedition is important for my personal growth and development	NS

b   The reputation of BSES, its history and that BSES was started by a real explorer.

c   Adventure and an opportunity to visit the icecap.

At the end of the expedition the analysis brought very different responses that did not correlate with expectations. The question regarding the influence that the expedition had on young people's lives brought response themes that are summarised as:

a   Appreciation of everyday luxuries such as running water and comfortable beds and an expectation of complaining less.

b   A commitment to do more outdoor activities.

c   Increases in confidence and independence.

d   Considerations of career choices sometimes leading to changes and for others providing affirmation.

e   Changes in environmental understanding and commitments to, for example, switch lights off.

Elements of the expedition experience that were considered to be important in leading to the learning were identified as:

a   Team building and the importance of being in one Fire for the entire expedition – through good and bad times!

b   Adventure phase and the opportunity to learn new skills and visit the icecap.

c   Being in a remote location away from civilisation.

d   Building strong friendships with people throughout the expedition.

These themes that emerged from the qualitative questions provided a rich insight into the YEs experiences and need further analysis to illustrate the complexity of the learning process. The analysis may prove to be useful in informing future directions and allow more accurate target marketing for expeditions as well as hopefully enabling leaders to improve their practice.

Clearly, a study such as this pre-post experimental design has its limitations in that it was simply a 'snapshot' of YE s feelings at two particular points in time. It adopted a 'black box' approach and the Social Science Fire investigation was our attempt to find out what caused these changes (what was going on inside the black box), or when they occurred.

Findings from Social Science Fire observation study

The Social Science Fire findings are grouped by the four focus areas of group dynamics which were the subject of the study: leadership; team working; communication; and group management.

Leadership

All of the Fires except for the Social Science Fire used the 'leader for a day' system. We found that the leader for the day was not apparent in any of the activities we asked the Fires to complete, and in one Fire those we asked who the leader for the day was did not know who it was that day. When asked to choose attributes of good leadership, the leaders and YEs chose similar values. The best and worst values were, respectively, confidence and selfishness. When asked who they would choose to be the leader if the blue barrel activity had been real, the YEs and Fire leaders often also chose the same person to be the leader. The person they chose they usually described as the quieter and more logical, respected person in the group. In the tasks that groups were asked to complete, Fire members engaged in different behaviours that had varying contributions to successful completion of the tasks. These included: jumping in to control the situation; being quiet or silent; being listened to; and listening to everyone else. By observing these behaviours and then asking questions after the activities, it was possible to identify some common themes about leadership that emerged from across all Fires. For example, dominance and a loud voice are not the key to good leadership or being seen as a good leader while listening to others and being listened to by others are. The quality of 'respect' is important, and is demonstrated by confidence, logic, consideration (listening) and selflessness.

Team working

The group that was observed at the beginning of the expedition had the widest range and most inconsistent scores across the six teamwork areas and the group that was observed at the end of the expedition had a smaller range and more consistent scores across the areas. Though direct comparisons between Fires cannot be made, these results suggest that the expedition experience has a positive effect on the development of effective team work. A surprising result was that each of the Fires scored themselves higher than the observation team. The reasons for this are not clear, but it suggests that the groups had confidence in their performance beyond what was observed and they believed they were doing well.

Communication

One of the most interesting findings related to verbal communication was that every Fire had only one or two dominant voices during the activities. Those dominant voices were listened to and led to decisions from other members of the Fire, even if what they were suggesting was not the 'best' idea (as confirmed by asking questions about their decisions after the activities) and they were not viewed as the best 'leader'. Consequently, those individuals who were quieter within the Fire were ignored, even if they had better ideas than those with dominant voices and were considered better leaders (again, as confirmed by asking questions after completion of the activities). It was also noted that the later the

Social Science Fire visited the other Fires throughout the expedition, the more established the dominant voices were; but it was also noted that every individual in the Fire was more involved in the conversation and had more voice.

The Fire observed at the beginning of the expedition seemed not to engage in turn-taking across all members, and it was found that they talked over each other and ignored individual contributions. The Fire observed toward the end of the expedition appeared to be more bonded, demonstrated more respect for each other and was more visibly engaged in turn-taking. In each Fire, respect was demonstrated by how individuals listened and reacted to opinions of others. The more dominant voice did not necessarily gain more demonstrations of respect even if the dominant voice appeared to have more influence over final decisions. Though direct comparisons between Fires cannot be made, it was found (not surprisingly) that the longer each Fire had spent with each other when the observation took place, the more respect they demonstrated for each other.

Group management

This dynamic was about whether individuals were concerned with how the group completed the task and the focus was on group function and group issues. Observers were looking for how decisions were made (not what the decisions were); demonstrations of trust and relationships between group members; and methods used by the Fire leaders for managing the group. All Fires varied in their styles of group management. However, the Fire leaders' approach to group management had a significant effect on how the Fire members engaged in group management. Each of the four Fires had four different styles of group management, as follows:

1   leader driven and YE implemented: where the Fire leaders set up duty rotas and management systems and the YEs were then responsible for group chores and activities;
2   YE driven and YE implemented: where the YEs set up duty rotas and management systems and were responsible for completing group chores and activities;
3   leadership oriented: where the management of chores and choices were included in the remits of task leaders (i.e. food manager) or leader for a day;
4   group oriented: where the management of chores and choices emerged through group discussion. These four systems involved either up-front group management where the development of rotas and schedules led to fewer management decisions along the way, or on-going group management where responsibilities for tasks and group decisions were negotiated throughout the expedition experience.

Discussion

Questionnaire

From a methodological perspective the research design proved to be strong. Naturally, both qualitative and quantitative findings will have greater strength and generalisability if a larger sample size had been used (e.g. 500 respondents). We should acknowledge the common problem that pairing 'before' and 'after' ELQs could lead to the danger that exposure to the first ELQ is going to alter the reaction to the second (Clegg, 1990). However, given that five weeks intervened between the pre- and post-expedition surveys, we believe that this effect would have been minimal. Although the open-ended questions produced rich and encouraging data, they are also limited by the somewhat varied level of literacy skills between YEs from different socio-economic backgrounds and we recognise that those who wrote more on their questionnaires would increase the dominance of certain themes (inevitable in such a small study). The ELQ appears to be transferable to other expedition organisations who wish to understand more deeply their practice through increasing their knowledge of participants' perspectives on their experiences. Although we do not recommend the unconsidered adoption of any research instrument, we do hope that other expedition organisations will seek to learn from our research process; after all, there is little point in doing research of this nature if others in the sector are not able to benefit from it.

Further, we feel that with some carefully considered, but relatively minor modifications, the ELQ could be used in different contexts where some kind of assessment of changes in aspects of young people's self-confidence, leadership, teamwork, time management, environmental attitudes, life direction/career and other such skills are needed. The ELQ may be adaptable to other situations where young people might take part in programmes such as sail training (e.g. McCulloch *et al.*, 2010; Norris and Weinman, 1996) or Outward Bound-type programmes. However, before promoting expeditions as a universal panacea there are some further considerations. First, these findings should not be compared to those from studies based on non-voluntary programmes. When measuring self-concept, Hunter (1984) found that young offenders taking part in outdoor rehabilitation programmes as conscripted participants produced worse scores at the end of the study while controls showed no change. In contrast, the YEs on this expedition chose to go themselves. They completed an application form and were interviewed. Second, if the changes observed using the ELQ are short lived, the expedition experience becomes a purely recreational pursuit, devoid of educational worth. The authors are currently studying the longer-term influences of expeditions and hope to report on this in the future. Finally, there is a need to determine if these outcomes apply to other age groups and populations besides those between the ages of 17 and 21 years.

Another critical issue is the duration of the expedition and the severity of the challenge in relation to participants' capabilities and levels of motivation. This expedition was five weeks, and was chosen to maximise the chance of observing an effect. It may be likely that a one- or two-week expedition would be too brief for the changes seen here to occur. An opportunity for further research lies in determining an optimum length for this kind of expedition (which balances adventure, science and/or community projects), and if changes seen are dependent on the length of the expedition or on the experiences within it. Comparison studies across other expeditions of differing duration and severity, run by different organisations and in different locations would be a helpful way of investigating these elements more systematically.

Social science study

All of the elements of the observation study carried out during the expedition were interdependent and related. For example, characteristics of good group management were also necessary for effective team work. Elements of good communication and leadership contributed to effective group functioning, and the concepts of leadership and management were often blended together by Fire leaders in their descriptions of different group management styles and methods for organising the activities of the group.

The process of conducting the research highlighted certain shortcomings of the approach and ways in which they could be addressed in future research. By meeting with each of the Fires at different times in the expedition, their conception of leadership within the Fire, for example, would have been affected by how long the group had been together and what phase of the expedition they were in (that is if they were doing their science, adventure or changeover). The Social Science Fire also gained skill and confidence as researchers over time and the way they asked their questions and the data they chose to record may have changed during the course of the expedition. The type of activity is likely to have an impact on the results – that is our blue barrel activity was contrived and not a 'real' expedition activity, so the consequences of success or failure or the ways in which the tasks were approached or completed were not 'real'. Since we observed different Fires at different times in the expedition and not the same Fire at different times, it is impossible to be certain about whether group skills evolved over the course of the expedition. Though it also might have been useful to identify whether one style of group management was more effective or successful than the others, because it was not possible (within this research design) to observe all Fires at the same time in the expedition, it was not possible provide direct comparisons of the effectiveness of different group management styles between Fires.

Conclusions

Thirty-two participants who completed an expedition learning questionnaire before and after a five-week Greenland expedition self-reported statistically significant changes (<0.005) in the following statements: feeling important responsibilities to their home community; skills to resolve conflicts; ability to speak their mind in group situations; that people can rely on them; confidence and seeing solutions to most situations. Changes that were significant at the $p < 0.01$

level included the following: good at listening to other's points of view and ability to set personal goals and make plans to achieve them. Changes significant at the $p<0.025$ level were these statements: awareness of ways everyday choices affect the natural environment; and awareness of how their behaviour was perceived by others. Finally, changes significant at the $p<0.05$ significant level included these statements: consciousness in relation to carbon footprint, food miles and recycling; and understanding the ways in which everyday consumer choices affect people's lives in other countries.

Analysis of the pre-expedition open-ended questions identified that adventure and physical aspects of the expedition were the main attraction, followed by making new friends and learning about group work and becoming an 'independent individual and being able to look after myself'. The attractions to BSES, rather than to other organisations were: science work in a remote environment that could otherwise not be visited alone; the reputation of BSES; the organisation's history and that BSES was started by a real explorer; adventure; an opportunity to visit the icecap. At the end of the expedition the analysis brought very different responses that did not correlate with expectations. The question regarding the influence that the expedition had on young peoples' lives brought response themes that including some that can be anticipated (appreciation of everyday luxuries such as running water and comfortable beds and an expectation of complaining less; a commitment to do more outdoor activities) and some that may be more surprising or require further exploration to gain a sound grasp of their meaning (increases in confidence and independence; considerations of career choices sometimes leading to changes and for others providing affirmation; and changes in environmental understanding and commitments). Elements of the expedition experience that were considered to be important in leading to the learning were identified as: team building and the importance of being in one Fire for the entire expedition – through good and bad times; the adventure phase and the opportunity to learn new skills and visit the icecap; being in a remote location away from civilization; and building strong friendships with people throughout the expedition. The ability to work successfully as part of a team and to build strong friendships has been identified by numerous employers as key skills which they seek (e.g. Holmes, 2001; Knight and Yorke, 2003). It therefore seems that an expedition such as this may develop these key skills in young people.

The findings from Social Science Fire observation study are grouped in these categories: leadership; team working; communication; and group management. The social science research projects were useful in identifying the appetite for and interest expressed by the YEs and the Fire leaders in gaining insights into the effect of an expedition experience. An expedition is an environment rich with data about how individuals and groups act and interact. Creating shared meaning among those who share the experience through disciplined enquiry is an excellent research opportunity. With youth development as the *raison d'être* for BSES, it is natural for the expedition science to explore how and why youth development, learning and change occur as a result of the expedition experience. In line with the findings from the ELQ approach, the Social Science Fire observation study highlighted team working as a key skill developed on the expedition. Also, the importance of leadership, communication and group management were imphasised, and these again are skills which employers seek (e.g. Tomlinson, 2007, 2008, 2010). So, both approaches, the ELQ and the Social Science Fire observation study have arrived at very similar conclusions which, we believe, demonstrate the potential for expeditions to develop values and skills sought by employers, be they in the adventure tourism/education industry, or elsewhere.

In this chapter we have offered a summary of some research on an expedition; an adventure experience which sits at the juncture of adventure tourism, youth development and non-formal education. In doing so, we have tried to illustrate the challenges of conducting research about the value of such experiences. We expect that readers can identify a host of methodological challenges to this type of research and we want to point out some of the key challenges we believe will be useful to concentrate on to develop a cumulative body of literature in this area. First, we recognise the difficulty of experimental design, and in this case the problematic aspects of the ELQ. Though it is based on previous work, it is not sufficiently grounded in the extant literature to be sure that it is not missing out on measuring some aspects of the expedition experience and outcomes. Perhaps more importantly, given the limited use of ELQ in small groups, there is considerable work needed to check internal validity (i.e. we do not know that it measures what it claims to measure). Validating ELQ or locating a similar already validated instrument will allow further similar studies to develop this area further.

The criteria for assessing the value of qualitative work differ from those for quantitative work and there are a whole host of different qualitative approaches that could be combined to provide a much richer insight into the expedition experience. The qualitative study here was also undertaken as a pedagogical strategy since one of the Fires was learning about social sciences research. While one of the primary challenges of qualitative research is to consider the individual interpretations inevitably involved in comments about, for example, confidence and independence, that is particularly true when the researchers are 'learning by doing'. It is tempting to take a phenomenological approach and claim that such terms are whatever they mean to the individual but this does little to progress a meaningful and shared understanding of the effect and impact of an experience.

Finally, we have not explored in this paper how the pre and post test impacted on the observational study and vice versa. All of these issues highlight, among other things, the complexity of research in the social sciences. While it is tempting to collect data (more data is always alluring) in order to progress a meaningful understanding and contribution to literature in this area, some work needs to be done to create a theoretical and conceptual framework to inform what might count as useful evidence about an experience, whose views and opinions matter and what purposes research does, can and should serve.

Notes

1 www.bses.org.uk, accessed 23 December 2011.
2 www.bses.org.uk/AboutUs.aspx, accessed 1 January 2012.

References

Abram, D. (1996) *The Spell of the Sensuous*, New York: Vintage Books.

Adaval, R. and Wyer, R.S. (1998) The role of narratives in consumer information processing, *Journal of Consumer Psychology*, 7(3): 207–245.

Adventure Travel Society (1999) *The Importance of Adventure Travel and Ecotourism*, formerly online at: www.adventuretravel.com/seminar_home.htm [accessed 8 August 1999].

Aggarwal, V.S., Handa, M. and Ajay Singh, K. (2011) Satisfaction level of adventure tourists in India: an empirical study of perception of tourists and other stakeholders, *International Journal of Leisure and Tourism Marketing*, 2(2): 92–110.

Akama, J.S. and Kieti, D.M. (2003) Measuring tourist satisfaction with Kenya's wildlife safari: a case study of Tsavo West National Park, *Tourism Management*, 24(1): 73–81.

Alexandris, K., Kouthouris, C. and Meligdis, A. (2006) Increasing customers' loyalty in a skiing resort, *International Journal of Contemporary Hospitality Management*, 18(5): 414–425.

Allison, P. (2002) Values, narrative and authenticity: A study of youth expeditions in the 1990s, unpublished PhD dissertation, University of Strathclyde.

Allison, P. (2001) School trips and youth expeditions: Time for a united front? *Horizons*, 16(1): 15–17.

Allison, P. (2000) *Research from the Ground Up: Post Expedition Adjustment*, Ambleside: Brathay Hall Trust.

Allison, P. and Beames, S. (2010) Feature article: The changing geographies of overseas expeditions, *International Journal of Wilderness*, 16(3): 35–42.

Allison, P., Davis-Berman, J. and Berman, D. (2011) Changes in latitude, changes in attitude: analysis of the effects of reverse culture shock – a study of students returning from youth expeditions, *Leisure Studies*, DOI: 10.1080/02614367.2011.619011.

Allison, P. and Pomeroy, E. (2000) How shall we 'know'? Epistemological concerns in research in experiential education, *Journal of Experiential Education*, 23(2): 91–98.

Allison, P., Stott, T.A., Felter, J. and Beames, S. (2011) Overseas youth expeditions, in M. Berry and C. Hodgson (eds) *Adventure Education*, London: Routledge.

Allison, P. and Telford, J. (2005) Turbulent times: Outdoor education in Great Britain 1993–2003, *Australian Journal of Outdoor Education*, 9(2): 21–30.

Allison, P. and Von Wald, K. (2010) Exploring values and personal and social development: learning through expeditions, *Pastoral Care in Education*, 28(3): 219–233.

Alreck, P. and Settle, R.B. (2002) Gender effects on internet, catalogue, and store shopping, *Journal of Database Management*, 9(1): 150–162.

Anderson, E.W., Fornell, C. and Lehman, D.R. (1994) Customer satisfaction, market share, and profitability: findings from Sweden, *Journal of Marketing*, 58(3): 53–66.

Arabatzis, G. and Grigoroudis, E. (2010) Visitors' satisfaction, perceptions and gap analysis: The case of Dadia–Lefkimi–Souflion National Park, *Forest Policy and Economics*, 12(3): 163–172.

Archer, D.J. and Griffin, A.R. (2005) *A Study of Visitor Use and Satisfaction in Mungo National Park*, Gold Coast, Australia: Sustainable Tourism Cooperative Research Centre.

Ashforth, B.E. and Humphrey, R.H. (1993) Emotional labor in service roles: the influence of identity, *The Academy of Management Review*, 18(1): 88–115.

Baker, D.A. and Crompton, J.L. (2000) Quality, satisfaction and behavioural intentions, *Annals of Tourism Research*, 27(3): 785–804.

Banff Mountain Festival World Tour (2012), *Banff Mountain Festival World Tour*, online, available at: www.banff-uk.com/index.htm [accessed 10 March 2012].

Barclay, C.R. (1996) Autobiographical remembering: narrative constraints on objectified selves, in D. Rubin (ed.) *Remembering our Past: Studies in Autobiographical* Memory, Cambridge: Cambridge University Press.

Barkham, P. (2006) A bigger splash a bit more cash, *Guardian*, 17 July, online, available at: www.guardian.co.uk/travel/2006/jul/17/travelnews. watersportsholidays.unitedkingdom 1 [accessed 18 August 2006].

Barret, J. and Greenaway, R. (1995) *Why Adventure?* Coventry: Foundation for Outdoor Adventure.

Baudrillard, J. (1983) *Simulations*, New York: Semiotics.

Bauer, A. (2011) Marketing adventure tourism – what works and what doesn't, in K. O'Connell, M. Palma Fahey, S.T. Ruane and K. Onderdonk Horan (eds) *Tourism and Hospitality Research in Ireland: Current Challenges and Future Opportunities*, Galway/Shannon: College of Business, Public Policy and Law (NUI) Galway in conjunction with Shannon College of Hotel Management.

Bauman, Z. (1991) *Modernity and Ambivalence*, Cambridge: Polity.

Bauman, Z. (2001) *The Individualised Society*, Cambridge: Polity.

Baumeister, R.F. (1986) *Identity: Cultural Change and the Struggle for Self*, New York: Oxford University Press.

Baumeister, R.F. (1991) *Escaping the Self: Alcohlism, Spirituality, Masochism and Other Flights from the Burden of Selfhood*, New York: Basic Books.

Beal, B. (1995) Disqualifying the official: an exploration of social resistance through the subculture of skateboarding, *Sociology of Sport Journal*, 12(3): 252–267.

Beal, B. and Crosset, T. (1997) The use of 'subculture' and 'subworld' in ethnographic works on sport: a discussion of definitional distinctions, *Sociology of Sport Journal*, 14(1): 73–85.

Beames, S. (2003) Overseas youth expeditions, in B. Humberstone, H. Brown and K. Richards (eds) *Whose Journeys?* Penrith: Institute for Outdoor Learning.

Beames, S. (2004a) Critical elements of an expedition experience, *Journal of Adventure Education and Outdoor Learning*, 4(2): 145–157.

Beames, S. (2004b) Overseas youth expeditions: A rite of passage? *Australian Journal of Outdoor Education*, 8(1), 29–36.

Beames, S. (2005) Expeditions and the social construction of the self, *Australian Journal of Outdoor Education*, 9(1): 14–22.

Beames, SB. and Stott, T.A. (2008) Raleigh International pilot study report: summary of findings on how participants benefited from a 10-week expedition to Costa Rica, Report presented to Raleigh International, March.

Bechhofer, F. and Paterson, L. (2000) *Principles of Research Design in the Social Sciences*, London: Routledge.

Beck, U. (1992) *Risk Society: Towards a New Modernity*, London: Sage.

Beedie, P. (2008) Adventure tourism as a new frontier in leisure, *World Leisure Journal*, September, 50(3): 202–227.

Beedie, P. (2010) *Mountain Based Adventure Tourism: Lifestyle Choice and Identity Formation*, Saarbrucken: Lambert Academic Publishing.

Beedie, P. and Hudson, S. (2003) Emergence of mountain-based adventure tourism, *Annals of Tourism Research*, 30(3): 625–643.

Beeh, E.J. (1999) Adventure vs. ecotourism: environmental impact of so-called ecotourism activities, *E: The Environmental Magazine*, May/June, online, available at: www.emagazine.com/author/emagazine/P2150.

Belsey, C. (2002) *Poststructuralism: A Very Short Introduction*, Oxford: Oxford University Press.

Bentley, T.A. and Page, S.J. (2001) Scoping the extent of adventure tourism accidents, *Annals of Tourism Research*, 28(3): 705–726.

Bentley, T.A. and Page, S.J. (2008) A decade of injury monitoring in the New Zealand adventure tourism sector: a summary risk analysis, *Tourism Management*, 29(5): 857–869.

Bentley, T.A., Cater, C. and Page, S.J. (2010) Adventure and ecotourism safety in Queensland: operator experiences and practice, *Tourism Management*, 31(5): 563–571.

Bentley, T.A., Page, S.J. and Laird, I.S. (2001) Accidents in the New Zealand adventure tourism industry, *Journal of Safety Science*, 38(1): 31–48.

Berkowitz, E.N. (2006) *Essentials of Health Care Marketing*, Sudbury: Jones and Bartlett Publishers.

Bernhardt, K.L., Donthu, N. and Kennett, P.A. (2000) A longitudinal analysis of satisfaction and profitability, *Journal of Business Research*, 47(2): 161–171.

Biesta, G.J.J. (1994) Education as practical intersubjectivity: towards a critical-pragmatic understanding of education, *Educational Theory*, 44(3): 299–317.

Birkett, W. (1983) *Lakeland's Greatest Pioneers: 100 Years of Rock Climbing*, London: Robert Hale.

BMC (British Mountaineering Council) (2003) Participation statistics, online, available at: www.thebmc.co.uk/participation-in-climbing-mountaineering [accessed 25 September 2012].

BMC (British Mountaineering Council) (n.d.) *BMC Community*, online, available at: http://community.thebmc.co.uk [accessed 17 November 2011].

Booms, B. and Bitner, M. (1981) Marketing strategies and organisation structures for service firms, in J. Donnelly and W. George (eds) *Marketing of Sevices*, Chicago, IL: American Marketing Association.

Bottenburg, M. and Salome, L. (2010) The indoorisation of outdoor sports: an exploration of the rise of lifestyle sports in artificial settings, *Leisure Studies*, 29(2): 143–160.

Botterill, D. (1987) Dissatisfaction with a construction of satisfaction, *Annals of Tourism Research*, 14(1): 139–141.

Bourdieu, P. (2001 [1986]) *Distinction: A Social Critique of the Judgement of Taste*, trans. R. Nice, London: Sage.

Brady, M.K. and Cronin, J.J. (2001) Some new thoughts on conceptualising perceived service quality: a hierarchical approach, *Journal of Marketing*, 65(3): 34–49.

Brandt, A. (2004) Extreme classics: the 100 greatest adventure books of all time, *National Geographic*, online, available at: www.nationalgeographic.com/adventure/0404/adventure_books.html [accessed 16 February 2012].

British Educational Research Association (2004) *Revised Ethical Guidelines for Educational Research*, Macclesfield: BERA.

Brookes, A. (2003a) A critique of neo-Hahnian outdoor education theory, part one: challenges to the concept of 'character building', *Journal of Adventure Education and Outdoor Learning*, 3(1): 49–62.

Brookes, A. (2003b) A critique of neo-Hahnian outdoor education theory, part two: 'The fundamental attribution error' in contemporary outdoor education discourse, *Journal of Adventure Education and Outdoor Learning*, 3(2): 119–132.

Brown, M. (2002) The facilitator as gatekeeper: a critical analysis of social order in facilitation sessions, *Journal of Adventure Education and Outdoor Learning*, 2(2): 101–112.

Brown, M. (2009) Reconceptualising outdoor adventure education: Activity in search of an appropriate theory, *Australian Journal of Outdoor Education*, 13(2): 3–13.

Brown, M. (2010) Transfer: outdoor adventure education's Achilles heel? Changing participation as a viable option, *Australian Journal of Outdoor Education*, 14(1): 13–22.

Bruner, J.S. (1986) *Actual Minds, Possible Worlds*, Cambridge, MA: Harvard University Press.

Bryman, A. (1999) The Disneyization of society, *The Sociological Review*, 47(1): 25–47.

Bryman, A. (2004) *The Disneyization of Society*, London: Sage.

Buckley, R. (2003) Adventure tourism and the clothing, fashion and entertainment industries, *Journal of Ecotourism*, 2(2): 126–134.

Buckley, R. (2007) Adventure tourism products: price, duration, size, skill, remoteness, *Tourism Management*, 29(4): 1428–1433.

Buckley, R. (2012) Rush as a key motivation in skilled adventure tourism: resolving the risk recreation paradox, *Tourism Management*, 33(4): 961–970.

Buckley, R. (ed.) (2006) *Adventure Tourism*, Oxford: CABI.

Buckley, R. and Cater, C. (2007) *Adventure Tourism*, Wallingford: CABI.

Buckley, R., Cater, C., Zhong, L. and Chen, T. (2008) Shengtai Luyou: A Chinese perspective on ecotourism, *Annals of Tourism Research*, 35(4): 945–968.

Bullock, N. (2011) Mountains for sale, *Summit Magazine*, 63: 32–36.

Burnes, B. (2004) Kurt Lewin and the planned approach to change: a re-appraisal, *Journal of Management Studies*, 41(6): 977–1002.

Burns, R.C., Graefe, A.R. and Absher, J.D. (2003) Alternate measurement approaches to recreational customer satisfaction: satisfaction-only versus gap scores, *Leisure Sciences*, 25(4): 363–380.

Callander, M. and Page, S.J. (2003) Managing risk in adventure tourism operations in New Zealand: a review of the legal case history and potential for litigation, *Tourism Management*, 24(1): 13–23.

Campbell, E., Greenwood, C. and Yeoman, I. (2007) *Visit Scotland: What Will Activity and Adventure Tourism Look Like in 2015?* Edinburgh: Visit Scotland.

Campbell, J. (1990) *Transformation of Myth Through Time*, New York: Harper and Row.

Campbell, J. (2008) *The Hero with a Thousand Faces*, 3rd edition, Oakland, CA: New World Library.

Carman, J.M. (1990) Consumer perceptions of service quality: an assessment of the SERVQUAL dimensions, *Journal of Retailing*, 66(1): 33–55.

Carspecken, P.F. (1996) *Critical Ethnography in Educational Research: A Theoretical and Practical Guide*, New York: Routledge.

Castoriadis, C. (1998) *The Imaginary Institution of Society*, trans. K. Blamey, Cambridge, MA: MIT Press.

Cater, C. (2000) Can I play too? Exclusion and inclusion in adventure tourism, *North West Geographer*, 3(2): 50–60.

Cater, C. (2005) Looking the part: the relationship between adventure tourism and the outdoor fashion industry, in C. Ryan, S. Page and M. Aicken (eds) *Taking Tourism to the Limits*, London: Elsevier.

Cater, C. (2006a) World adventure capital, in R. Buckley (ed.) *Adventure Tourism*, Oxford: CABI, pp. 429–442.

Cater, C. (2010) Any closer and you'd be lunch!: interspecies interactions as nature tourism at marine aquaria, *Journal of Ecotourism*, 9(2): 133–148.

Cater, C. (2013) Nature bites back: impacts of the environment on tourism, in A. Holden and D. Fennell (eds) *Routledge Handbook of Tourism and the Natural Environment*, London: Routledge.

Cater, C. and Smith, L. (2003) New country visions: adventurous bodies in rural tourism, in P. Cloke (ed.) *Country Visions*, London: Pearson.

Cater, C.I. (2006b) Playing with Risk? Participant perceptions of risk and management implications in adventure tourism, *Tourism Management*, 27(2): 317–325.

Cater, C.I. (2007) Adventure tourism: will to power? in A. Church and T. Coles (eds) *Tourism, Power and Space*, Abingdon: Routledge,

Cater, C.I. (2008) The life aquatic: scuba diving and the experiential imperative, *Journal of Tourism in Marine Environments*, 5(4): 233–244.

Cave, A. (2011) *Andy Cave Blog*, online, available at: www.andycave.co.uk/blog/ [accessed 30 November 2011].

Chance, J. (2001) *The Lord of the Rings: The Mythology of Power*, revised edition, Lexington, KY: University Press of Kentucky.

Chang, J. and Samuel, N. (2004) Internet shopper demographics and buying behaviour in Australia, *Journal of the American Academy of Business*, 5(1/2): 171–176.

Chase, R. and Priest, S. (1990) Effective communication for the reflective outdoor leaderm *Journal of Adventure Education and Outdoor Leadership*, 7(1): 7–12.

Chatwin, B. (1987) *The Songlines*, London: Jonathan Cape.

Chi, C.G. and Gursoy, D. (2009) Employee satisfaction, customer satisfaction, and financial performance: an empirical examination, *International Journal of Hospitality Management*, 28(2): 245–253.

Chon, K. and Singh, A. (1995) Marketing resort to 2000: review of trends in the USA, *Tourism Management*, 16(6): 463–469.

Christiansen, D.R. (1990) Adventure tourism, in J.C. Miles and S. Priest (eds) *Adventure Education*, State College, PA: Venture Publishing.

Christopher, J.C. and Hickinbottom, S. (2008) Positive psychology, ethnocentrism, and the disguised ideology of individualism, *Theory and Psychology*, 18(5): 563–589.

Clegg, F. (1990) *Simple Statistics: A Course Book for the Social Sciences*, Cambridge: Cambridge University Press.

Cloke, P. and Perkins, H.C. (2002) Commodification and adventure in New Zealand tourism, *Current Issues in Tourism*, 5(6): 521–549.

Cloutier, R. (2003) The business of adventure tourism, in S. Hudson (ed.) *Sport and Adventure Tourism*, New York: Haworth Hospitality Press.

Cobley, P. (2001) *Narrative*, London: Routledge.

Cohen, S. and Taylor, L. (1992) *Escape Attempts: The Theory and Practice of Resistance to Everyday Life*, London: Routledge.

Connor, J. (1999) *Creagh Dhu Climber: The Life and Times of John Cunningham*, Bury St Edmunds: Ernest Press.

Conway, M.A. and Pleydell-Pearce, C.W. (2000) The construction of autobiographical memories in the self-memory system, *Psychological Review*, 107: 261–288.

Cook, L. (1999) The 1944 Education Act and outdoor education: from policy to practice, *History of Education*, 28(2): 157–172.

Cooley, A. (1999) Against commoditization: backpacking culture, *NCSU Ethnographic Field School in Costa Rica*, online, available at: http://faculty.chass.ncsu.edu/ wallace/ Cooley.PDF [accessed 20 March 2012].

Corvo, P. (2010) The pursuit of happiness and the globalised tourist, *Social Indicators Research*, 102(1): 93–97.

Cravens, D.W., Hills, G.E. and Woodruff, R.B. (1987) *Marketing Management*, Scarborough: Irwin.

Crompton, J.L. and Love, L.L. (1995) The predictive validity of alternative approaches to evaluating quality of a festival, *Journal of Travel Research*, 34(1): 11–24.

Cronin, J.J. and Taylor, S.A. (1992) Measuring service quality: a re-examination and extension, *Journal of Marketing*, 56(3): 55–68.

Cronin, J.J. and Taylor, S.A. (1994) SERVPERF versus SERVQUAL: reconciling performance-based and perceptions-minus-expectations measurement of service quality, *Journal of Marketing*, 58(1): 125–131.

Crosby, A. (1981) A critical look: The philosophical foundations of experiential education, *Journal of Experiential Education*, 4(1): 9–15.

Crowley, C., Harre, R. and Tagg, C. (2002) Qualitative research and computing: methodological issues and practices in using QSR NVivo and NUD*IST, *International Journal of Social Research Methodology*, 5(3): 193–197.

Csikszentmihalyi, M. (1990) *Flow: The Psychology of Optimal Experience*, New York: Harper and Row.

Csikszentmihalyi, M. and Csikszentmihalyi, I.S. (1990) Adventure and the flow experience, in J.C. Miles and S. Priest (eds) *Adventure Education*, State College, PA: Venture Publishing, pp. 149–155.

Cummins, R. (2009) The influence of tourism on the subjective wellbeing of host communities, *Exploring Wellbeing Seminar*, Melbourne, Australia: Victoria University.

Curran, J. (1999) *High Achiever: The Life and Times of Chris Bonington*, London: Constable.

Curtis, B. and Pajaczkowska, C. (1994) Getting there: travel, time and narrative, in G. Robertson, M. Mash, L. Tickner, J. Bird, B. Curtis and T. Putnam Robertson (eds) *Travellers' Tales: Narratives of Home and Displacement*, Abingdon: Routledge.

Dann, G. (1977) Anomie, ego-enhancement and tourism, *Annals of Tourism Research*, 4(4): 184–194.

Davis, H. and McLeod, S.L. (2003) Why humans value sensational news: an evolutionary perspective, *Evolution and Human Behaviour*, 24(3): 208–216.

De Botton, A. (2003) *The Art of Travel*, London: Penguin.

De Bruycker, L. (2007) Perception of local children towards tourists visiting Bruges, *Journal for Applied Anthropology*, 3: 157–162.

Delandshere, G. (2002) Assessment as inquiry, *Teachers College Record*, 104(7): 1461–1484.

Deleuze, G. (1983) *Nietzsche and Philosophy*, trans. H. Tomlinson, London: Continuum.

Deleuze, G. (1988) *Spinoza: Practical Philosophy*. trans R. Hurley, San Francisco, CA: City Light Books.

Desforges, L. (2000) Travelling the world: identity and travel biography, *Annals of Tourism Research*, 27(4): 926–945.

Devesa, M., Laguna, M. and Palacios, A. (2010) The role of motivation in visitor satisfaction: Empirical evidence in rural tourism, *Tourism Management*, 31(4): 547–552.

Dewey, J. (1916) *Democracy and Education*, New York: Free Press.

Dewey, J. (1922) *Human Nature and Conduct: An Introduction to Social Psychology*, New York: Henry Holt and Co.

Dewey, J. (1938) *Experience and Education*, New York: Macmillan.

Dholakia, R.R. and Uusitalo, O. (2002) Switching to electronic stores: consumer characteristics and the perception of shopping benefits, *International Journal of Retail and Distribution Management*, 30(10): 459–469.

Dickens, L. and Watkins, K. (1999) Action research: rethinking Lewin, *Management Learning*, 30(2): 127–140.

Diener, E. (2009) *The Science of Well-Being: The Collected Works of Ed Diener*, New York: Springer.

Diener, E., Wirtz, D., Tov, W., Kim-Prieto, C., Choi, D.-W., Oishi, S. and Biswas-Diener, R. (2010) New well-being measures: short scales to assess flourishing and positive and negative feelings, *Social Indicators Research*, 97(2): 143–156.

Dittmar, H., Beattie, J. and Friese, S. (1995) Gender identity and material symbols: objects and decision considerations in impulse purchases, *Journal of Economic Psychology*, 16(1): 491–502.

Dittmar, H., Long, K. and Meek, R. (2004) Buying on the internet: gender differences in online and conventional buying motivations, *Journal of Sex Roles*, 50(5/6): 423–444.

Dobson, J. (2006) Sharks, wildlife tourism, and state regulation, *Tourism in Marine Environments*, 3(1): 15–23.

Donne, K. (2009) ADVENTUREQUAL: an extension of the SERVQUAL conceptual gap model in young people's outdoor adventure, *International Journal of Sport Management and Marketing*, 6(3): 253–276.

Donnelly, P. (1981) Towards a definition of sport subculture, in M. Hart and S. Birell (eds) *Sport in the Sociocultural Process*, Dubuque: IA: Wm. C. Brown.

Donnelly, P. (1993) Subcultures in sport: resilience transformation, in A.G. Ingham and J.W. Loy (eds) *Sport in Social Development: Traditions, Transitions and Transformations*. Champaign, IL: Human Kinetics.

Donnelly, P. (2003) The great divide sport climbing vs. adventure climbing, in R.E. Rinehart and S. Sydnor (eds) *To the Extreme: Alternative Sports, Inside and Out*, Albany, NY: State University of New York Press.

Donnelly, P. and Young, K. (1988) The construction and confirmation of identity in sport subcultures, *Sociology of Sport Journal*, 5(3): 223–240.

Douglas, M. (1992) *Risk and Blame: Essays in Cultural Theory*, London: Routledge.

Drasdo, H. (1996) *The Ordinary Route*, Berwick: The Ernest Press.

Duckworth, A.L., Steen, T.A. and Seligman, M.E.P. (2005) Positive psychology in clinical practice, *Annual Review of Clinical Psychology*, 1: 629–651.

Dundes, A. (ed.) (1989) *Little Red Riding Hood: A Case Book*, Madison WI: The University of Wisconsin Press.

Eassom, S. (1993) Leisure, health and happiness: in praise of hedonism, in C. Brackenridge (ed.) *Body Matters: Leisure Images and Lifestyles*, Brighton: Leisure Studies Association.

Edensor, T. (2001) Performing tourism, staging tourism: (re)producing tourist space and practice tourist studies, *Tourist Studies*, 1(1): 59–81.

Ekinci, Y. (2003) Which comparison standard should be used for service quality and customer satisfaction? *Journal of Quality Assurance in Hospitality and Tourism*, 4(3): 61–75.

Elias, N. and Dunning, E. (1986) *The Quest for Excitement in Leisure: Sport and Leisure in the Civilising Process*, London: Blackwell.

Engel, E. (2009) in *Encyclopaedia Britannica online encyclopaedia 2009*, online, available at: www.britannica.com/EBchecked/topic/187452/Ernst-Engel#ref=ref86426 [accessed 10 July 2009].

Engeström, Y. (2001) Expansive learning at work: toward an activity theoretical reconceptualization, *Journal of Education and Work*, 14(1): 133–156.

European Communities (2003) *A Manual for Evaluating the Quality Performance of Tourist Destinations and Services*, online, available at: http://ec.europa.eu/enterprise/sectors/tourism/files/studies/evaluation_quality_performance/qualitest_manual_en.pdf [accessed 27 March 2012].

Ewert, A. (1989) *Outdoor Adventure Pursuits: Foundations, Models, and Theories*, Scottsdale, AZ: Publishing Horizons.

Eyler, J. (2009) The power of experiential education, *Liberal Education*, 95(4): 24–31.

Fáilte Ireland (2007) *Tourism Product Development Strategy 2007–2013*, Dublin: Fáilte Ireland.

Falco-Mammone, F. (2007) *Beach Images: More Than Just Sun, Sea, Sand and Sex*, Proceedings of the 17th Annual CAUTHE Conference, Sydney, NSW: University of Technology Sydney.

Fallon, P. and Schofield, P. (2003) 'Just trying to keep the customer satisfied': a comparison of models used in the measurement of tourist satisfaction, *Journal of Quality Assurance in Hospitality and Tourism*, 4(3/4): 77–96.

Faullant, R., Matzler, K. and Füller, J. (2008) The impact of satisfaction and image on loyalty: the case of Alpine ski resorts, *Managing Service Quality*, 18(2): 163–178.

Fennell, D. (1999) *Ecotourism: An Introduction*, London: Routledge.

Fennell, D. (2003) *Ecotourism*, 2nd edition, London/New York: Routledge.

Fennell, D.A. and Eagles, P.F.J. (1990) Ecotourism in Costa Rica: a conceptual framework, *Journal of Park and Recreation Administration*, 8(1): 23–34.

Fenwick, T.J. (2001) *Experiential Learning: A Theoretical Critique from Five Perspectives*. Columbus, OH: ERIC Clearinghouse on Adult, Career, and Vocational Education.

Fick, G.R. and Brent Richie, J.R. (1991) Measuring service quality in the travel and tourism industry, *Journal of Travel Research*, 30(2): 2–9.

Fiennes, R. (2007) *Mad, Bad and Dangerous*, London: Hodder and Stoughton Ltd.

File, K.M. and Prince, R.A. (1996) A psychographic segmentation of industrial family businesses, *Journal of Industrial Marketing*, 25(3): 223–234.

Fine, G.A. (1979) Small groups and culture creation: the ideoculture of little league baseball teams, *American Sociological Review*, 44(5): 733–745.

Fletcher, R. (2010) The emperor's new adventure: public secrecy and the paradox of adventure tourism, *Journal of Contemporary Ethnography*, 39(1): 6–33.

Fluker, M.R. and Turner, L.W. (2000) Needs, motivations and expectations of a commercial white-water rafting experience, *Journal of Travel Research*, 38(2): 380–389.

Foucault, M. (1990) *The Will to Knowledge: The History of Sexuality Volume 1*, trans. R. Hurley, London: Penguin.

Frash, R.E., Antun, J.M. and Hodges, H.E. (2008) Family life cycle segmentation for foodservice marketing: an exploratory case study, *Journal of Restaurant and Foodservice Marketing*, 11(4): 382–397.

Fredrickson, B.L. (2001) The role of positive emotions in positive psychology: the broaden-and-build theory of positive emotions, *American Psychologist*, 56(3): 218–226.

Frison-Roche, R. (1996) *A History of Mountain Climbing*, Paris: Flammarion.

Frost, W. and Hall, C.M. (2009) *Tourism and National Parks: International Perspectives on Development, Histories and Change*, London/New York: Routledge.

Furedi, F. (2007) *Culture of Fear: Revisited*, London: Continuum.

Garbarino, E. and Strahilevitz, M. (2004) Gender differences in the perceived risk of buying online and the effect of receiving a site recommendation, *Journal of Business Research*, 57(7): 768–775.

Gardner, D. (2008) *Risk: The Science and Politics of Fear*, London: Virgin Books.

Geertz, C. (1973) *The Interpretation of Cultures*, New York: Basic Books.

Gelder, K. and Thornton, S. (eds) (1997) *The Subcultures Reader*, London: Routledge.

George, R. (2008) *Marketing South African Tourism and Hospitality*, 3rd edition, Cape Town: Oxford University Press.

Giddens, A. (1990) *The Consequences of Modernity*, Cambridge: Polity.

Gieryn, T. (2000) Place in sociology, *Annual Review of Sociology*, 26: 463–496.

Gilbert, D. and Abdullah, J. (2004) Holidaytaking and the sense of well-being, *Annals of Tourism Research*, 31: 103–121.

Goffman, E. (1959) *The Presentation of Self in Everyday Life*, Harmondsworth: Penguin.

Golomb, J. (1995) *In Search of Authenticity: From Kierkegaard to Camus*, London: Routledge.

Gondek, M.F. (2008) Wilderness, leadership, and gender: the experience of being a wilderness instructor, a phenomenological study, unpublished doctoral dissertation, Pacifica Graduate Institute, Carpinteria, CA.

Gray, D. (1993a) *Slack: The Fun of Climbing*, Dewsbury: Joseph Ward.

Gray, D. (1993b) *Tight Rope! The Fun of Climbing.* Berwick: The Ernest Press.

Gray, D.E. (2004) *Doing Research in the Real World*, London: Sage.

Green, M. (1980) *Dreams of Adventure, Deeds of Empire: A Wide-Ranging and Provocative Examination of the Great Tradition of the Literature of Adventure*, London: Routledge.

Gregory, D. (1994) *Geographical Imaginations*, Oxford: Blackwells.

Greider, T. and Garkovich, L. (1994) Landscapes: the social construction of nature and the environment, *Rural Sociology*, 59(1): 1–24.

Greig, A., Taylor, J. and MacKay, T. (2007) *Doing Research with Children*, London: Sage.

Grey, T. (1984) The expedition experience, *Adventure Education*, March/April: 17–18.

Grey, T. (1998) How it all began: 25 years of young exploring, *Horizons*, 2: 26–27.

Griffiths, J. (2007) *Wild: An Elemental Journey*, London: Hamish Hamilton.

Grönroos, C. (1984) A service quality model and its marketing implications, *European Journal of Marketing*, 18(4): 36–44.

Gruber, M., Kane, K., Flack, L., Abbotoy, J., Recchio, J., Williamson, K., Horan, K. and McCarthy, P. (2003) A 'perfect day' work redesign in a chemotherapy and infusion center, *Oncology Nursing Forum*, 30(4): 567.

Gursoy, D. and Swanger, N. (2007) Performance-enhancing internal strategic factors and competencies: impacts on financial success, *Hospitality Management*, 26(1): 213–227.

Gyimothy, S. and Mykletun, R.J. (2004) Play in adventure tourism: the case of arctic trekking, *Annals of Tourism Research*, 31(4): 855–878.

Habermas, J. (1984) *The Theory of Communicative Action*, Cambridge: Polity.

Habermas, J. (1991) *The Structural Transformation of the Public Sphere*, Cambridge: Polity.

Hahn, K. (1934) The practical child and the bookworm, *The Listener*, 28 November: 39–41.

Hahn, K. (1960) *The Moral Equivalent of War (Outward Bound)*, address at the annual meeting of the Outward Bound Trust, 20 July, London: Outward Bound Trust, available from Kurt Hahn Archive, Salem International College, Schloss Spetzgart, 88662 Überlingen, Germany.

Hales, R. (2006) Mountaineering, in R. Buckley (ed.) *Adventure Tourism*, Oxford: CABI, pp. 260–285.

Hall, S. and du Gay, P. (1996) *Questions of Cultural Identity*, London: Sage.

Hallowell, R. (1996) The relationships of customer satisfaction, customer loyalty, and profitability: an empirical study, *International Journal of Service Industry Management*, 7(4): 27–42.

Han, S.Y., Um, S. and Mills, A. (2005) The development of on-site experience measurement scale, *The 11th APTA Conference-New Tourism for Asia-Pacific*, Busan, Korea: Dong-A University, pp. 14–22.

Hankinson, A. (1988) *A Century on the Crags: The History of Rock Climbing in the Lake District*, Frome: Butler and Tanner Ltd.

Hanson, G.D., Rauniyar, G.P. and Herrmann, R.O. (1994) Using consumer profiles to increase the U.S. market for seafood: implications for aquaculture, *Journal of Aquaculture*, 127(4): 303–316.

Hardwell, A. (2009) Authentic experience: the importance of climbing to indoor only climbers, in J. Ormrod and B. Wheaton (eds) *On the Edge: Leisure Consumption and the Representation of Adventure Sports*, Brighton: Leisure Studies Association.

Hardwell, A.G. (2007) Detraditionalization and differentiation in UK rock climbers, unpublished PhD thesis, University of Central Lancashire.

Harewood, J., Chinula, T., Talbot, V., Carillet, J.-B. and Sorokin, M. (2006) *Lonely Planet: Vanuatu and New Caledonia*, Singapore: Lonely Planet Publications Pty Ltd.

Hargreaves, J. (1986) *Sport, Power and Culture: A Social Historical Analysis of Popular Sports in Britain*, London: Polity.

Hattie, J., Marsh, H.W., Neill, J.T. and Richards, G.E. (1997) Adventure education and Outward Bound: out-of-class experiences that make a lasting difference, *Review of Educational Research*, 67(1): 43–87.

Hayami, A. and Okada, A. (2005) Population and households' dynamics: a mountainous district in northern Japan in the Shûmon Aratame Chô of Aizu, 1750–1850, *Journal of the History of the Family*, 10(3): 195–229.

Health Systems Trust (2007) *Average Household Size*, online, available at: http://indicators.hst.org.za/healthstats/6 [accessed 15 August 2009].

Hebdige, D. (1987) *Subculture: The Meaning of Style*, London: Routledge.

Hennig, C. (2002) Tourism: enacting modern myths, in G.M. Dann (ed.) *The Tourist as a Metaphor of the Social World*, Wallingford: CABI.

Hermans, H.J.M. (1996) Voicing the self: from information processing to dialogical interchange, *Psychological Bulletin*, 119(1): 31–50.

Hetherington, K. (1996) Identity formation, space and social centrality, *Theory, Culture and Society*, 13(4): 33–52.

Heywood, I. (1994) Urgent dreams: climbing rationalization and ambivalence, *Leisure Studies*, 13(3): 179–194.

Heywood, I. (2006) Climbing monsters: excess and restraint in contemporary rock climbing, *Leisure Studies*, 25(4): 455–467.

Hobson, J.A. (1994) *The Chemistry of Conscious States*, London: Little, Brown.

Holmes, L. (2001) Reconsidering graduate employability: the 'graduate identity' approach, *Quality in Higher Education*, 7(2): 111–119.

Hom Cary, S. (2004) The tourist moment, *Annals of Tourism Research*, 31(1): 61–77.

Hopkins, D. and Putnam, R. (1993) *Personal Growth Through Adventure*, London: David Fulton.

Hotelstars Union (2009) *Classification Criteria 2010–2014*, online, available at: www. hotelstars.eu/userfiles/files/en/downloads/Criteria_2010-2014.pdf [accessed 16 March 2012].

Howat, G., Crilley, G. and McGrath, R. (2008) A focused service quality, benefits, overall satisfaction and loyalty model for public aquatic centres, *Managing Leisure*, 13(3/4): 139–161.

Hsu, C.H., Kang, S.K. and Wolfe, K. (2002) Psychographic and demographic profiles and niche market leisure travellers, *Journal of Hospitality and Tourism Research*, 26(1): 3–22.

Huang, M. (2010) Hiking the 100 mountains: how individuals move from a beginner to a specialist in mountain hiking activity in Taiwan, PhD upgrade presentation, Aberystwyth University, Wales.

Hudson, S. (2002) *Sport and Adventure Tourism*, London: Routledge.

Hudson, S. and Beedie, P. (2006) From Inuits in skin boats to Bobos on the high seas: the commodification of sea kayaking through tourism, *Tourism in Marine Environments*, 2(2): 65–77.

Hudson, S., Hudson, P. and Miller, G.A. (2004) The measurement of service quality in the tour operating sector: a methodological comparison, *Journal of Travel Research*, 42(3): 305–312.

Hunt, J. (1990) Philosophy of adventure education, in J.C. Miles and S. Priest (eds) *Adventure Education*, State College, PA: Venture Publishing.

Hunter, I.R. (1984) Impact of voluntary selection procedures on the reported success of outdoor rehabilitation programmes, *Therapeutic Recreation Journal*, 18(3): 38–44.

Inglis, F. (2000) *The Delicious History of the Holiday*, London: Routledge.

Ingold, T. (1993) The temporality of the landscape, *World Archaeology*, 25(2): 152–174.

INSIGHTS (2003) Adventure tourism typology, cited in E. Campbell, C. Greenwood, and I. Yeoman (2007) *Visit Scotland: What Will Activity and Adventure Tourism Look Like in 2015?* Edinburgh: Visit Scotland.

IPPR (Institute of Public Policy Research) (2009) *Rallying Together: An IPPR Report for Raleigh International Trust*, London: Institute of Public Policy Research.

Jackson, S. (1992) Athletes in flow: a qualitative investigation of flow states in elite figure skaters, *Journal of Applied Sport Psychology*, 4(2): 161–180.

Jackson, S.A. and Eklund, R.C. (2004) *The Flow Scales Manual*, Morgantown, WV: Fitness Information Technology.

Jang, S.C. and Ham, S. (2009) A double-hurdle analysis of travel expenditure: baby boomer seniors versus older seniors, *Tourism Management*, 30(3): 372–380.

Jayawickreme, E., Pawelski, J., Seligman, M. and Auxier, R. (2008) Happiness: positive psychology and nussbaum's capabilities approach, in R. Auxier (ed.) *Library of Living Philosophers: The Philosophy of Martha Nussbaum*, Chicago, IL: Open Court.

Jenks, C. (2005) *Subculture: The Fragmentation of the Social*, London: Sage.

Jennings, G.R., Lee, Y-S., Ayling, A., Cater, C., Ollenburg, C. and Lunny, B. (2008) *What Do Quality Adventure Tourism Experiences Mean for Adventure Travellers and Providers? An Industry Report to the Gold Coast Adventure Travel Group*, online, available at: http://businessgc.com.au/uploads/QTE%20Report.pdf [accessed 8 March 2012].

Johnston, B.R. and Edwards, T. (1994) The commodification of mountaineering, *Annals of Tourism Research*, 21(3): 459–477.

172   *References*

Johnston, M.E. (1989) Peak experiences: challenge and danger in mountain recreation in New Zealand, unpublished PhD thesis Lincoln University, New Zealand.

Jones, A. (2004) *Review of Gap Year Provision. DfES Research Report 555*, online, available at: www.rgs.org/NR/rdonlyres/3147D7BD-5359-4387-BAC9-CEC80EC7D85F/0/AndrewJonesforDfES2003.pdf [accessed 14 September 2012].

Jones, T. and Milburn, G. (1988) *Cumbrian Rock: 100 Years of Climbing in the Lake District*, Manchester: Pic Publications.

Joplin, L. (2008) On defining experiential education, in K. Warren, D. Mitten and T.A. Loeffler (eds) *Theory and Practice of Experiential Education*, Boulder, CO: Association for Experiential Education.

Jung, K. (1990) *The Archetypes and the Collective Unconscious*, 2nd edition, Princeton, NJ: Princeton University Press.

Kaldec, A. (2007) *Dewey's Critical Pragmatism*, Lanham, MD: Lexington Books.

Kennedy, A. (1992) *The Expedition Experience as a Vehicle for Change in the Inner City*, Penrith: Adventure Education.

Kerry County Council (2009) *Kerry County Development Plan 2009–2015*, online, available at: www.kerrycoco.ie/en/allservices/planning/codevelopmentplan [accessed 20 April 2012].

Khan, M. (2003) ECOSERV: ecotourists' quality expectations, *Annals of Tourism Research*, 30(1): 109–124.

Kiewa, J. (2002) Traditional climbing: metaphor of resistance or metanarrative of oppression? *Leisure Studies*, 21(2): 145–161.

Klein, D. (1980) Work, leisure and recreational risk, in R.L. Bury (ed.) *Risk and Accidents in Outdoor Recreation Areas: Selected Papers*, College Station, TX: Texas A&M University, pp. 103–121.

Kler, B.K. and Tribe, J. (2012) Flourishing through scuba: understanding the pursuit of dive experiences, *Tourism in Marine Environments*, 8(1/2): 19–33.

Knight, P.T. and Yorke, M. (2003) Employability and good learning in higher education, *Teaching in Higher Education*, 8(1): 3–16.

Kolb, D. (1984) *Experiential Learning: Experience as the Source of Learning and Development*, Englewood Cliffs, NJ: Prentice-Hall.

Korth, B. (2005) Choice, necessity, or narcissism? A feminist does feminist ethnography, in G. Troman, B. Jeffrey and G. Walford (eds) *Methodological issues and practices in ethnography*, Bingley: Emerald.

Korth, B. (2007) The leaps of faith in social science: study of the imagined in the discourse of the real, *International Journal of Qualitative Methods*, 6(1): 69–94.

Kotler, P. (2000) *Marketing Management: The Millennium Edition*, Upper Saddle River, NJ: Prentice-Hall Inc.

Kotler, P., Bowen, J.T. and Makens, J.C. (2006) *Marketing for Hospitality and Tourism*, 4th edition, Upper Saddle River, NJ: Pearson Education Inc.

Kouthouris, C. and Alexandris, K. (2005) Can service quality predict customer satisfaction and behavioural intentions in the sport tourism industry? An application of the SERVQUAL model in an outdoors setting, *Journal of Sport Tourism*, 10(2): 101–111.

Kozak, M. (2001) A critical review of approaches to measure satisfaction with tourist destinations, in J.A. Mazanec, G.I. Crouch, J.R. Brent Ritchie and A.G. Woodside (eds) *Consumer Psychology of Tourism, Hospitality and Leisure, Vol. 2*, Oxford: CABI.

Kreeft, P.J. (2005) *The Philosophy of Tolkien: The Worldview Behind The Lord of the Rings*, San Francisco, CA: Ignatius Press.

Krueger, R.A. (1994) *Focus Groups: A Practical Guide for Applied Research*, Thousand Oaks, CA: Sage Publications.

Kurtz, D.L. (2008) *Principles of Contemporary Marketing*, international student edition, Mason, OH: Thomson Learning Academic.

Kurtz, J. (2006) Journal assignment on motivation, setting goals and finding meaning, *Psychology 403: The Psychology of Happiness Subject Handout*, Charlottesville, VA: University of Virginia.

Kvale, S. (1996) *An Introduction to Qualitative Research Interviewing*, London: Sage.

LaPage, W.F. (1969) Campground marketing: the heavy-half strategy – USDA forest service research note, Upper-Darby, PA: North-Eastern Forest Experiment Station.

Laing, J.H. and Crouch, G.I. (2011) Frontier tourism: retracing mythic journeys, *Annals of Tourism Research*, 38(4): 1516–1534.

Langer, E.J. and Moldoveanu, M. (2000) The construct of mindfulness, *Journal of Social Issues*, 56(1): 1–9.

Lash, S. and Urry, J. (1994) *Economies of Signs and Space*, London: Sage.

Last, A. (1997) Causes and solutions to incidences of climbing, unpublished master's thesis, Sheffield Hallam University.

Latour, B. (1988) *The Pasteurisation of France*, London: Harvard University Press.

Lave, J. and Wenger, E. (1991) *Situated Learning: Legitimate Peripheral Participation*, Cambridge: Cambridge University Press.

Laviolette, P. (2011) *Extreme Landscapes of Leisure, Not a Hap-Hazardous Sport*, Farnham: Ashgate.

Laws, E. (1991) *Tourism Marketing: Service and Quality Perspective*, London: Stanley Thornes.

Layard, R. (2005) *Happiness: Lessons Form a New Science*, London: Allen Lane.

le Breton, D. (2000) Playing symbolically with death in extreme sports, *Body Society*, 6(1): 1–11.

Lee, G., Morrison, A.M. and O'Leary, J.T. (2006) The economic value portfolio matrix: a target market selection tool for destination marketing organizations, *Tourism Management*, 27(4): 576–588.

Lefebvre, H (1991) *The Production of Space*, New York: Wiley-Blackwell.

Legoherel, P. (1998) Toward a market segmentation of the tourism trade: expenditure levels and consumer behaviour instability, *Journal of Travel Research*, 29(4): 12–18.

Lewis, N. (2000) The climbing body, nature and the experience of modernity, *Body and Society*, 6(3/4): 58–80.

Lewis, N. (2004) Sustainable adventure: embodied experiences and ecological practices within British climbing, in B. Wheaton (ed.) *Understanding Lifestyle Sports: Consumption, Identity and Difference*, London, Routledge.

Lim, F.K.G. (2008) Of reverie and emplacement: spatial imaginings and tourism encounters in Nepal Himalaya, *Inter Asia Cultural Studies*, 9(3): 375–394.

Lin, C.F. (2002) Segmenting customer brand preference: demographic or psychographic, *Journal of Product and Brand Management*, 11(4): 249–268.

Lonely Planet (2010) *World's 10 Happiest Places*, online, available at: www.lonely-planet.com/vanuatu/travel-tips-and-articles/54565 [accessed 10 July 2012].

Lorimer, H. and Lund, K. (2003) Performing facts: finding a way over Scotland's mountains, *The Sociological Review*, 51(2): 121–134.

Loverseed, H. (1997) The adventure travel industry in North America, *Travel and Tourism Analyst*, 6(1): 87–104.

Loynes, C. (1998) Adventure in a bun, *Journal of Experiential Education*, 21(1): 35–39.

Loynes, C. (1999a) Development training in the United Kingdom, in J.C. Miles and S. Priest (eds) *Adventure Programming*, State College, PA: Venture Publishing.

Loynes, C. (1999b) Once upon a time, paper presented at the National Outdoor Education Conference, Perth, Australia.

Luhmann, N. (1996) Complexity, structural contingencies and value conflicts, in P. Heelas, S. Lash and P. Morris (eds) *Detraditionalization*, Oxford: Blackwell.

Lupton, D. (1999) *Risk*, London: Routledge.

Lyng, S. (1990) A social psychological analysis of voluntary risk taking, *American Journal of Sociology*, 95(4): 851–886.

Lyotard, J.F. (1984) *The Postmodern Condition: A Report on Knowledge*, Manchester: Manchester University Press.

Macbeth, J. (2005) The 'Pals' the 'Professionals' and the 'Conformers': the meaning of football in the lives of women footballers in Scotland, in, J. Magee, A. Bairner, and A. Tomlinson (eds) *The Bountiful Game? Football Identities and Finances*, Oxford: Meyer and Meyer Sport.

MacCannell, D. (1976) *The Tourist*, London: Macmillan.

MacCannell, D. (1992) *Empty Meeting Grounds: The Tourist Papers*, London: Routledge.

Macfarlane, R. (2003) *Mountains of the Mind*, London: Granta.

Macfarlane, R. (2007) *The Wild Places*, London: Granta.

Maffesoli, M. (2000) *The Time of Tribes: The Decline of Individualism in Mass Society*, London: Sage.

Mannell, R.C. and Iso-Ahola, S.E. (1987) Psychological nature of leisure and tourism experience, *Annals of Tourism Research*, 14(3): 314–331.

Marchart, O. (2004) Bridging the micro-macro gap: is there such a thing as a post-subcultural politics? in D. Muggleton and R. Weinzierl (eds) *The Post Subcultural Reader*, Oxford: Berg.

Maritime Safety Authority (1995) *Whitewater Rafting Customer Research; Quantitative and Qualitative Research Findings*, Wellington: MSA.

Martilla, J.A. and James, J.C. (1977) Importance-performance analysis, *Journal of Marketing*, 41(1): 77–79.

Martin, B.A.S. (2003) The influence of gender on mood effects in advertising, *Journal of Psychology and Marketing*, 20(3): 249–273.

Massey, D. and Jess, P. (1995) *A Place in the World: Places, Cultures and Globalisation*, Oxford: Oxford University Press.

Massumi, B. (2002) *Parables for the Virtual: Movement, Affect, Sensation*, Durham, NC/London: Duke University Press.

May, J. (1996) In search of authenticity off and *on* the beaten track, *Environment and Planning D: Society and Space*, 14(6): 709–736.

Mazumdar, T. and Papatla, P. (1995) Gender differences in price and promotion response, *Pricing Strategy and Practice: An International Journal*, 3(1): 21–33.

McAdams, D.P. (1985) *Power, Intimacy, and the Life Story: Personological Inquiries into Identity*, New York: The Guilford Press.

McAdams, D.P. (2001) The psychology of life stories, *Review of General Psychology*, 5(2): 100–122.

McCulloch, K., McLaughlin, P., Allison, P., Edwards, V. and Tett, L. (2010) Sail training as education: more than mere adventure, *Oxford Review of Education*, 36(6): 661–676.

McDougall, G.H. and Levesque, T. (2000) Customer satisfaction with service: putting perceived value into the equation, *Journal of Services Marketing*, 14(5): 392–410.

McGillivray, D. and Frew, M. (2007) Capturing adventure: trading places in the symbolic economy, *Annals of Leisure Research*, 10(3): 54–78.

Mehmetoglu, M. and Engen, M. (2011) Pine and Gilmore's concept of experience economy and its dimensions: an empirical examination in tourism, *Journal of Quality Assurance in Hospitality and Tourism*, 12(4): 237–255.

Merchant, S. (2011) Negotiating underwater space: the sensorium, the body and the practice of scuba-diving, *Tourist Studies*, 11(3): 215–234.

Messner, R. (1975) *Le 7è degree*, Paris: Arthaud.

Meyers-Levy, J. and Sternthal, B. (1991) Gender differences in the use of message cues and judgments, *Journal of Marketing Research*, 28(1): 84–96.

Miles, J. and Priest, S. (1999) *Adventure Programming*, PA: Venture Publishing.

Mintel (2010) *Activity Holidays – UK – 2010*, London: Mintel Oxygen.

Morgan, D.J. (2000) Adventure tourism activities in New Zealand: perceptions and management of client risk, *Tourism Recreation Research*, 25(3): 79–89.

Morgan, M., Lugosi, P. and Brent Ritchie, J.R. (2010) *The Tourism and Leisure Experience*, Bristol: Channel View Publications.

Mortlock, C. (1984) *The Adventure Alternative*, Milnthorpe: Cicerone Press.

Mory, E.H. (2004) Feedback research revisited, in D. Jonassen (ed.) *Handbook of Research on Educational Communications and Technology*, 2nd edition, London: Macmillan.

Moscardo, G. (2010) The shaping of tourist experience: the importance of stories and themes, in M. Morgan, P. Lugosi and J.R. Brent Ritchie (eds) *The Tourism and Leisure Experience*, Bristol: Channel View Publications.

Mostafa, M.M. (2009) Shades of green: a psychographic segmentation of the green consumer in Kuwait using self-organizing maps, *Journal of Expert Systems with Applications*, 36(8): 11030–11038.

Murray, D. and Howat, G. (2002) The relationships among service quality, value, satisfaction, and future intentions of customers at an Australian sports and leisure centre, *Sport Management Review*, 5(1): 25–43.

Mykletun, R.J. (2009) Celebration of extreme playfulness: Ekstremsportveko at Voss, *Scandinavian Journal of Hospitality and Tourism*, 99(2/3): 146–176.

Mykletun, R.J., Crotts, J.C. and Mykletun, A. (2001) Positioning an island destination in the peripheral area of the Baltics: a flexible approach to market segmentation, *Tourism Management*, 22(5): 493–500.

Nadkarni, D. (2007) *Vanuatu: Tourism Booms But Could Do Better*, online, available at: www.islandsbusiness.com/islands_business/index_dynamic/containerName ToReplace=MiddleMiddle/focusModuleID=18186/overideSkinName=issueArticle-full.tpl [accessed 10 July 2012].

Nawijn, J. (2011) Determinants of daily happiness on vacation, *Journal of Travel Research*, DOI: 0047287510379164.

Nawijn, J. and Mitas, O. (2011) Resident attitudes to tourism and their effect on subjective well-being: the case of Palma De Mallorca, *Journal of Travel Research*, DOI: 10.1177/0047287511426482.

Nawijn, J., Marchand, M.A., Veenhoven, R. and Vingerhoets, A.J. (2010) Vacationers happier, but most not happier after a holiday, *Applied Research in Quality of Life*, 5(1): 35–47.

Neill, J.T. (2000) The life effectiveness questionnaire: a tool for measuring change, unpublished manuscript, University of Canberra, Australia.

Neill, J.T., Marsh, H.W. and Richards, G.E. (2003) The life effectiveness questionnaire:

development and psychometrics, unpublished manuscript, University of Western Sydney, NSW, Australia.

Nerlich, M. (1987) *Ideology of Adventure*, Minneapolis, MN: University of Minnesota.

Neumann, M. (1992) The trail through experience: finding self in the recollection of travel, in C. Ellis and M.G. Flaherty (eds) *Investigating Subjectivity: Research on Lived Experience*, Newbury Park, CA: Sage, pp. 176–201.

Nevis Range (2011) *Employment at Nevis Range*, online, available at: www.nevisrange.co.uk/jobs.asp [accessed 1 November 2011].

NZMSC (New Zealand Mountain Safety Council) (1993) *Managing Risks in Outdoor Activities*, Wellington: NZMSC.

Nicol, R. (2002) Outdoor education: research topic or universal value? Part one, *Journal of Adventure Education and Outdoor Learning*, 2(1): 29–41.

Norris, R.M. and Weinman, J.A. (1996) Psychological change following a long sail training voyage, *Personality and Individual Differences*, 21(2): 189–194.

Noy, C. (2004) This trip really changed me: backpackers' narratives of self-change, *Annals of Tourism Research*, 31(1): 78–102.

Noy, C. (2007) The poetics of tourist experience: an autoethnography of a family trip to Eliat, *Journal of Tourism and Cultural Change*, 5(3): 141–157.

O'Brien, B. (2010) *Kerry Activity Tourism Strategy 2010–2014*, Cahersiveen: South Kerry Development Partnership/Fáilte Ireland.

OECD (2006) *Glossary of Statistical Terms*, online, available at: http://stats.oecd.org/glossary/detail.asp?ID=5150 [accessed 12 March 2012].

Ogilvie, K. (2000) Duke of Edinburgh Award expeditions: fings ain't wot they used to be! *Horizons*, 11: 16–19.

Oh, H. (1999) Service quality, customer satisfaction, and customer value: a holistic perspective, *Hospitality Management*, 18(1): 67–82.

Oh, H., Fiore, A.M. and Jeoung, M. (2007) Measuring experience economy concepts: tourism applications, *Journal of Travel Research*, 46(2): 119–132.

Oliver, S. (2006) Moral dilemmas of participation in dangerous leisure activities, *Leisure Studies*, 25(1): 95–109.

O'Neill, M.A., Williams, P., MacCarthy, M. and Groves, R. (2000) Diving into service quality: the dive tour operator perspective, *Managing Service Quality*, 10(3): 131–140.

Outdoors and Health Network (2012) online, available at: www.outdoorshealthnetwork.co.uk/project-outputs [accessed 14 September 2012].

Outward Bound USA (ed.) (2008) *Outward Bound Instructor Manual*, Golden, CO: Outward Bound USA.

Pacific Peoples Partnership (n.d.) *Map of the South Pacific Islands*, online, available at: www.pacificpeoplespartnership.org/media/pacific_map.jpg [accessed 19 March 2012].

Page, S., Steele, W. and Connell, J. (2006) Analysing the promotion of adventure tourism: a case study of Scotland, *Journal of Sport and Tourism*, 11(1): 51–76.

Page, S.J. and Bentley, T.A. (2001) Scoping the extent of adventure tourism accidents, *Annals of Tourism Research*, 28(3): 705–726.

Page, S.J. and Connell, J. (2006) *Tourism: A Modern Synthesis*, 2nd edition, South Melbourne: Thompson Learning.

Page, S.J. and Dowling, R.K. (2001) *Ecotourism*, London: Prentice-Hall.

Page, S.J., Bentley, T.A. and Walker, L. (2005) Scoping the nature and extent of adventure tourism operations in Scotland: How safe are you? *Tourism Management*, 26(3): 381–397.

Panicucci, J. (2007) Cornerstones of adventure education, in D. Prouty, J. Panicucci, and

R. Collinson (eds) *Adventure Education: Theory and Applications*, Champaign, IL: Human Kinetics.

Panksepp, J. (2005) Affective consciousness: core emotional feelings in animals and humans, *Consciousness and Cognition*, 14(1): 30–80.

Papadimitriou, D. and Karteroliotis, K. (2000) The service quality expectations in private sport and fitness centers: a re-examination of the factor structure, *Sport Marketing Quarterly*, 9(3): 157–164.

Parasuraman, A., Berry, L. and Zeithaml, V. (1991) Refinement and reassessment of the SERVQUAL scale, *Journal of Retailing*, 67(4): 420–450.

Parasuraman, A., Zeithaml, A. and Berry, L. (1985) A conceptual model of service quality and its implications for further research, *Journal of Marketing*, 49(4): 41–50.

Parasuraman, A., Zeithaml, V. and Berry, L. (1988) SERVQUAL: a multiple-item scale for measuring consumer perceptions of service quality, *Journal of Retailing*, 64(1): 12–40.

Passier, H. and Jeuring, J. (2004) Ontology based feedback generation in design-oriented e-learning systems, *Proceedings of the IADIS International conference, e-society, Volume II*, Ávila, Spain, 16–19 July.

Patton, M.Q. (2002) *Qualitative Research and Evaluation Methods*, 3rd edition, Thousand Oaks, CA: Sage.

Pearce, D. and Cant, R. (1981) *The Development and Impact of Tourism in Queenstown*, Man and Biosphere Report No. 7, Christchurch: University of Canterbury.

Pearce, P.L. (2011) *Tourist Behaviour and the Contemporary World*, Bristol: Channel View Books.

Pearce, P.L. and Moscardo, G. (2004) Assessing market convergence and divergence: studies of visitors to Australia's Great Barrier Reef, in R. MacLellan, T. Baum, A. Goldsmith, J. Kokkranikal, E. Losekoot, S. Miller, A. Morrison, D. Nickson, J.S. Taylor and K. Thompson (eds) *Tourism State of the Art II Conference*, University of Strathclyde, Glasgow, 27–30 June, Glasgow: The Scottish Hotel School, University of Strathclyde.

Pease, A. and Pease, B. (2001) *Why Men Don't Listen And Women Can't Read Maps: How We're Different And What To Do About It*, New York: Broadway.

Perrin, J. (2004) *The Villain*, London: Hutchinson.

Phillimore, J. and Goodson, L. (eds) (2004) *Qualitative Research in Tourism: Ontologies, Epistemologies and Methodologies*, London: Routledge.

Phillips R. (1997) *Mapping Men and Empire: A Geography of Adventure*, London: Routledge.

Pike, E. and Beames, S. (2007) A critical interactionist analysis of 'youth development' expeditions, *Journal of Leisure Studies*, 26(2): 147–159.

Pine, J.B., II, and Gilmore, J.H. (1999) *The Experience Economy: Work Is Theatre and Every Business a Stage*, Cambridge, MA: Harvard Business School.

Pizam, A. and Reichel, A. (1979) Big spenders and little spenders in US tourism, *Journal of Travel Research*, 18(2): 42–43.

Polkinghorne, D. (1988) *Narrative Knowing and the Human Sciences*, Albany, NY: State University of New York Press.

Pomfret, G. (2006) Mountaineering adventure tourists: a conceptual framework for research, *Tourism Management*, 27(1): 113–123.

Poon, A. (1993) *Tourism Technology and Competitive Strategy*, Wallingford: CABI.

Price, T. (2000) *Travail So Gladly Spent*, St. Edmundsbury: Ernest Press.

Priest, S. (1990) The adventure experience paradigm, in J. Miles and S. Priest (eds) *Adventure Education*, State College, PA: Venture Publishing.

Priest, S. and Bunting, C. (1993) Changes in perceived risk and competence during white-water canoeing, *Journal of Applied Recreation Research*, 18(4): 265–280.

Priest, S. and Gass, M. (1997) *Effective Leadership in Adventure Programming*, Champaign, IL: Human Kinetics.

Quay, J. (2003) Experience and participation: relating theories of learning, *Journal of Experiential Education*, 26(2): 105–116.

Ransome, A. (2010) *The History of Story-Telling: Studies in the Development of Narrative*, Charleston, SC: Nabu Press.

Ratho (2011) *Things To Do*, online, available at: www.eica-ratho.com/content/things-to-do-/2423 [accessed 1 November 2011].

Richards, G. (1996) Skilled consumption and UK ski holidays, *Tourism Management*, 17(1): 25–34.

Rickinson, M., Dillon, J., Teamey, K., Morris, M., Choi M.Y., Sanders, D. and Benefield, P. (2004) *A Review of Research on Outdoor Learning*, Shrewsbury: National Foundation for Educational Research and King's College London.

Ricoeur, P. (1984) *Time and Narrative*, Chicago, IL: University of Chicago Press.

Riley, R. (1995) Prestige-worthy tourism behaviour, *Annals of Tourism Research*, 22(3): 630–649.

Ritzer, G. (1993) *The McDonaldization of Society*, Thousand Oaks, CA: Pine Forge Press.

Ritzer, G. (1997) *The McDonaldization Thesis*, London: Sage.

Roberts, J. (2008) From experience to neo-experiential education: variations on a theme, *Journal of Experiential Education*, 31(1): 19–35.

Roberts, K. (1999) *Leisure in Contemporary Society*, Wallingford: CABI.

Rogoff, B. (1993) Children's guided participation and participatory appropriation in sociocultural activity, in R.H. Wozniak and K.W. Fischer (eds) *Development in Context: Acting and Thinking in Specific Environments*, Hillsdale, NJ: Lawrence Erlbaum Associates.

Rojek, C. (1993) *Ways of Escape: Modern Transformations in Leisure and Travel*, Basingtoke: Macmillan.

Roy, S. (2011) *The Psychology of Fantasy*, online, available at: www.futurehealth.org/populum/page.php?f=The-Psychology-of-Fantasy-by-Saberi-Roy-100901-178.html [accessed 1 July 2012].

Rubens, D. (1999) Effort or performance: keys to motivated learners in the outdoors, *Horizons*, 4: 26–28.

Rudolph, J.W., Simon, R., Rivard, P., Dufresne, R.L. and Raemer, D.B. (2007) Debriefing with good judgment: combining rigorous feedback with genuine inquiry, *Anesthesiology Clinics*, 25(2): 361–376.

Rudra, S. (2008) *Market Segmentation, Targeting and Positioning*, online, available at: www.scribd.com/doc/6356725/market-segmentation-targeting-positioning-by-Subha-Rudra [accessed 15 August 2009].

Rust, R.T., Zahorik, A.J. and Keiningham, T.L. (1995) Return on quality (ROQ): making service quality financially accountable, *Journal of Marketing*, 59: 58–70.

Ryan, C. (1995) *Researching Tourist Satisfaction: Issues, Concepts, Problems*, New York: Routledge.

Sanjuán, P. (2011) Affect balance as mediating variable between effective psychological functioning and satisfaction with life, *Journal of Happiness Studies*, 12(3): 373–384.

Sarup, M. and Raja, T. (1996) *Identity, Culture and the Postmodern World*, Edinburgh: Edinburgh University Press.

Saussure, F. (2011) *Course in General Linguistics*, trans. W. Baskin, New York: Columbia University Press.

Scheffler, I. (1974) *Four Pragmatists: A Critical Introduction to Peirce, James, Mead, and Dewey*, New York: Routledge.

Schiebe K. (1986) Self narratives and adventure, in T. Sarbin (ed.) *Narrative Psychology: The Storied Nature of Human Conduct*, New York: Praeger.

Schimmack, U. (2003) Affect measurement in experience sampling research, *Journal of Happiness Studies*, 4(1): 79–106.

Schmitt, B. (1999) *Experiential Marketing: How to Get Customers to Sense, Feel, Think, Act, Relate to Your Company and Brands*, New York: Free Press.

Schneider, B. (1991) Service quality and profits: can you have your cake and eat it, too? *Human Resource Planning*, 14(2): 151–157.

Scott, D. (1994) Trekking commentary, *High Mountain Sports*, 134: 56–59.

Scott, J. (2000) Is it a different world to when you were growing up? Generational effects on social representations and child-rearing values, *British Journal of Sociology*, 51(2): 355–376.

Seaman, J. (2007) Taking 'things' into account: learning as kinaesthetically-mediated collaboration, *Journal of Adventure Education and Outdoor Learning*, 7(1): 3–20.

Seaman, J. (2008) Experience, reflect, critique: the end of the 'learning cycles' era, *Journal of Experiential Education*, 31(1): 3–18.

Seaman, J. (2009) Balancing evidence and authenticity in research on experiential education and youth development in diverse settings, *Journal of Experiential Education*, 31(3): 425–430.

Seaman, J. and Coppens, A.D. (2006) Repertoire of practice: reconceptualizing instructor competency in contemporary adventure education, *Journal of Adventure Education and Outdoor Learning*, 6(1): 25–37.

Seaman, J. and Nelson, P.J. (2011) An overburdened term: Dewey's concept of experience as curriculum theory, *Journal of Education and Culture*, 27(1): 5–25.

Sedmak, G. and Mihalič, T. (2008) Authenticity in mature seaside resorts, *Annals of Tourism Research*, 35(4): 1007–1031.

Seigworth, G.J. and Gregg, M. (2010) An inventory of shimmers, in M. Gregg and G.J. Seigworth (eds) *The Affect Theory Reader*, Durham, NC/London: Duke University Press.

Seligman, M.E.P. (2002) *Authentic Happiness: Using the New Positive Psychology to Realize Your Potential for Lasting Fulfillment*, New York: Free Press.

Seligman, M.E.P. (2011) *Flourish*, Sydney, NSW: Random House.

Seremetakis, C.N. (ed.) (1994) *The Senses Still: Perception and Memory as Material Culture in Modernity*, Chicago, IL: University of Chicago Press.

Silverman, D. (2010) *Doing Qualitative Research*, London: Sage.

Simmel, G. (1997 [1991]) The adventure, in D. Frisby and M. Featherstone (eds) *Simmel on Culture*, London: Sage.

Singer, J.A. (1995) Seeing one's self: locating narrative memory in a framework of personality, *Journal of Personality*, 63(3): 429–457.

Singer, J.A. and Salovey, P. (1993) *The Remembered Self*, New York: Free Press.

Smith, A. (2011) *The Frozen Planet*, BBC television documentary.

SNEWS (2004) *Stowell Takes Helm of Adventure Travel Trade Association*, 18 October, online, available at: www.snewsnet.com/cgi-bin/snews/02122.html [accessed 1 April 2006].

Snoshop (2011) *Snoshop*, formerly online at: www.snoshopuk.com [accessed 10 November 2011].

Snozone (2011) *Sno-bar*, formerly online at: www.snozoneuk.com/v/scotland/ activities/ sno-bar [accessed 10 November 2011].

Spotts, D.M. and Mahoney, E.M. (1991) Segmenting visitors to a destination region based on the volume of their expenditure, *Journal of Travel Research*, 29(4): 24–31.

Stamboulis, Y. and Skayannis, P. (2003) Innovation strategies and technology for experience-based tourism, *Tourism Management*, 24(1): 35–43.

Stamou, A.G. and Paraskevopoulos, S. (2003) Ecotourism experiences in visitors' books of a Greek Reserve: a critical discourse analysis perspective, *Sociologia Ruralis*, 43(1): 34–55.

Steger, M.F., Frazier, P., Oishi, S. and Kaler, M. (2006) The Meaning in Life Questionnaire: assessing the presence of and search for meaning in life, *Journal of Counseling Psychology*, 53(1): 80–93.

Stonehouse, B. and Crosbie, K. (1995) Tourist impacts and management in the Antarctic Peninsula Area, in C.M. Hall and M.E. Johnston (eds) *Polar Tourism: Tourism in the Arctic and Antarctic Regions*, Chichester: Wiley.

Stott, T.A. and Hall, N.E. (2003) Changes in aspects of students' self-reported personal, social and technical skills during a six-week wilderness expedition in arctic Greenland, *Journal of Adventure Education and Outdoor Learning*, 3(2), 159–169.

Stott, T.A., Allison, P., Felter, J. and Beames, S. (in review) The educational value of expeditions: a literature review and thematic analysis, *British Educational Research Journal*.

Strategic Business Insights (2012) *VALS™*, online, available at: www.strategicbusinessinsights.com/vals [accessed 25 September 2012].

Strauss, A.L. and Corbin, J.M. (1990) *Basics of Qualitative Research: Grounded Theory Procedures and Techniques*, Newbury Park, CA: Sage.

Stynes, D.M. and Mahoney, E.M. (1980) *Michigan Downhill Ski Market Study: Segmenting Active Skiers. Research Report 391*, East Lansing, MI: Michigan University Agricultural Experiment Station.

Su, C.-H. and Sun, L.-H. (2007) Taiwan's hotel rating system: a service quality perspective, *Cornell Hotel and Restaurant Administration Quarterly*, 48(4): 392–401.

Sugiyama, M.S. (2001) Food, foragers and folklore: the role of narrative in human subsistence. *Evolution and Human Behaviour*, 22(4): 221–240.

Sung, H.H. (2004) Classification of adventure travellers: behaviour, decision-making and target markets, *Journal of Travel Research*, 42(1): 343–356.

Sung, H.H., Morrison, A.M., Hong, G.S. and O'Leary, J.T. (2001) The effects of household and trip characteristics on trip types: a consumer behavioural approach for segmenting the U.S. domestic leisure travel market, *Journal of Hospitality and Tourism Research*, 25(1): 46–67.

Swarbrooke, J., Beard, C., Leckie, S. and Pomfret, G. (2003) *Adventure Tourism: The New Frontier*, Kidlington: Butterworth-Heinemann.

Taplin, R.H. (2012a) Competitive importance-performance analysis of an Australian wildlife park, *Tourism Management*, 33(1): 29–37.

Taplin, R.H. (2012b) The value of self-stated attribute importance to overall satisfaction, *Tourism Management*, 33(2): 295–304.

Tarrant, M.A. and Smith, E. (2002) The use of a modified importance-performance framework to examine visitor satisfaction with attributes of outdoor recreation settings, *Managing Leisure*, 7(2): 69–82.

Tejada-Flores, L. (1978) Games climbers play, in K. Wilson (ed.) *The Games Climbers Play*, London: Diadem.

Thesiger, W. (1959) *Arabian Sands*, London: Longmans.

Thomas, N. (1987) Accessible adventure in 'Swallows and Amazons', *Anthropology Today*, 3(5): 8–11.

Thompson, C.P., Skowronski, J.J., Larsen, S.F. and Betz, A.L. (1996) *Autobiographical Memory: Remembering What and Remembering When*, Mahwah, NJ: Erlbaum.

Thompson, K. (2007) *The Frodo Franchise: The Lord of the Rings and Modern Hollywood*, Los Angeles, CA: University of California Press.

Thompson, S. (2010) *Unjustifiable Risk: The Story of British Climbing*, Milnthorpe: Cicerone.

Thrift, N. (2004) Intensities of feeling: towards a spatial politics of affect, *Geografiska Annaler*, 86(1): 57–78.

Tian-Cole, S., Crompton, J. and Willson, V. (2002) An empirical investigation of the relationships between service quality, satisfaction and behavioral intentions among visitors to a wildlife refuge, *Journal of Leisure Research*, 34(1): 1–24.

TIG (2010) *Adventure Tourism in Scotland, Market Analysis Report, April 2010*, by Paul Easto and Caroline Warburton, n.p.: Tourism Innovation Group.

Timothy, D.J. (2001) *Tourism and Political Boundaries*, London: Routledge.

Tomkins, S. (1987) Script theory, in J. Aronoff, A.I. Rabin and R.A. Zucker (eds) *The Emergence of Personality*, New York: Springer, pp. 147–216.

Tomlinson, J. and Leigh, E. (1996) *Extreme Sports: In Search of the Ultimate Thrill*, London: Carlton.

Tomlinson, M. (2007) Graduate employability and student attitudes and orientations to the labour market, *Journal of Education and Work*, 20(4): 285–304.

Tomlinson, M. (2008) The degree is not enough: students perceptions of the role of higher education credentials for graduate work and employability, *British Journal of Sociology of Education*, 29(1): 49–61.

Tomlinson, M. (2010) Investing in the self: structure, agency and identity in graduates' employability, *Education, Knowledge and Economy*, 4(2): 73–88.

Tonge, J. and Moore, S.A. (2007) Importance-satisfaction analysis for marine-park hinterlands: a Western Australian case study, *Tourism Management*, 28: 768–776.

Tuan, Y. (2003) *Space and Place: The Perspective of Experience*, Minneapolis, MN: University of Minnesota Press.

Tucker, H. and Kane, M.J. (2004) Adventure tourism: the freedom to play with reality, *Tourist Studies*, 4(3): 217–234.

Turner, V. (1982) *From Ritual to Theatre: The Human Seriousness of Play*, New York: PAJ Publications.

Turner, V. (1986) *The Anthropology of Performance*, New York: PAJ Publications.

Tversky, B. (2002) What do sketches say about thinking? *Papers from the AAAI Spring Symposium on Sketch Understanding*, R. Davis, J. Landay and T. Stahovich, Program Cochairs, Menlo Park, CA: AAAI, pp. 148–151.

UNWTO (2003) *Quality in Tourism*, online, available at: http://sdt.unwto.org/en/content/quality-tourism [accessed 12 March 2012].

Urbain, J.-D. (1989) The tourist adventure and his images, *Annals of Tourism Research*, 16(1): 106–118.

Urry, G. (2010) Research diary: 6–7 November, Bristol: University of Bristol.

Urry, J. (1995) *Consuming Places*, London: Routledge.

Urry, J. (2000) *Sociology Beyond Societies: Mobilities for the Twenty-first Century*, London: Routledge.

Vanuatu National Statistics Office (2012) *Statistics Update: International Migration – January 2012*, Port Vila: Vanuatu National Statistics Office.

Vanuatu Tourism Office (2012) *Discover What Matters: Vanuatu*, online, available at: http://vanuatu.travel [accessed 1 July 2012].

Varley, P. (2006a) Confecting Adventure and Playing with Meaning: the Adventure Commodification Continuum. *Journal of Sport and Tourism*, 11(2): 173–194.

Varley, P. (2006b) Adventurers in Bohemia: Temporary Adventure Communities in the 'Forgotten Ground' of Late Modernity. Paper presented to the Leisure Studies Association Annual Conference, Making Space: Leisure, Tourism and Renewal.

Varley, P.J. (2011) Sea kayakers at the margins: the liminoid character of contemporary adventures, *Leisure Studies*, 30(1): 85–98.

Veal, A.J. (2005) *Business Research Methods: A Managerial Approach*, 2nd edition, Sydney, NSW: Addison.

Veevers, N and Allison, P. (2011) *Kurt Hahn: Inspirational, Visionary, Outdoor and Experiential Educator*, Rotterdam: Sense Publications.

Vernon, F. (2011a) The experience of co-instructing on extended wilderness trips: a phenomenological inquiry, *Journal of Experiential Education*, 33(4): 374–378.

Vernon, F. (2011b) Whose responsibility is it? The hierarchical contract in co-instruction, *Proceedings from Symposium on Experiential Education Research*, Jacksonville, Florida, November.

Wainwright, M. (2011) Potholers break through the final Three Counties link, *The Guardian*, 7 November, online, available at: www.guardian.co.uk/uk/the-northerner/2011/nov/07/caving-potholing-three-counties-system-gaping-gill-white-scar-caves-edouard-martel [accessed 29 November 2011].

Waldfogel, J. (2008) The median voter and the median consumer: local private goods and population composition, *Journal of Urban Economics*, 63(2): 567–582.

Walle, A.H. (1997) Pursuing risk or insight: marketing adventures, *Annals of Tourism Research*, 24(2): 265–282.

Wang, N. (1999) Rethinking authenticity in tourism experience, *Annals of Tourism Research*, 26(2): 349–370.

Warde, A. (2002) Setting the scene: changing conceptions of consumption, in S. Miles, A. Anderson and K. Meetham (eds) *Changing Consumers: Markets and Meanings*, London: Routledge.

Warren, K., Mitten, D. and Loeffler, T.A. (eds) (2008) *Theory and Practice of Experiential Education*, Boulder, CO: Association for Experiential Education.

Watts, F.N, Apps, J. and East M.P. (1993b) Personality change produced by expedition stress: a controlled study, *Personality and Individual Differences*, 15(5): 603–605.

Watts, F.N, Cohen, J. and Toplis, R. (1994) Personality and coping strategies on a stressful expedition, *Personality and Individual Differences*, 17(5): 647–656.

Watts, F.N, Webster, S.M., Morley, C.J. and Cohen, J. (1992) Expedition stress and personality change, *British Journal of Psychology*, 83(3): 337–341.

Watts, F.N, Webster, S.M., Morley, C.J and Cohen, J. (1993a) Cognitive strategies in coping with expedition stress, *European Journal of Personality*, 7(4): 255–266.

Weber, K. (2001) Outdoor adventure tourism: a review of research approaches, *Annals of Tourism Research*, 28(2): 360–377.

Weed, M. (2008) *Sport and Tourism: A Reader*, Abingdon: Routledge.

Weiermair, K. and Fuchs, M. (1999) Measuring tourist judgment on service quality, *Annals of Tourism Research*, 26(4): 1004–1021.

Weinzierl, S. and Muggleton, D. (eds) (2004) *The Post-subcultures Reader*, Oxford: Berg.

Wells, C. (2001) *A Brief History of British Mountaineering*, Sheffield: The Mountain Heritage Trust.

Westphal, R. (2011) We have the Fjells, but you have character ... A comparative study of personal and social development (PSD) within the discourses of outdoor education in Great Britain and Friluftsliv in Norway, unpublished doctoral thesis, University of Edinburgh, Scotland.

Wheaton, B. (2000) 'Just do it': consumption commitment, and identity in the windsurfing culture, *Sociology of Sport Journal*, 17(3): 254–276.

Wheaton, B. (2004) Introduction: mapping the lifestyle sport-scape, in B. Wheaton (ed.) *Understanding Lifestyle Sports: Consumption, Identity and Difference*, London: Routledge.

Whisman, S.A. and Hollenhorst, S.J. (1998) A path model of whitewater boating satisfaction on the cheat river of West Virginia, *Environmental Management*, 22(1): 109–117.

Wilber, K. (1995) *Sex, Ecology, Spirituality: The Spirit of Evolution*, Boston, MA: Shambala Publications.

Wilcoxon, F. and Wilcox, R.A. (1964) *Some Rapid Approximate Statistical Procedures*, New York: Lederle Laboratories.

Wiley, J.W. (1991) Customer satisfaction: a supportive work environment and its financial costs, *Human Resource Planning*, 14(2): 117–127.

Wilks, J. and Page, S.J. (2003) *Managing Tourist Health and Safety in the New* Millennium, London: Pergamon.

Williams, P. and Soutar, G.N. (2009) Value, satisfaction, and behavioural intentions in an adventure tourism context, *Annals of Tourism Research*, 36(3): 413–438.

Williams, R., Higgins, P., Humberstone, B. and Loynes, C. (1998) *Outdoor Education in Britain – Outdoor, Adventure And Experiential Learning: A Wealth Of European Concepts*. Report of the third European congress of the European Institute for Outdoor Adventure Education and Experiential Learning, Marburg: European Institute for Outdoor Adventure Education.

Wilson, E. and Harris, C. (2006) Meaningful travel: women, independent travel and the search for self and meaning, *Tourism*, 54(2): 161–172.

Wilson, E.O. (1993) Biophilia and the conservation ethic, in S. Kellert and E.O. Wilson (eds) *The Biophilia Hypothesis*, Washington, DC: Island Press and Shearwater Books.

Wilson, K. (1998) A future for traditional values, *The Alpine Journal*, 103(357): 175–188.

Wilson, R.M.S. and Gilligan, C. (2005) *Strategic Marketing Management: Planning, Implementation and Control*. Kidlington: Butterworth-Heinemann.

Winchester, H., McGuirk, P. and Everett, K. (1999) Schoolies week as a rite of passage, in E.K. Teather (ed.) *Embodied Geographies; Spaces Bodies and Rites of Passage*, London: Routledge.

Woicik, P.A., Stewart, S.H., Pihl, R.O. and Conrod, P.J. (2009) The substance use risk profile scale: a scale measuring traits linked to reinforcement-specific substance use profiles, *Journal of Addictive Behaviours*, 34(12): 1042–1055.

Woodside, A.G., Cook, V.J. and Mindak, W. (1987) Profiling the heavy traveller segment, *Journal of Travel Research*, 25(3): 9–14.

Woodside, A.G., Sood, S. and Miller, K.R. (2008) When consumers and brands talk: Storytelling theory and research in psychology and marketing, *Psychology and Marketing*, 25(2): 97–145.

WorldAtlas.com (n.d.) *Vanuatu Outline Map*, online, available at: www.worldatlas.com/webimage/countrys/oceania/outline/vu.htm [accessed 18 April 2012]

Worsley, T.C. (1985) *Flannelled Fool*, London: The Hogarth Press.

Wu, C.H.-J. and Liang, R.-D. (2011) The relationship between white-water rafting experience formation and customer reaction: a flow theory perspective, *Tourism Management*, 32(2): 317–325.

Wurdinger, S. (1996) *Philosophical Issues in Adventure Education*, Dubuque, IA: Kendall Hunt.

Xscape (2011) Homepage, online, available at: http://xscape.co.uk/braehead [accessed 1 November 2011].

Yee, R.W.Y., Yeung, A.C.L. and Cheng, T.C.E. (2011) The service-profit chain: an empirical analysis in high-contact service industries, *International Journal of Production Economics*, 130(2): 236–245.

Young, J. (1997 [1971]) The subterranean world of play, in K. Gelder and S. Thornton (eds) *The Subcultural Reader*, London: Routledge.

Yüksel, A. and Rimmington, M. (1998) Consumer-satisfaction measurement, *Cornell Hotel and Restaurant Administration Quarterly*, 39(6): 60–70.

Ziegler, J. Dearden, P. and Rollins, R. (2012) But are tourists satisfied? Importance-performance analysis of the whale shark tourism industry on Isla Holbox, Mexico, *Tourism Management*, 33(3): 692–701.

Zipes, J.D. (1993) *The Trials and Tribulations of Little Red Riding Hood*, New York: Routledge.

Zweig, P. (1974) *The Adventurer*, Princeton, NJ: Princeton University Press.

Index